FROM SIN
TO SALVATION

FROM SIN
TO SALVATION

THE ASCENT
OF THE SOUL

John S. Hatcher, PhD

Bahá'í
PUBLISHING

Wilmette, Illinois

Bahá'í Publishing
401 Greenleaf Avenue, Wilmette, Illinois 60091

19   18   17   16   4   3   2   1

Library of Congress Cataloging-in-Publication Data

Names: Hatcher, John S., 1940–author.
Title: From sin to salvation : the ascent of the soul / John S Hatcher, PhD.
Description: Wilmette, Illinois : Bahá'í Publishing, [2016] | Includes
    bibliographical references.
Identifiers: LCCN 2015050634 | ISBN 9781618511027 (pbk. : acid-free paper)
Subjects: LCSH: Bahai Faith—Doctrines.
Classification: LCC BP365 .H3225 2016 | DDC 297.9/322—dc23
LC record available at http://lccn.loc.gov/2015050634

Book design by Patrick Falso
Cover design by Misha Maynerick Blaise

for my special teachers

Mrs. Kirkpatrick (4th Grade)
Grady L. Randolph (Critical Thinking)
William S. Hatcher (Bahá'í Faith)
Winston Evans (Bahá'í Faith)
Edgar H. Duncan (Medieval Literature)
John Crowe Ransom (Poetry)
John J. Compton (Philosophy)
Robert H. West (Shakespeare)
Ken Grimmer (Farming)
Lucia C. Hatcher (Humility)

CONTENTS

ACKNOWLEDGMENTS

First, I would like to express my appreciation to my wife Lucia who did the initial editing of this work. I also want to thank the personnel at the Bahá'í Publishing Trust — the general manager and my dear friend Tim Moore, and editors Bahhaj Taherzadeh and Chris Martin. Most importantly, I want to express my immense gratitude to Nilufar Gordon whose editorial contributions to this book were creative and totally indispensable.

PART 1:
SOME MAJOR AXIOMS ABOUT REALITY

1 / FUNDAMENTAL AXIOMS ABOUT REALITY

The word of God is as clear as the sun. This is a spiritual argument, but it cannot be presented to the material philosophers at the outset. Rather, we must first present the rational arguments and only afterwards the spiritual ones.

—'Abdu'l-Bahá, *Some Answered Questions*, no. 50.6

The concept of sin is dependent on a context in which there exists some systematic notion of value. Such a notion depends on an overall view of the nature and purpose of human existence; and any vision of human purpose necessarily derives from an understanding of the nature and purpose of reality as a whole.

The undeniable logic of this sequence requires that before we can consider the various concepts of sin, we must first describe the concept of reality we will employ for the purposes of this discussion and, beyond that, the rational basis on which it rests. After setting forth the logical underpinnings, we can, as the epigraph for this chapter suggests, proceed to the "spiritual arguments" for this view of the purpose of reality. Once we have accomplished this initial objective, we can then proceed to the major focus of this book— namely, trying to understand the nature of "sin" (wrongdoing), "Satan" (the cause of wrongdoing), "damnation" (the consequence of wrongdoing), and "salvation" (the cure for wrongdoing).

THEORIES OF REALITY: CHANCE VERSUS DESIGN

We are all aware of the adversarial relationship between science and religion, especially regarding theories of reality and its origin. Religious views about the origin and nature of reality most often theorize that reality is the product of design by a Creator. At the heart of this theory is the belief that God, the Creator of the universe, decided to fashion a being in His own image (Genesis 1:26).* While this idea is usually assumed to imply spiritual capacities—an essentially spiritual reality (the soul) from which emanate powers and capacities such as free will, discernment, self-consciousness, and so on—one might also infer from this theory that the "image" includes having the soul associate with a physical form (the body) that must navigate a physical environment in order to educate and test the human soul for its continued and more expansive experience in the entirely spiritual environment of the afterlife.

The scientific or materialist antithesis of this theory of reality is that no metaphysical dimension exists, that reality came into being by the pure chance of a random cause-and-effect process. Many scientists believe that the origin of physical reality began *ab ovo* with a "Big Bang," a spontaneous or instantaneous explosion of matter about sixteen billion years ago, before which there was nothing, or perhaps a very compact, dense, really hot conglomeration of "stuff" that suddenly needed to expand and cool off for a while.

Between the extremes of these theories about reality are various combinations. For example, some believe that there is a metaphysical aspect to it but that this expression of reality has no influence on the physical realm, and vice versa. Alternate theories synthesize parts from both extremes in a variety of combinations. There is a spectrum of views from those that are more materialist in orientation (but concede that there might be some metaphysical aspect to reality), to those that are spiritually or metaphysically based (but accept the idea that God may employ physical processes to bring about spiritual objectives). Similarly, some theists believe that our physical lives and actions have no direct effect on our metaphysical

---

* This and all further biblical citations are from *The King James Version.*

4

or afterlife experience, while others believe that our afterlife experience is precisely geared to how well we respond to our challenges and opportunities during the course of the foundational, or preparatory, physical portion of our lives. But here, too, we find room for a variety of views between these two alternatives.

While our examination of theories concerns the nature of reality in all its manifold expressions, we will focus on the reality of the human being and those aspects of reality that might have some influence on theories of value—how we can or should live our lives. For example, we may or may not agree with theories regarding the origin of the cosmos, the evolution of human beings, or precisely when a fertilized egg becomes a human being, but for the purposes of this examination of concepts such as virtue and vice, Satan and salvation, we do need to arrive at some rational and useful theory about the origin and nature of human virtue and the extent to which we have willful control over our own character. We also need to establish a process by which we can evaluate our individual humanity in terms of a theory of value.

If we are to consider sin—its nature, origin, consequences, and cure—it is imperative that we first establish the theory of reality we will be employing as the foundation for our study. Otherwise, our observations may well be baseless or insubstantial. But right away we run into a problem—there are presently no commonly shared views about the nature, structure, and purpose of reality. Not even those whom we might think would possess some degree of objectivity and reliability—scientists, philosophers, and theologians in academia—can agree among themselves about reality, especially regarding discrete categories of questions.

This is one of the many paradoxes we face in our contemporary perspective. However exquisitely knowledgeable we may become with specific technologies—the GPS, the iPod, the iPad, etc.—we are still left pondering how creation began. For example, despite all our technological prowess, we still do not know what the source of human self-awareness is, whether or not there is an afterlife, or whether life on our planet is the result of random chance or some organic process set in motion by divine guidance. In short, while we have acquired the ability to know an incredible amount about very discrete parts of it, our answers to the questions about the totality of reality remain ambiguous and vague.

This dilemma might seem superbly ironic, but it means that you or I just may have as much right as anybody else to discover a theory that suits our independent investigation of available answers to the central issues regarding reality: Who am I? Do I have an inherent purpose and, therefore, inherent responsibilities? Is my thought under my willful control, or is this "I" merely an illusion created by the "microprocessors" in the lobes of my brain? Is my sense of "self" dependent on the health of my physical body, or will I endure as a cognitive being beyond the decline and decomposition of my mortal frame and aging brain?

THE COLLECTIVE STUDY OF REALITY

For a moment, let us pretend that collaboration and cooperation among the various areas of study were suddenly possible. Let us imagine that all the brilliant minds decided to combine their talents and love of learning to discover and then describe reality. And let us pretend, purely for the purposes of a brief analogy, that these assembled individuals determined that reality, whatever it might be, is hanging from the limb of a large oak tree in a dark, almost impenetrable forest, and that it is discernible only on Tuesday nights.*

After a period of extensive consultation, this imaginary crew of great minds gathers on a Tuesday night with very powerful flashlights and cameras, then sets out to find the oak tree so that they might see reality and determine collectively what it looks like and how it works. The deeper into the woods they go, the darker it gets, so that when they reach the great oak, it is too dark to see

* Usually, not much is happening in a forest on Tuesday nights.

anything without the extremely powerful flashlights they have designed especially for this venture.

One at a time, each shines the powerful beam of his light on this object hanging from a huge limb. They can see parts of it, but it is quite large, and they cannot get a sense of the entire thing. So they decide to spread out in a large circle. From these various perspectives, each gets a slightly different view of reality. Each describes to the others what he or she sees, but none of the descriptions seems to match—not the shape, the color, or any other aspect of "reality."

They gather in the dark, consult, and reach a consensus that if each of them takes a picture of what their light reveals, they can later assemble the single images into one coherent portrait of reality. Carefully they spread out in the circle again, shine their lights, and take the pictures one at a time so that the flash from the camera on one side of the circle does not interfere with the picture taken by the colleague on the opposite side. Once finished, they excitedly rush back through the woods and assemble at the lab where the pictures are printed out. Hurriedly they gather at a large round table in the same order they had been placed under the tree, and each one nervously slides his or her picture forward until all of the pieces are at last one large composite photograph of reality!

"Astounding!" says the theologist.

"Remarkable!" says the particle physicist.

"Totally unexpected!" says the astrophysicist.

"Just as I thought!" says the zoologist.

For there before them, assembled in a mosaic from all the photos, is a ginormous, exquisitely designed, grey African elephant. And what is more, the elephant is smiling, as if it *knew* it was having its picture taken (because it did).

WHY REALITY IS SO COY

As many readers probably noticed right away, this fictional parable is my own version of the ancient fable about different men describing an elephant as each examines a different part of the beast. In the original telling, the men are blind, and we may thus sympathize with their inherent disadvantage.* Still another way to tell the story is to recount the men and women as having allowed themselves to become blindfolded, as if some sage were trying to teach them a lesson about the path to enlightenment, or else as an example of how seekers after truth must not allow themselves to be close-minded in what they consider possible solutions to what they are examining. The theme of this parable is not so much the need for collaboration as it is an illustration of the organically whole, but infinitely varied, appearance of reality. It is also about another key to the quest for knowledge: the advantage of being able to discern the end in the beginning.

In this version of the story, the blindfolded men and women, who have never before encountered or even seen pictures of an elephant, are exhorted to examine the beast and then describe and discuss what they believe its nature to be. One feels the tail and asserts, "The elephant is skinny like a whip or a snake!" "No, it is thick, round, and straight like a tree trunk," says the second man as his hands feel the huge legs. "I beg your pardon, gentlemen, but I find the elephant to be entirely different—it is flat, thick, and leathery, rather like a very heavy blanket," says a woman who carefully examines one ear. And so the discourse proceeds as a fourth feels the tusk, and a fifth feels the massive side.

The wise teacher then guides the men to sit and discuss their findings so that they may come to a conclusion about the reality of this strange creation. They soon begin to quarrel about the nature, size, and texture of the elephant. Each discusses what empirical evidence has enabled him or her to conclude about the nature of the elephant. But as each reports his findings—certain that his or

---

* While the origin of this ancient fable is thought to be India, it has spread worldwide and become part of the lore of various religious and cultural traditions, including Hinduism, Buddhism, and Islam.

her examination had been objective, accurate, and thorough—all naturally refuse to accept what seem to be the contrary findings that the others have reached. Therefore, what had begun as a calm, rational, and collaborative effort to define reality quickly degenerates into an unruly quarrel.

Finally, the sage teacher has them remove their blindfolds and exhorts them to look over beneath a large banyan tree, where, to their amazement, an elephant is standing—a complex reality, to be sure, but one that is quite neatly assembled into one organic, coordinated, and happy being. Immediately they realize that each of them had been right; yet, because each one had been insistent that he or she had discovered the complete truth, each one had been entirely wrong. Each had correctly described a distinct part of reality, but because the group could not (or would not) collaborate and assemble their findings collectively, all were deprived of understanding the overall nature of the elephant's reality or how this reality could function as a single system.

THE IMPORTANCE OF KNOWING THE END IN THE BEGINNING

Another equally important "message" or theme of these two fables has to do with a Bahá'í axiom about attaining learning. Bahá'u'lláh states that knowledge and its acquisition are greatly assisted if one is able to discern "the end in the beginning" (Bahá'u'lláh, The Seven Valleys, p. 24). Or, to relate the axiom to our two stories, we can imagine how much more rapidly the knowledge of the elephant of reality would have been for both sets of seekers had they already been informed about the nature of reality, and understood something about the overall characteristics of the object of their search before they set out to understand it by examining discrete parts of it.

As a result of this initial understanding, they might not have quarreled or become stubborn and insistent about their own views. Rather, by understanding the "end result" in the "beginning of search," they would have immediately begun to cooperate in figuring out how the parts fit together, how reality as a whole is diverse in its parts but coherently designed as an organic creation.

Another useful parable about the quest for knowledge in relation to seeing the end in the beginning can be found in the writings of Bahá'u'lláh—the founder of the Bahá'í Faith, regarded by Bahá'ís as a Manifestation, or Messenger, of God. Among His many works, all of which are considered scripture by Bahá'ís, is The Seven Valleys, a portrayal of the mystical path that constitutes each person's journey toward spiritual enlightenment and edification.

Each of the seven valleys in the work represents a successive level of advancement, and each of these levels is attained by means of a specific type of endeavor and the application of a particular skill set. For example, the entire journey begins with striving through the Valley of Search, an effort that is characterized by persistence and patience. The next valley is Love, and traversing this stage of development requires one to be vulnerable and receptive to the attraction of the "Beloved"—the presence of Whom is the goal of the spiritual quest.

The journey then proceeds through the successive stages of Knowledge, Unity, Contentment, Wonderment, and concludes with the Valley of True Poverty and Absolute Nothingness. But the parable about the value of discerning the "end" in the "beginning" occurs in third valley, the Valley of Knowledge. Bahá'u'lláh implies that in traversing the Valley of Knowledge, we will greatly benefit from acquiring the ability to understand the nature of the object of our quest if we are to avoid distractions and obstacles along the way:

> There was once a lover who had sighed for long years in separation from his beloved, and wasted in the fire of remoteness. From the rule of love, his heart was empty of patience, and his body weary of his spirit; he reckoned life without her as a mockery, and time consumed him away. How many a

day he found no rest in longing for her; how many a night the pain of her kept him from sleep; his body was worn to a sigh, his heart's wound had turned him to a cry of sorrow. He had given a thousand lives for one taste of the cup of her presence, but it availed him not. The doctors knew no cure for him, and companions avoided his company; yea, physicians have no medicine for one sick of love, unless the favor of the beloved one deliver him.

At last, the tree of his longing yielded the fruit of despair, and the fire of his hope fell to ashes. Then one night he could live no more, and he went out of his house and made for the marketplace. On a sudden, a watchman followed after him. He broke into a run, with the watchman following; then other watchmen came together, and barred every passage to the weary one. And the wretched one cried from his heart, and ran here and there, and moaned to himself: "Surely this watchman is Izra'il, my angel of death, following so fast upon me; or he is a tyrant of men, seeking to harm me." His feet carried him on, the one bleeding with the arrow of love, and his heart lamented. Then he came to a garden wall, and with untold pain he scaled it, for it proved very high; and forgetting his life, he threw himself down to the garden.

And there he beheld his beloved with a lamp in her hand, searching for a ring she had lost. When the heart-surrendered lover looked on his ravishing love, he drew a great breath and raised up his hands in prayer, crying: "O God! Give Thou glory to the watchman, and riches and long life. For the watchman was Gabriel, guiding this poor one; or he was Isráfíl, bringing life to this wretched one!" (Bahá'u'lláh, The Seven Valleys, pp. 20–23)

As with any parable, there are various levels of allegorical meaning to this story. For example, the quest for the Beloved might represent a seeker's search for union with God. In a more literal, romantic interpretation, the story might symbolize one's quest for earthly love. But, inasmuch as the story is set in Bahá'u'lláh's depiction of the acquisition of knowledge, the more obvious symbolism would seem to point to our quest for knowledge of reality in all its forms.

In this sense, the primary message symbolized in the lover's quest is that the journey toward understanding is greatly assisted if we, as seekers, comprehend at the outset the characteristics of what it is we are seeking, as well as the nature of the challenges we will likely encounter along the way. Otherwise, we may mistakenly perceive the discomfiture of our journey as a sign that we are taking the wrong path, and we might subsequently cease our search or else go in the wrong direction. In this story, however, we see that the seeker's means for escape from discomfort are blocked by an unseen force that is subtly directing him precisely where he needs to go to attain his objective—the acquisition of knowledge or, in a more mystical and spiritual interpretation, the reunion with the Beloved of his heart (a sense of nearness to God).

To explore a commonplace example of how we might apply this allegorical fable to the quest for knowledge, we might find useful the well-known example of our advancement from the Ptolemaic to the Copernican theory of reality regarding our solar system. We proceeded from what seemed perfectly obvious, that the heavenly bodies—the Sun, the Moon, the stars—appear to move around the Earth in both the daytime and the nighttime. Little by little, calculations about the period or cycle of each of these planets and stars were determined, and over time theology and science constructed reality accordingly. Earth was appropriately the center of creation, and man, just as appropriately, was the ruler of Earth.

Problems arose when the skills and mechanisms for viewing the heavens became more accurate, and the theory that Earth is the center of creation no longer seemed to work so well. But confident in their theory—or attached to it and fearful of theorizing something contrary to what those in authority had made part of religious dogma—scientists tried to contrive explanations for those observations that seemed to challenge or undermine the Ptolemaic assumption. For example, to explain how Mars could be closer to the Earth at one time of the year than another, or how it seemed to have a retrograde motion at times, the theory was proposed that Mars must be rotating in small circular patterns, which, in turn, rotated around the Earth in epicycles.

We need not examine all the details about how problems mounted in trying to account for findings that contradict a geocentric theory of reality; suffice it to say that the Copernican heliocentric theory—that the Sun is the center of our solar system—resolved all the convoluted tampering that had to be imposed on the Ptolemaic system to enable it to describe reality. Simply stated, the Copernican view disentangled the increasingly complex description of the universe needed to vindicate geocentricism. Consequently, the law of parsimony (also called Ockham's Razor, the axiom that the simplest and most reasonable answer is most probably the correct one) overcame all the objections of those who had a vested interest in keeping the knowledge of reality staid and veiled in traditional philosophical and religious beliefs.

This example of a transition from one common accepted theory of reality to a more accurate one serves to demonstrate a number of critical axioms about the quest for knowledge of reality. For one thing, we realize that the truth about reality—at least as we understand it at any given point in time—is always relative, always a partial view of an endless process of an ever more expansive and comprehensive vision. Thus the heliocentric theory of reality is accurate so long as we are limiting our view of reality to our solar system, but it is hardly a complete or sufficient description of reality once we expand our quest for knowledge beyond this relatively discrete portion of the infinite cosmos.

A second axiom we can infer from this transition or evolution in our knowledge about reality is that, over time, truth will emerge from the clash of theories and opinions simply because the ultimate test of any theory of reality is that it works. The accurate theory is the one that does the most efficient job of describing reality and how it functions. Therefore, any theory must be embraced with a certain degree of flexibility to allow for the fact that, as more information is gathered, we will come to appreciate that every theory describes only a portion of this amazing "elephant" that is reality. In time, each theory will need to be combined with other complementary theories in order to give way to still more inclusive theories of reality, especially if reality is infinite.

A third axiom we can usefully infer from this one example about the journey in the progression of knowledge is that problems and challenges should be viewed as sources of progress in our understanding, rather than as roadblocks or deterrents to learning. Viewed appropriately, a stumbling block in our quest to understand reality is simply valuable feedback urging us to gauge more carefully what our next step should be, even as the guards blocking the doorways in Bahá'u'lláh's analogy force the lover to take the right path.

But getting back to the central thesis of Bahá'u'lláh's message about the lover seeking his beloved, we can now appreciate that to know ahead of time a handful of verities about the process and the nature of the endless quest for our understanding about reality can put us far ahead of where we would otherwise be. We may never have the ability to see the entirety of the "end" in the "beginning" of our quest, but we can, at the very least, have some valuable insights about paths we need not take.

For example, the Bahá'í writings state that there is a purposeful and abiding correspondence between the spiritual and material (metaphysical and physical) dimensions of reality, yet there is a fundamental and changeless distinction between the two types of existence: everything that is essentially spiritual in nature is noncomposite, and thus eternal, whereas everything material is composite and will in time decompose: "Verily the body is composed of physical elements, and every composite must needs be decomposed. The spirit, however, is a single essence, fine and delicate, incorporeal, everlasting, and of God" ('Abdu'l-Bahá, *Selections from the Writings of 'Abdu'l-Bahá*, no. 143.1).

From these axioms, we can easily derive several other important axioms regarding what we can know before we set out on our journey to learn about reality. For example, if material reality is composite, then there can be no such thing as space, at least not in the sense of some portion of material reality that is a complete void. Another axiom we can infer is that if all material reality is composite, then there can be no final, discrete, and indivisible "God Particle."

Likewise, if we know prior to our quest that physical reality is infinite in time, space, and plentitude, then we already know that however big a single "Big Bang" might have been, we, who are viewing this ongoing expansion of the universe from the inside of one of its many galaxies, are unable to appreciate the possibility of other Big Bangs in the past, present, and future. Given the axiom of an infinite universe, we might well consider each Big Bang as a cell in an infinite body, bringing forth life according to its predetermined capacity, and then decomposing or going out of existence when its usefulness has ended.

Perhaps these and other verities will be discovered in time, whether or not they are presently accepted as accurate. Nevertheless, our understanding of reality will advance far more rapidly if we accept this vision of the "end" result as we proceed through these beginning stages of our attempt to understand the universe as a single organic construct. For even though matter is infinitely divisible and infinitely additive, and even though matter has always existed, we know that in the material expression of reality there can be no absolute void because anything material is necessarily filled with particles of "stuff." Likewise, we know that there is a metaphysical dimension of reality, that the physical and metaphysical expressions of reality are exact counterparts of each other, and that there is a precise interplay between these twin expressions of reality. In short, if we accept these axioms at the outset, then we have some important clues about reality before we set off into the woods with flashlights in hand. We will no longer be clueless about that elephant in the tree.

This brings us to the central message Bahá'u'lláh seems to be imparting, in His analogy about the lover's quest, about the nature of knowledge. Bahá'u'lláh completes this story with two statements about what the lover should have learned from his experience, or at least what we, the reader, should learn. The first explains the "moral" at the level of the story. He states that the lover "had found many a secret justice in this seeming tyranny of the watchman, and seen how many a mercy lay hid behind the veil. Out of wrath, the guard had led him who was athirst in love's desert to the sea of his loved one, and lit up the dark night of absence with the light of reunion. He had driven one who was afar, into the garden of nearness, had guided an ailing soul to the heart's physician" (Bahá'u'lláh, The Seven Valleys, p. 23).

Bahá'u'lláh then extrapolates this lesson learned into a broader sort of verity about the nature of seeking knowledge, or at least the attitude with which one should approach the quest. He observes that if we know the end of our quest in the beginning, we are at a great advantage in our journey: "Now if the lover could have looked ahead, he would have blessed the watchman at the start, and prayed on his behalf, and he would have seen that tyranny as justice; but since the end was veiled to him, he moaned and made his plaint in the beginning. Yet those who journey in the garden land of knowledge, because they see the end in the beginning, see peace in war and friendliness in anger" (Bahá'u'lláh, The Seven Valleys, pp. 23–24).

If we apply this wisdom to mankind's quest to understand the nature and operation of the cosmos, we can imagine how much more rapidly our advancement in science (and religion) would have been had we known from the beginning that the sun is the center of the solar system. Even if we did not understand how or why this is true, we might have saved ourselves centuries of bickering and oppression.

THE COLLABORATION BETWEEN PHYSICAL
AND METAPHYSICAL PROPERTIES OF REALITY

Long ago, the study of reality split between those who examine the existence of the spiritual/metaphysical aspects of reality, and those whose study focuses entirely on the physical dimension. But if, as the Bahá'í teachings affirm, both aspects of reality exist, and both work in harmony as collaborative expressions of a single organic creation, then all branches of learning are, in the long run, inherently valuable, true, and indivisibly related to one another: "The spiritual world is like unto the phenomenal world. They are the exact counterpart of each other. Whatever objects appear in this world of existence are the outer pictures of the world of heaven" ('Abdu'l-Bahá, *The Promulgation of Universal Peace*, p. 12). Furthermore, if this "beginning" thesis is correct, then all branches of learning will, in the long run, discover this integration and work collaboratively to advance human understanding. But how much faster this process could take place if this and other equally important foundational verities about reality were already known and accepted!

This is the same assumption we make when we approach an examination of human nature in relation to concepts of morality. But at this point, let us consider another major thesis or core Bahá'í belief about reality—that the twin dimensions or aspects of reality we presently understand (the physical and the metaphysical) are "the exact counterpart of each other" ('Abdu'l-Bahá, *The Promulgation of Universal Peace,* p. 12). The manifest or material world is a sensibly perceptible expression of the concealed realm of the spirit. Indeed, as we will discuss later, our experience in the physical realm is devised precisely to train our essential reality (our self or "soul") in order to prepare it for the continuation of life in the realm of the spirit.

Another even more fascinating axiom about these twin expressions of reality is that, from the point of view of the spiritual realm, these are twin dimensions of a single reality. There is no division between the two, only the illusion of separation from the perspective of the physical point of view: "Those souls who are pure and unsullied, upon the dissolution of their elemental frames, hasten away to the world of God, and that world is within this world. The people of this world, however, are unaware of that world, and are even as the mineral and the vegetable that know nothing of the world of the animal and the world of man" ('Abdu'l-Bahá, *Selections from the Writings of 'Abdu'l-Bahá*, no. 163.6).

TWIN ASPECTS OF THE HUMAN REALITY

In order that we might benefit from discerning the end in the beginning of our discourse about the human reality—the soul and moral principles—let us now establish some of the principal verities about the "self" or "soul" from the Bahá'í texts. We might expedite our journey by establishing those concepts about the human reality that have a direct bearing on theories of morality as they relate to human nature and purpose. By this means we may avoid wandering astray, going down blind alleys, or mistaking some foxfire for the light of truth.

First and foremost, the Bahá'í teachings describe human reality as possessing both physical and metaphysical attributes. The primary or essential human reality is a metaphysical essence, the soul or spirit. But this reality takes its beginning when it emanates from God during the course of physical conception of the individual, whereupon it establishes an associative relationship with the physical organism that is the human body.* This relationship is so aligned that, on a subjective level, we are, for the most part, unable to distinguish

---

* The following quotations illustrate this concept:

"No revelation from God has ever taught re-incarnation; this is a man-made conception. The soul of man comes into being at conception." (Shoghi Effendi, in *Lights of Guidance*, p. 536)

"Secondly, the rational soul, or the human spirit, does not subsist through this body by inherence—that is to say, it does not enter it; for inherence and entrance

between our physical self and our essentially spiritual reality except, perhaps, in moments of meditation and reflection.

From the Bahá'í perspective, this concealed, collaborative relationship between the spiritual and the physical expressions of reality establishes the basis for the central objective in our education during our earthly existence. We are guided by the Manifestations—the Prophets or Teachers sent by God throughout human history—to discover and develop our spiritual nature and powers through a process of physical exercises and relationships, even as we collectively are challenged to discern the divine purpose and spiritual meaning underlying physical reality:

> Know thou that every created thing is a sign of the revelation of God. Each, according to its capacity, is, and will ever remain, a token of the Almighty. Inasmuch as He, the sovereign Lord of all, hath willed to reveal His sovereignty in the kingdom of names and attributes, each and every created thing hath, through the act of the Divine Will, been made a sign of His glory. (Bahá'u'lláh, *Gleanings*, no. 93.1)

---

are characteristics of bodies, and the rational soul is sanctified above this. It never entered this body to begin with, that it should require, upon leaving it, some other abode. No, the connection of the spirit with the body is even as the connection of this lamp with a mirror. If the mirror is polished and perfected, the light of the lamp appears therein, and if the mirror is broken or covered with dust, the light remains concealed" ('Abdu'l-Baha, *Some Answered Questions*, no. 66.3).

Whatever is in the heavens and whatever is on the earth is a direct evidence of the revelation within it of the attributes and names of God, inasmuch as within every atom are enshrined the signs that bear eloquent testimony to the revelation of that Most Great Light. Methinks, but for the potency of that revelation, no being could ever exist. How resplendent the luminaries of knowledge that shine in an atom, and how vast the oceans of wisdom that surge within a drop! (Bahá'u'lláh, *Gleanings*, no. 90.1)

The authoritative Bahá'í texts assert that everything in creation manifests the attributes of the Creator (God); therefore, the twin dimensions of our personal reality have been devised for the explicit purpose of educating us to recognize the Creator and to benefit from our relationship with God. Or stated in more common terms, the Creator, being inherently loving and knowledgeable about the bounty of the gifts He wishes to bestow, desires, like a loving parent, to share His love with a being capable of understanding that love, of benefitting and utilizing this gift, and thence actively or willfully participating in a love relationship capable of infinite progression and refinement.

As human souls, we thus begin our existence operating in association with a mortal body. Through this indirect relationship with spiritual reality, and with our purpose to discover the "Beloved" veiled from us during our earthly life, we are challenged to become willful participants in our own education by discovering and reciprocating this love relationship. But as any seasoned teacher can attest, knowledge cannot be imposed—the student must desire to acquire the tools for learning. Likewise, as any parent fully appreciates, a loving relationship cannot be imposed because it must be bilateral.

It is precisely in this context that Bahá'u'lláh, speaking on God's behalf, states the following profound axiom about this love relationship: "Love Me, that I may love thee. If thou lovest Me not, My love can in no wise reach thee. Know this, O servant" (Bahá'u'lláh, The Hidden Words, Arabic, no. 5). Obviously this statement does not mean that God will refuse to love us unless we instigate this relationship. God's love is already extant and unconditional. The obvious intent of this axiom is that while God's love for us may not be contingent on our response, that love and its bountiful effects "can in no wise reach" us unless we are receptive. To use a commonplace analogy, the phone is forever ringing, but we must willingly pick up the receiver and participate in a bilateral dialogue for a relationship to take place.

Therefore, the object of concealing the one aspect of reality while revealing the other is to encourage us to develop the capacity for discernment, judgment, and willful participation in our own advancement. In another statement of the rationale for this veiling of metaphysical reality, Bahá'u'lláh implies that were we able to behold the concealed realm of the spirit, we would not be able to withhold ourselves from attaining that reality: "Didst thou behold immortal sovereignty, thou wouldst strive to pass from this fleeting world. But to conceal the one from thee and to reveal the other is a mystery which none but the pure in heart can comprehend" (Bahá'u'lláh, The Hidden Words, Persian, no. 41).

While this verse undoubtedly contains various levels of meaning, one major purpose it discloses is that underlying the purposeful concealment of metaphysical reality is the prompting in each of us of the desire to strive for knowledge and enlightenment by gradually uncovering the gems of wisdom concealed in earthly garb. For example, the wise teacher will often withhold answers from a class to encourage students to acquire the tools with which to discover them for themselves.

THE DIVINE EDUCATORS

Because the Creator is a loving, benign, and forgiving Teacher, He has not left us to our own devices in this educational process. He has instilled in our souls an inherent love for, and attraction

21

to, anything that reminds us of that Divine Source from which we emanated as a spiritual essence. More directly, as Administrator of this educational system, He has periodically sent us Teachers (Messengers, Prophets, or what Bahá'u'lláh alludes to as "Manifestations of God") Whose explicit job it is to educate us by degrees—individually and collectively—about the nature of reality and how we can best advance our knowledge, enhance our own refinement, and collectively promulgate an "ever-advancing civilization" (Bahá'u'lláh, *Gleanings,* no. 109.2).

The Bahá'í writings refer to these specialized Teachers as Manifestations because They both instruct us about the object of our life's journey (establishing a love relationship with God) and model how that process can best take place by "manifesting" or demonstrating through example the attributes and spiritual skills by which our life's journey can best be pursued. Though concealed from any sort of obvious physical indication of Their identity or station, these Manifestations are sent whenever human society is in need of another stage in the incremental progress of civilization toward the ultimate goal of fashioning a global community organized and run according to spiritual principles. Christ alludes to this objective as creating the Kingdom of God in an earthly form: "Thy kingdom come, Thy will be done in earth, as it is in heaven" (Matthew 6:10).

The Manifestations are thus distinguished by being spiritually immaculate (perfect expressions of all divine attributes exemplified in human form) and infallible in Their guidance. Through Their writings or utterances, each bequeaths a "revelation" (the "Book" or the "Word of God") that serves as sufficient guidance for a specific period of time—generally referred to in the Bahá'í writings as a "dispensation," or "era," or, poetically, as a "Day." Thus allusions to the "Day of Noah" would refer to the dispensation during which the revelation of Noah guided the peoples to whom He appeared. The Bahá'í writings interpret allusions in the Qur'án to the "Day of Days" or the "Day of Resurrection" as referring to the climactic period in which we are presently living, a period during which humankind will collectively begin to understand fully the process of progressive revelation (how all religions throughout history are really stages in the unveiling of a single coherent religion) and will subsequently establish a world community founded on principles of collective justice and universal suffrage at every level, whether in the community, in a state or territory, or at the level of a global commonwealth.

The Bahá'í teachings thus view the motivating force in human history as the advent of these successive Teachers, each of Whom reiterates the changeless concepts of what it means to be a spiritual human being, while simultaneously advancing the individual and social practices by which spiritual attributes can be implemented in private character and public interaction. As civilization progresses and the efficacy of the previous revelation is weakened and its teachings perverted by its followers, a subsequent Teacher must then be sent to instigate the next stage of our collective development.

Each succeeding revelation, therefore, contains a reiteration of the changeless spiritual principles of human virtue articulated by all the previous Manifestations, plus updated guidance regarding human comportment geared to the newly emerging physical and social condition of humanity. So it is that the attributes which constitute the "good person" remain more or less the same, even though the emphasis on particular virtues may shift or become more amply explicated according to the exigencies of the new "Day."

Stated in more common terms, the new guidance brought with the advent of a new Manifestation might be understood as containing two categories of information. The first is more advanced knowledge about reality through teachings related to both the spiritual and physical dimensions of reality. The second is an updated body of laws geared to befit an evolved social reality and, more often than not, a more complex panoply of social structures and relationships to respond to the needs of a more advanced and more expansive stage of human civilization. ('Abdu'l-Bahá, *The Promulgation of Universal Peace*, pp. 553–54).

One example of how the evolving law complies with and upholds advancing understanding and social conditions is the gradual unfoldment of guidance regarding the equality of women and men. As the Bahá'í writings note, women and men have always been equal in spiritual station and intellectual capacity, as well as in the eyes of God ('Abdu'l-Bahá, *The Promulgation of Universal Peace*, pp. 242–243), but not until the advent of Bahá'u'lláh in the mid-nineteenth century could this reality be explicitly articulated and laws revealed to uphold and implement gender equality in every aspect of the life of society.

The reason for the "delay" in revealing this aspect of reality is fairly obvious but perhaps worth reciting. In terms Bahá'u'lláh Himself cites, there is a "timeliness" involved with the revealed guidance, a wisdom that only the Manifestation can understand in full: "How great the multitude of truths which the garment of words can never contain! How vast the number of such verities as no expression can adequately describe, whose significance can never be unfolded, and to which not even the remotest allusions can be made! How manifold are the truths which must remain unuttered until the appointed time is come! Even as it hath been said: 'Not everything that a man knoweth can be disclosed, nor can everything that he can disclose be regarded as timely, nor can every timely utterance be considered as suited to the capacity of those who hear it'" (Bahá'u'lláh, *Gleanings*, no. 89.3).

Until the modern era, power through the ages was largely derived from physical strength. With the onset of the modern age, power and capacity derived less from the physical strength of the individual and more frequently from newly invented machines. Therefore, while the "end" in this beginning was the gradual recognition of the equality of women and men, the Manifestations of the past did not think it timely to reveal explicit and binding information about this principle of reality until civilization was ready to understand it and capable of implementing it: "The world in the past has been ruled by force, and man has dominated over woman by reason of his more forceful and aggressive qualities both of body and mind. But the balance is already shifting; force is losing its dominance, and mental alertness, intuition, and the spiritual qualities of love and service, in which woman is strong, are gaining ascendancy. Hence the new age will be an age less masculine and more permeated with the feminine ideals, or, to speak more exactly, will be an age in which the masculine and feminine elements of civilization will be more evenly balanced" ('Abdu'l-Bahá, cited in *Compilation of Compilations,* vol. 2, no. 2116, p. 369).

THE THEME OF OUR LESSON FOR THIS "DAY"

In the context of the progressive enlightenment about reality, the central theme of the teachings of Bahá'u'lláh is focused on the unity of humankind as expressed in His blueprint for the creation of a global commonwealth that will accommodate and secure the equality of rights for all the citizens of planet Earth.

Here again, this is not a new objective. The reality or destiny of human civilization has always been world unity and a global commonwealth. This has been the "end" or objective toward which we have been striving by incremental stages. But once the "Day" arrived when both the need and the means were concomitant, the Manifestation (Bahá'u'lláh) was mandated by the Creator to teach us the details about this objective and, just as importantly, to provide us with explicit instructions about how to create the foundational institutions necessary for planetary governance.

Of course, because human civilization is an "ever-advancing" organic process, we will never achieve some final stage of development, whether materially or spiritually. However refined and spiritual human society may become, we can always advance further. This principle of spiritual evolution is equally applicable to us individually. While the physical apparatus of our body peaks around twenty years of age, our essential reality—our conscious soul—has by then barely begun its progress, at least potentially. This is a major axiom about reality from the Bahá'í perspective— that we never attain some final stage of advancement, whether in this life or in the afterlife: "as the perfections of man are infinite, he can also advance in these perfections after his ascension from this world" ('Abdu'l-Bahá, *Some Answered Questions*, no. 24.7).

For though we will never become anything other than a human soul, our essential reality—our soul or self—is ever the source of our personal reality and is capable of infinite progress and refinement. The journey of the human soul is thus endless, yet, in terms of our analogy about seeing the "end" in the "beginning," we are able to comprehend the fundamental objective of this journey early on, even while still in our formative years.

The Bahá'í teachings also affirm that the revelation of Bahá'u'lláh constitutes the most recent guidance from God, even though the educational process of humankind will never cease; there will never be a final Manifestation. As the Manifestation sent to usher in this critical stage in the maturation of humankind, Bahá'u'lláh has revealed guidance geared to the needs of this present age. And while this age does not represent a final point of progress, it does represent a critical turning point that has been anticipated by every previous Manifestation and religion.

As with any organic creation, the condition of maturity is the stage at which an organism has developed all the powers and capacities it needs in order to achieve its inherent purpose. For a fruit tree, maturation is the stage where it is capable of producing fruit. For the human being, it is the stage when we become responsible for our own actions, knowledgeable about our inherent purpose, and actively involved in pursuing spiritual and intellectual development as expressed overtly in service to others.

It is because our global community at long last finds this objective understandable and achievable that the Bahá'í writings attest that this is the period which all previous Manifestations were anxiously awaiting and for which They prepared Their followers.

> Great indeed is this Day! The allusions made to it in all the sacred Scriptures as the Day of God attest its greatness. The soul of every Prophet of God, of every Divine Messenger, hath thirsted for this wondrous Day. All the divers kindreds of the earth have, likewise, yearned to attain it. No sooner, however, had the Daystar of His Revelation manifested itself in the heaven of God's Will, than all, except those whom the Almighty was pleased to guide, were found dumbfounded and heedless. (Bahá'u'lláh, *Gleanings*, no. 7.2)

Therefore, while this dispensation is hardly the "end" of our collective development, this "Day" of Bahá'u'lláh marks the culmination of all previous preparation and the attainment of the age-old objective of all previous revelations—the Kingdom of God manifest in a global polity.

We are thus living in a period of immense transition from the end of one era to the beginning of another. Already humankind is striving to establish some of the foundational characteristics of a global community. Among these are the gradual construction of a world commonwealth of nations, a global economy, universal suffrage, and a universal and lasting peace secured by a voluntary international pact. The most salient feature of this last goal will be an accord affirming that all nations will collectively deter any attempt by an aggressor nation or territory to oppress or to war against a neighboring territory or nation:

> On the societal level, the principle of collective security enunciated by Bahá'u'lláh (see *Gleanings from the Writings of Bahá'u'lláh*, CXVII) and elaborated by Shoghi Effendi (see the Guardian's letters in *The World Order of Bahá'u'lláh*) does not presuppose the abolition of the use of force, but prescribes "a system in which Force is made the servant of Justice," and which provides for the existence of an international peace-keeping force that "will safeguard the organic unity of

the whole commonwealth." (editorial note in Bahá'u'lláh, The Kitáb-i-Aqdas: The Most Holy Book, pp. 240–41)

In conclusion, from the Bahá'í perspective of reality, creation is an organic design whose purpose is to foster and train souls—a process that has neither beginning nor end. The integration, under the hand of the Creator, between the physical and metaphysical dimensions of this ceaseless and infinite creation is constant, unremitting, purposeful, and altruistic. Or, as we have already implied, once our blindfolds have been removed, we will witness, revealed before us, one organic reality with infinite variations and conditions.

2 / PUBLIC AND PRIVATE VIRTUE

Not by the force of numbers, not by the mere exposition of a set of new and noble principles, not by an organized campaign of teaching—no matter how worldwide and elaborate in its character—not even by the staunchness of our faith or the exaltation of our enthusiasm, can we ultimately hope to vindicate in the eyes of a critical and skeptical age the supreme claim of the Abhá Revelation. One thing and only one thing will unfailingly and alone secure the undoubted triumph of this sacred Cause, namely, the extent to which our own inner life and private character mirror forth in their manifold aspects the splendor of those eternal principles proclaimed by Bahá'u'lláh.

—Shoghi Effendi, *Bahá'í Administration,* p. 66

Now that we have discussed some features of the Bahá'í concept of the nature and purpose of reality in general and of human reality in particular, we can begin in earnest to discuss meaningfully what might be considered detrimental to that reality. For however else we might define "sin," on the broadest level it must involve some sort of action that is harmful. And if the concept of what is harmful derives from our belief in the purpose of reality, then we need to understand the logical relationship between our actions and our objectives, both as individuals and as a social collective.

In an ideal society, we would want to have some consistency regarding our views about all of these concerns. For example, while maintaining tolerance for diverse opinions, we would want the attributes of the "good citizen" to be more or less identical to those of the "good person." Likewise, we would want the model of the "good citizen" to be replicated in the overall vision of the "good society." Finally, we would expect any concept of immorality or sin to be consonant with, and reflected in, social mores and civil codes regarding ethical behavior. Ideally, we would want the motive force for both individual and social morality to be enforced by our mutual desire to create a healthy, felicitous, and secure environment.

THE CODIFICATION OF VIRTUE AND VICE

While anyone at any time in human history could provide a general assessment about who are the "good people" and who are the "bad" or "sinful people," numerous cultures, kingdoms, and empires codified virtues and vices, most of which derived from evolving religious traditions.

Until fairly recently, we in the West were most familiar with the codification of virtue and sin that evolved within the Jewish and Christian religious traditions. And even though these two traditions have over time divided into myriad sects, each with its own attitude about moral laws and ethical codes, perhaps the most commonly shared view of sin in the West derives from the Ten Commandments of the Old Testament, Christ's "Sermon on the Mount" in the New Testament, and some of the specific guidance from the letters of St. Paul to the various Christian congregations.

As the Catholic Church evolved, another familiar codification of virtue became known as "the Seven Deadly Sins," as opposed to the seven virtues—the Four Cardinal Virtues and the Three Theological Virtues. Around the end of the sixth century, Pope Gregory formalized these sins as lust, gluttony, greed, sloth, wrath, envy, and pride. Though derived primarily from Plato's description of the virtuous citizen in his fictional republic, the Catholic Church adopted Plato's four cardinal virtues of prudence (good judgment), justice, self-restraint, and courage (Plato, *The Republic*, Book IV, Section II). To these, the Church later added the spiritual virtues of faith, hope, and charity (love) as articulated in St. Paul's oft-cited passage from his first letter to the believers at Corinth.*

The idea of the Seven Deadly Sins was artfully employed by Dante in his allegory *The Divine Comedy* (ca. 1321), in which the character (or persona) Dante tours Hell, Purgatory, and Paradise. In Hell (the Inferno), he views the successively more egregious sinners receiving ever more grievous physical punishment for their mortal sins. In his tour of Purgatory, he views those who have committed venial (forgivable) sins. The distinction between these two realms, however, is not so much the category of sin as the gravity of it.

While not a codification of virtues and vices per se, another tool for determining virtue is inherited from Aristotle's discussion of the Golden Mean in the *Nicomachean Ethics.* The same notion of moderation, discussed before him by Socrates and Plato, is sublimely simple and practical. From this viewpoint, virtue is an area of moderation between the extremes of two antithetical vices. For example, courage is the mean or balance between the vice of cowardice and the vice of foolhardiness.

The key to this philosophy or philosophical tool—whether articulated by Buddha, Confucius, or Thomas Aquinas—is that the "right path" or "virtuous choice" is most often a matter of existential judgment. In other words, rather than memorizing some exact code or canon of legalisms regarding every action we take, the individual must be constantly vigilant, constantly monitoring choices, and always aware that the "mean" or area of virtue may be shifting from situation to situation or from one moment to the next.

---

* "When I was a child, I spake as a child, I understood as a child, I thought as a child, but when I became a man, I put away childish things. For now we see through a glass, darkly, but then face to face. Now I know in part; but then shall I know even as also I am known. And now abideth faith, hope, charity, these three, but the greatest of these is charity" (I Corinthians 13:11–13).

What was a moderate choice yesterday in one situation may be an ill-advised choice today in another context. Therefore, while exercised in the context of moral concepts and standards of what constitutes the "good person," the Golden Mean does not dictate where virtue lies. It simply asserts that the virtuous choice should be guided by this concept of balance or moderation. One modern version of this principle that emerged in the 1960s was the concept of "situational ethics," though this notion that the context should guide us in determining moral choices is distinct from the utilitarian notion that the best choice is that which brings about the greatest good for the greatest number of people.*

Other cultures and religions have codified moral laws and civil laws based on these same moral imperatives. Judaism categorizes transgressions according to intentionality or motive, whether they are against God—violations of the Covenant and all laws attendant thereto—or whether they are sins or transgressions against others. But Judaic scripture acknowledges that while mankind is frail and thus vulnerable to sinful behavior, God is forgiving. Therefore, there are in Judaic law various methods by which believers can atone for sin or violations of law.

As with most tribal communities (such as the Hebrews when the main body of their laws were established), there is often little distinction between civil disobedience and personal immorality. The basis for the Jewish religion is the overriding concept of a coherent community that is effectively a theocracy. But because Judaism as a whole is presently so remote in time from its origins, its laws and concepts of sin are often regarded by believers as traditions more than as part of a theologically based covenant between the believer and God. Indeed, many Jews may consider themselves agnostics or

---

* See, Fletcher, Joseph. *Situation Ethics: The New Morality.* Louisville, KY: Westminster John Knox Press, 1997.

atheists, yet still good Jews according to their obedience to traditional observances that are more culturally than theistically based.

THE CONTEMPORARY DISCONNECT

As a world community, we do not seem to have attained anything approaching the synthesis of personal and social concepts of morality that existed in past cultures. We may not feel that we have any overall agreement between what constitutes these two sets of values—the good person as opposed to the good citizen. This is not so in Islamic cultures or in Hindu communities, where worship and religious practices are often the central organizing force in civil life and social order.

But the vast majority of the world has become dominated by economic concerns as the single gauge of a successful society. Indeed, it would not be incorrect to assert that the portions of the world that wield the greatest military might and economic power find it hard to understand, let alone empathize with, those Islamic movements that seek to realign governance with strict adherence to Islamic law and doctrine as assembled over time in the Sharia. And yet the ongoing violent struggles among Middle Eastern states that formerly seemed quite content with their westernized economies (for example, Egypt, Turkey, Iraq, Iran) demonstrate the dissatisfaction among a vast number of Muslims with the western notion of the "separation of church and state." They wish to utilize the Sharia for both secular and sacred guidance.

THE EVOLVING SENSE OF REALITY
AND THE MORAL PERSPECTIVE

While we would presently be hard put to establish any universally applicable response to the question about the nature of sin, perhaps, as a point of beginning, we can at least agree that we have in our collective sensibilities some notion (whether inherent or learned) that "sin" is a violation of fundamental moral expectations we have about how the "good person" or the "decent person" should behave. Furthermore, we could probably also agree that these moral assessments apply to both personal morality and public civil codes.

But if, in addition to this obvious use of our moral sensibilities, we also believe in a metaphysical dimension of reality, including a soul that is our "essential self," then we are forced to conclude that we cannot segregate the virtues of the inner self from their expression in our public persona. We would find it totally absurd to accept the idea of a spiritually enlightened thief, a benevolent murderer, or an immoral model citizen whom we consider to be the pillar of society.

As we have noted, in the less complex forms of society we may find little distinction between the social and the religious perspectives. Religious beliefs are integrated into the fabric of social practices. Whether in ceremonials of maturation, betrothals, burials, or preparation for hunting or war, a holistic religious or spiritual perspective underlies almost every action, regardless of whether or not the endeavor is overtly "spiritual" or whether it concerns an individual, a family, or the entire tribal community.

In many ways, this integration might correctly be viewed as a healthy and coherent society. There is no conflict between civil or social attitudes and religious beliefs and practices. Neither is there any distinction between the moral perspective and expectations of the individual and the body politic. In all probability, fewer internal conflicts arise about whether to accede to social pressure or to the inner voice of the spirit. The worldview, restricted though it might be in such a society, is likewise holistic, and virtually all aspects of daily life are collaborative expressions of the goals of life in general.

The obvious problem with this tribal model, as history has demonstrated, is the inability of this system to work outside the province of its own community—it has no effective tools for collaborating with the "other." And if there are no permanently assigned boundaries to tribal communities, problems emerge when one tribe bumps up against another tribe. Hence, the chronicles of most tribal communities recount one war after another. A second major problem is the emergence of "tribalism"—the deeply held and central belief that one's own tribe is necessarily superior to all other tribes—once "other tribes" are encountered. A third inescapable problem arises from the fact that a tribal community—one that does not wish to accept any established territorial boundaries and that has not developed agriculture and other essential tools for a stable community life—is often based on a hunter-gatherer or nomadic existence where the tribe lives off the land over a vast and varied area. Here again, tribal war is inevitable.

Even if a tribal community settles in a defined area and develops all the tools necessary for continuity and stability, another problem emerges with growth and development. Such a community will naturally require more complex governance, and, alas, such a community will become a prime target for those tribes that have not advanced to this more complex condition. In short, with relatively few human resources, a tribe will be hard-pressed to maintain both a consistent agricultural workforce and a strong and ready warrior class.

For these and other reasons that are also obvious in any study of tribal communities, it is not hard to appreciate that the tribal model is effective for only a particular stage early in the evolution of a people or culture. The tribal mentality is thus not inherently good or bad, any more than a stage in our personal development can be so characterized. In our childhood, we are necessarily totally dependent on parental love, guidance, protection, and provisions. In our early teenage years, we enter a period of tenuous balance between our desire and need to develop tools and behavioral patterns of limited independence, and our continuing need for some degree of parental assistance.

We could describe other intermediary stages of personal development, but the point is that none of these stages is simple, complete, or permanent. Until we achieve maturity, we appreciate that every stage is necessarily a process that, to be successful, must be fluid and susceptible to constant monitoring, and receptive to adjustments of rules and to the degree of authority imposed or accepted. Even once we have attained maturity we remain a work in progress, forever attempting to improve our knowledge and refine our character, even though we have completed the preparatory stages essential for this transition to a certain degree of autonomy.

These same observations hold true for the development of governance in the evolution of community building. As civilizations become more advanced, with ever-growing populations, they require increasing levels of bureaucracy to accomplish collective goals, and consequently, a more complex social infrastructure. New systems and methodologies must be adopted to meet the needs of an ever more complex web of interdependence among the individuals and communities within the city-state, nation-state, or empire.

The same causes of conflict that result in tribalism also run through the chronicle of human civilization as a whole. When complex and ever-expanding social entities encroach on neighboring territories, debates about boundaries or natural resources are often the result. Analogous to the maturation of the individual, these conflicts constitute advancing stages of evolution prior to what will eventually result in the inevitable emergence of a peaceful global community that will characterize the maturation of human history on planet Earth. Once this goal has been attained, the growth of our world commonwealth will be a process of continuous refinement rather than a major transformation of structure.

Shoghi Effendi makes a profound observation in this regard when he asserts that the global commonwealth designed by Bahá'u'lláh is the furthermost expression of governance for our planetary community, even though it is capable of infinite refinement:

The emergence of a world community, the consciousness of world citizenship, the founding of a world civilization and culture—all of which must synchronize with the initial stages in the unfoldment of the Golden Age of the Bahá'í Era—should, by their very nature, be regarded, as far as this planetary life is concerned, as the furthermost limits in the organization of human society, though man, as an individual, will, nay must indeed as a result of such a consummation, continue indefinitely to progress and develop. (Shoghi Effendi, *The World Order of Bahá'u'lláh,* p. 163)

3 / BREAKING THE LAW

Think not that I am come to destroy the law, or the prophets: I am not come to destroy, but to fulfill. For verily I say unto you, till heaven and earth pass, one jot or one tittle shall in no wise pass from the law, till all be fulfilled. Whosoever therefore shall break one of these least commandments, and shall teach men so, he shall be called the least in the kingdom of heaven, but whosoever shall do and teach them, the same shall be called great in the kingdom of heaven. (Matthew 5:17–19)

So long as there is a general accord about human purpose and the social infrastructures necessary to assist and secure that purpose, most problems can be worked out in any given society. More intense problems emerge when a social order or civilization needs to embrace a greater diversity of peoples as well as divergent beliefs about moral or organizational principles. As was the case with Ptolemy's inadequate, geocentric description of the cosmos, the social contract now has to become more sophisticated and advanced to accommodate the increased complexity of reality. And if the social contract becomes more complex without becoming more accurate, it will, like the Ptolemaic theory, become more convoluted and ineffectual. It will also quickly become subject to collapse as the bulwarks of its foundation become fragile or dysfunctional.

Because reality as originally described has changed, a completely new approach to order must be introduced that can accommodate the revised, expanded, and more complex understanding of reality. In such a case, the solution to conflict becomes predicated on the ability of those in charge to step back, to extricate themselves from attachment to the archaic and traditional views and systems that no longer work effectively, and thereby to become receptive to an entirely new perception of reality.

This is precisely what Bahá'u'lláh did in the midst of the warfare among empires in the mid-nineteenth century. He presented a blueprint for a global commonwealth to supplant or coordinate what would emerge as the intense post-colonial nationalism of the twentieth century. Doubtless at the time, the epistles of Bahá'u'lláh were received with scorn by such lofty figures as Napoleon III (foremost monarch of his day in the West), Nicolaevich Alexander II (Czar of Russia), Francis Joseph (emperor of Austria and king of Hungary), Pope Pius IX, Sultán 'Abdu'l-'Azíz (head of the Ottoman Empire), Kaiser Wilhelm I (the Prussian king), and Násiri'd-Dín Sháh (king of Persia). But by the end of the nineteenth century, these emperors and their empires had fallen, or soon would.

Early into the twentieth century, Bahá'u'lláh's concept of a global commonwealth was no longer an alien or aberrant notion. Technology had united the diverse peoples of the world. The League of Nations was proposed in 1918 after the stark horrors of World War I. This drive for an effective solution to global warfare evolved over thirty years and emerged in 1945, after the gruesome inhumanity of World War II, as the United Nations.

Violent upheavals, foretold clearly by Bahá'u'lláh, had convincingly taught humankind what reason and forewarning could not—that the world had reached maturity, at least structurally: the world was becoming a single, interdependent community. Bahá'u'lláh had provided the blueprint for how this physical, social fact could become a collaborative and coherent system based on collective justice so that a permanent peace could eventually be secured. Currently, the wisdom of His forewarnings and major parts of His detailed solutions to establishing a global community, which only decades ago may have seemed too idealistic or farfetched and shocking, are generally acknowledged as being urgently needed, even if the source of these ideas is not yet recognized.

For example, as a world community, we are all too aware that war anywhere has the potential to ignite conflict everywhere. The polarization of forces in the Cold War that immediately followed on the heels of World War II left the world with an uneasy peace that, on several occasions, came within a hair's breadth of escalating into a world-engulfing holocaust.* Now, with the breakdown of that polarization, we actually have a more complex and increasingly dangerous world in which many nations are capable of instigating global warfare, and where no single power can provide economic or military security for what has emerged as a bewildering conglomeration of conflicts and contentions.

Not unexpectedly, the more our global community becomes destabilized amidst the panoply of conflicts and terrorism, the more we also come to realize more fully and profoundly that we are one people on a single planet and that all of us desire the same essential objectives—peaceful neighborhoods; opportunities for education and employment; freedom from oppression and prejudice; and the fundamental necessities for survival, such as housing, potable water, clothing, affordable sources of energy, food, and healthcare. Ask people in any neighborhood or village in any country in the world and their answers will most likely be the same. Strange, then, that the ordinary peoples of the world can be in agreement while the political structures devised to uphold and assist them to achieve their desires are presently the most incorrigible, resistant, and ostensibly insurmountable obstacles in the path of our desperate need for collaborative change.

To state a very complex matter in a series of obvious axioms, the world's moral perspective has become totally out of sync with

---

* The Cuban Missile Crisis in the fall of 1962 was the most well-documented instance in which nuclear warfare between the US and the USSR was within minutes of being instigated.

both its scientific advancements and its social structures. Diverse views of reality about metaphysics and physics, about governance and human rights, about God and His sequence of religions, are all suddenly bumping up against one another. Few, if any, methods remain to discover or establish a refuge—some place or some way of life impervious to, or secure from, what is taking place in the world at large. The microcosm and the macrocosm have become so interwoven that a moral but responsible citizen can no longer in good conscience attempt to remain oblivious to the needs of his or her fellow-citizens, whether they be next door in our securely gated community or on the other side of the world.

ESCALATION IN THE WAR BETWEEN SCIENCE AND RELIGION

The dissonance that presently permeates our atmosphere is not new, nor is it the beginning of the disconnect or discord between concepts of morality and the scientific / technological perspectives about reality. But the exponential advances in technology in the nineteenth and twentieth centuries have made these battles increasingly relevant to the entire parade of world affairs, as well as to our own individual lives. Instead of taking place within a single community, nation, or culture, the battles about the moral perspective of the human condition and human purpose have become matters at the center of world tensions overall.

Consider, for example, past coherence between moral and civil codes. The Judaic law of the Sabbath forbidding work may have been devised to impose on landowners the requirement that slaves or bound laborers be given a day of relief from the physical demands of manual labor. But since this law was part of a religious code, violation was considered a "sin" against God. In other words, this law was "fear of God" translated into "fear of civil-legal reprisal."

But the law itself did not emanate from the spontaneous sympathy of the wealthy for the plight of the disenfranchised masses, nor from some mass demonstrations by the working class. An appreciation of spiritual equality and the fundamental civil rights of human beings was the more lofty rationale for the law, but prior to gaining an awareness of this spiritual motive, societies observed the law out of fear of punishment—a first step in this education about the inextricable connection between moral principle and social ordinance, or, more lofty still, the link between the twin aspects of reality: the physical and the spiritual.

Therefore, when Christ and His disciples seemed to be breaking the law of the Sabbath, first by harvesting some ears of corn to eat as they roamed the hills, and later that same day when Christ healed a man's hand, the Pharisees considered Christ as having "sinned" and also as being liable for civil prosecution because, though Judaea was occupied by Romans, the Jewish Sanhedrin was a theocratic government operating within the purview of Pontius Pilate, the Roman prefect responsible for the province of Judaea under Emperor Tiberius:

> And he entered again into the synagogue; and there was a man there which had a withered hand. And they watched him, whether he would heal him on the sabbath day; that they might accuse him. And he saith unto the man which had the withered hand, "Stand forth." And he saith unto them, "Is it lawful to do good on the sabbath days, or to do evil? to save life, or to kill?" But they held their peace. And when he had looked round about on them with anger, being grieved for the hardness of their hearts, he saith unto the man, "Stretch forth thine hand." And he stretched *it* out, and his hand was restored whole as the other. And the Pharisees went forth, and straightway took counsel with the Herodians against him, how they might destroy him. (Mark 3:1–6)

Unlike Judaic society, Christian civilization—if any particular territory or period in history could be so designated with complete accuracy—emerged within a culture already formed, within a Roman social order that had a highly developed social and civil contract and infrastructure. For a time, this was a propitious coalescence for both the religion and the government. Sophisticated as the Roman Empire was, socially and technologically, it had almost no effective form of unified religious belief immediately prior to Christianity other than worship of the emperor himself, together with some remnants of the polytheism it had inherited from ancient Greece.

Thus, when Emperor Constantine seized upon the vibrancy and energy of the emerging religious fervor of Christianity in the fourth century (325 CE), this act may have been to some extent a desperate political attempt (ultimately a futile one) to reunite an empire that had lost its sense of pride and unity of purpose. But while during the next few centuries the Germanic tribes from the north would overpower the empire, this somewhat arbitrary confluence of "church" and "state" greatly affected, and in the long run "afflicted," the evolution of Christian doctrine and dogma (Brown, *The Rise of Western Christendom*).

Of course, this alliance occurred three hundred years after the advent of Christ, and Constantine's son tried to reverse this trend. Furthermore, according to the Muslim and the Bahá'í view of history, no more than three hundred years later, the religion Christ had revealed had become so perverted from those spiritual principles He had articulated and manifested, so deteriorated in form and function, that God apparently thought it timely to send forth another Manifestation with a new revelation.

The year 622 CE marks the beginning of Islam with Muhammad's emigration from Mecca to Medina. And while He explicitly vindicated Christ's station and teachings, Muhammad also brought new concepts of moral law and social order, thereby continuing where Christ left off, just as Christ had promised that the Comforter (Paraclete) would do:

Nevertheless I tell you the truth. It is expedient for you that I go away, for if I go not away, the Comforter will not come

44

unto you. But if I depart, I will send him unto you. . . . I have yet many things to say unto you, but ye cannot bear them now. Howbeit when he, the Spirit of truth, is come, he will guide you into all truth, for he shall not speak of himself, but whatsoever he shall hear, that shall he speak, and he will shew you things to come. He shall glorify me, for he shall receive of mine, and shall shew it unto you. (John 6:7–14)*

Muhammad's teachings specifically rectify the most crucial perversion of Christ's teachings, which would also become the most pernicious source of schism between the western and eastern churches: the matter of Christology—the question of the essential station and nature of Christ. Muhammad asserted that Christ was a Manifestation or Prophet of God, not God incarnate, whereas most of Christianity (following the Council of Nicaea in 325 CE) had determined that Christ was God incarnate. Muhammad also rejected the inference on the part of Christian clerics that the station of Christ as Messiah was superior to, or distinct from, that of the previous Prophets or the ones Who would follow, such as Muhammad Himself.

For example, in discussing the continuity of the revealed law and guidance sent down by God to accord with the advancement of human civilization, Muhammad proclaims the following regarding the transition from the tribal law of retribution introduced by Moses to the law of forgiveness introduced by Christ:

> It was We who revealed the Law (to Moses); therein was guidance and light. By its standard have been judged the Jews,

---

* "His Holiness Christ made a covenant concerning the Paraclete [Comforter] and gave the tidings of His coming" ('Abdu'l-Bahá, in *Compilation of Compilations,* vol. 1, p. 114). "References in the Bible to 'Mt. Paran' and 'Paraclete' refer to Muhammad's Revelation" (Shoghi Effendi, *Letters from the Guardian to Australia and New Zealand,* p. 41).

by the Prophet who bowed (as in Islam) to Allah's Will, by the Rabbis and the doctors of Law: for to them was entrusted the protection of Allah's Book, and they were witnesses thereto: therefore fear not men, but fear Me, and sell not My Signs for a miserable price. If any do fail to judge by (the light of) what Allah hath revealed, they are (no better than) Unbelievers. We ordained therein for them: "Life for life, eye for eye, nose for nose, ear for ear, tooth for tooth, and wounds equal for equal." But if anyone remits the retaliation by way of charity, it is an act of atonement for himself. And if any fail to judge by (the light of) what Allah hath revealed, they are (no better than) wrongdoers.

And in their footsteps We sent Jesus the son of Mary, confirming the Law that had come before him. We sent him the Gospel. Therein was guidance and light, and confirmation of the Law that had come before him, a guidance and an admonition to those who fear Allah. Let the People of the Gospel judge by what Allah hath revealed therein. If any do fail to judge by (the light of) what Allah hath revealed, they are (no better than) those who rebel. (Qur'án 5:44–47)*

In this same vein later in Surah 5, Muhammad reveals how, like the Christians, the Jews also believed the law of God revealed to them was final and complete: "The Jews say: 'Allah's hand is tied up.' Be their hands tied up and be they accursed for the (blasphemy) they utter. Nay, both His hands are widely outstretched: He giveth and spendeth (of His bounty) as He pleaseth" (Qur'án 5:64).

Later in this same discussion, Muhammad warns that the Christians had overstepped the bounds of their own religion in concluding that Christ is God or that Christ is more than a Manifestation

---

* This and all further citations from the Qur'án are a synthesis of the translation of the work of Abdullah Yusuf Ali and my own work.

or Prophet: "Christ the son of Mary was no more than a Messenger; many were the Messengers that passed away before him" (Qur'án 5:75).

In keeping with this logic in His discussions about God's plan of progressive revelation, Muhammad reveals in another Surah the exact same fact about His own station: "Muhammad is no more than a Messenger: many were the Messengers that passed away before him" (Qur'án 3:144).

LAW AND ORDER AS ORGANIC CREATIONS

Underlying the entirety of this theme of the connection between individual behavior and social order—regardless of whether we are examining various governmental forms or any of those advocated by world religions—is the fact that the revelation of law, similar to our evolving enlightenment about reality as a whole, is an organic and progressive process. Consequently, when the Prophets say that the law of God will never pass away, They are referring to the essential need for law as well as to the process whereby laws are gradually unfolded as they become timely. Christ explains this concept immediately before He reveals His own updating of law in Matthew, chapters 5–7:

> Think not that I am come to destroy the law, or the prophets: I am not come to destroy, but to fulfill. For verily I say unto you, Till heaven and earth pass, one jot or one tittle shall in no wise pass from the law, till all be fulfilled. Whosoever therefore shall break one of these least commandments, and shall teach men so, he shall be called the least in the kingdom of heaven: but whosoever shall do and teach *them*, the same shall be called great in the kingdom of heaven. (Matthew 5:17–19)

But whereas the revelation of Muhammad advanced and consolidated personal and civil law, as well as the study of both physical and metaphysical aspects of reality, Christianity—during the same period of what is designated in Western history as the Dark Ages and the early and late Medieval Era—wandered far astray from almost every major teaching Christ had revealed.

During this same period of the decline of Western civilization, Christian institutions, and Christian theology, the influence of advanced thought introduced by Muslim scholars resulted in a more rigorous study of "natural philosophy," as well as revised interpretations of Christ's station, and a clear and coherent explication of the process whereby God educates humankind throughout history by means of a sequence of Vicegerents or divinely empowered Messengers.

But because Islam spread only as far as France in western Europe and was stopped by the Byzantine Empire at Constantinople in the East, Christianity continued to prevail in Europe. Its followers were largely oblivious to the theological teachings of Islam, though they did benefit indirectly from the advancement in learning that was disseminated through the influential centers of Muslim scholarship in Córdoba and throughout the Iberian Peninsula.

SCIENCE AND RELIGION IN WESTERN EUROPE

The western schism between science and religion had taken root in the Middle Ages, and the battle lines became ever more apparent. By the end of the fourteenth century and into the fifteenth century, Islam had breathed new life into ideas about social order and foundational theological concepts.* Wherever Islam spread,

---

* It had also infused into the collective minds of its followers the notion that social order, governance, and religion were most effective when synthesized into a single collaborative enterprise—a type of theocracy, but not anything like what passes today for the concept that Muhammad described and taught. For, like Christianity before it, Islam was doomed from the start when it effectively segregated governance and guidance from the core of teachings focused on the spiritual life of its adherents.

the model of social justice and the alliance of spiritual and civil law became implanted during what is regarded by most historians as the Golden Age of Islam.

In retrospect, therefore, we can see that the Christian religion was still being promulgated a thousand years past its "shelf life."* It possessed no scripturally based concept of social order. Neither did it possess a uniform social contract to support its core beliefs, other than the centralized authority of the pope as perpetrated through the monarchs under his sway.

Then, fifteen hundred years after Christ, and almost a thousand years after the appearance of Muhammad, several core beliefs of the Roman Church gave rise to the schism between the Catholic version of Christian belief and that of the instigators of the so-called Protestant rebellion. After the Reformation, initiated most famously by Martin Luther and John Calvin in the sixteenth century, Protestant sects and denominations established themselves. Their beliefs were based primarily on literalist applications of the epistolary guidance by Paul to the nascent Christian communities and congregations some fifteen hundred years earlier—his oxymoronic idea that there could be "antinomian"** institutions (Hatcher, *The Arc of Ascent*).

---

* From the Bahá'í view, a new Manifestation appears only after the previous revelation has become distorted and new problems have emerged that require an entirely different remedy to cure the ills of human society.

** "Anti-law": Paul preached against the idea that following a code of law, such as the Jewish laws, could be a means for attaining justification or salvation. Rather, he emphasized personal or individual belief and relationship with God through Christ as being the true path to redemption. The effective instigator of the Reformation, Martin Luther, rejected the idea, accordingly, that any religious institution or dogma or sacrament is necessary for this individual relationship to be established or maintained. Likewise, he concluded, it was God who could forgive sin, and no institution need serve as an intermediary for that request for forgiveness to be offered up.

This fact alone—the establishment of an institution whose founding principle is to reject the institutionalization of one's relationship with God—sowed the seeds of an exponential splintering of the Protestant movement into myriad sects and sub-sects. In many cases, a split would occur based on some slight variation in a ritual, such as baptism, while in other cases splintering would occur because of divergent interpretations of issues such as concepts of salvation, the station of Christ, the question of predestination, belief in the virgin birth, or ideas concerning the afterlife.

The end result of this widening gap between moral law and civil law in Western Europe is that during the Middle Ages—a thousand years after 325 CE, when the Christian religion became the state religion of the Roman Empire, though overrun in the coming centuries by non-Christian and pre-Christian tribes—there emerged two categories of law for two categories of offense. There were ecclesiastical courts to oversee the conduct of believers in relation to moral or religious law and its canon, and there were civil courts to oversee obedience to civil law, which had emerged largely from a synthesis of Roman law and Anglo-Saxon common law.

And while in time in the codification of Christian law there would emerge distinctions among categories of violation of law— venial sins versus mortal sins—this larger expression of division between the social contract and the religious contract was instrumental in virtually every contention and schism that would dog Christianity and ultimately result in the present-day war between science and religion, the separation between church and state, and the dissipation of Christian unity among thousands of individual sects, each with its particular leader and theological take on the most fundamental Christian beliefs.

THE PLAGUE OF COLONIZATION

Obviously, this same division regarding law and the study of reality was destined to spread throughout the territories Christian empires would invade, subdue, and colonize. The end result was the coerced conversion of native peoples. Those who survived the plagues of newly introduced European diseases, against which the indigenous peoples had no immunity, would most often be enslaved and forced to harvest the rich natural resources from their now-occupied homeland.

Over the course of time, remnants of indigenous cultural and religious practices would bring about revolution or, in some cases, more gradual struggles for independence. But during the course of Western history, the center of Christian power and authority in this process of conquest and colonization shifted successively from one European empire to another until almost every territory in the world was claimed by one of the several nations in this sequence of empire-building: Portugal, Spain, the Netherlands, France, Britain, and the United States.

While the motive of spreading the Christian Faith to save the souls of native peoples was touted, especially by the Catholic empires, the material benefits of colonialism were the obvious driving force underlying the arguments justifying all this decimation of indigenous peoples in the name of "God" and "country." And as any historian will readily acknowledge, this empire-building left in its wake the ruthless and "Godless" destruction of native peoples, of natural resources, and rich and diverse cultures. It likewise introduced an endemic, schizophrenic attitude among those cultures who were forced to assume the values and practices of this aberrant and contradictory version of almost everything Christ had originally taught about the supremacy of love over rules and rituals, and about the ascendancy of the lowly and the pure-hearted over wealthy, ruthless, and self-serving rulers.

The same distortion of religious law would occur more gradually and subtly within the Islamic empire as it rapidly spread throughout the nations of North Africa, the Middle East, and into Spain. Personal and civil law in Islam derive primarily from the

Qur'án itself or else from the traditions regarding Muhammad's sayings and the virtues He modeled in His own life. Consequently, there was less wiggle-room for the perversion of religious and civil codes—though internecine battles for power were ceaseless, as was the confluence of the secular with the sacred in terms of who was in charge.

The laws of Muhammad are clearly more numerous, more complex, and more explicit than those of Christ, and more au courant than those of Judaism, though foundational religious practices, such as prayer, fasting, and meditation are similar in every religion. Thus, while much of Sharia law is based on the authoritative utterances of Muhammad, Islam evolved over the centuries under various religious and political leaders from both the Sunni and Shia sects. As a result, certain laws were interpreted, amended, or, in some cases, simply invented to suit the preferences of those who believed they had authority. Among the most prominent of these were the judges (*qadis*), the religious leaders (*imams*), and the religious scholars (*ulama*). Islamic legal opinions also relied on parables or analogies taken either from the Qur'án or from incidences narrated about the life of the Prophet.

The schism or disconnect in Islam was thus not precisely between the spiritual teachings and the law, at least according to Shia doctrine and the Bahá'í view. Rather, it was the eventual weakening of the enlightenment that the Prophet had revealed, as well as the concept of social justice He had modeled, derived from the seeds of relentless and ruthless division perversely insinuated at the time of Muhammad's death.

While on His deathbed, Muhammad is said to have asked for a pen and paper, presumably to appoint His successor, even though He had made a public oral designation of His son-in-law and cousin, Ali, to lead the Faith upon His passing. Muhammad's expression of this succession is portrayed in the ḥadíth or tradition concerning the "two weighty things" that the Prophet bequeathed

His followers—the Book or Word of God (the Qur'án) and His family (the leadership under the authority of male lineal descendants). According to this tradition, called the hadíth of the pond of Khumm, Muhammad had openly appointed Ali as His successor, and the firstborn of Ali's male lineal descendants thereafter.

In spite of the fact that Ali was eventually elected as the fourth caliph, the governmental structure and process was contested and corrupted from the start. The result was that from its inception, Islam was divided into two distinct sects—the Shias, who believe in the succession of Ali and the other eleven Imams, and the Sunnis, who believe in the authority of the elected rule of the caliphate.

Because of this irreparable schism, each sect over time devised similar but distinct codes of law, as well as differing religious traditions and practices. Today we witness bloody warfare in Islamic countries in which these sects vie for power, as well as divisions about which laws of the Sharia are intended to be followed in the context of contemporary society.

The impact of this early schism in Islam was compounded over time, as neither sect was fully governed according to the values of the Prophet. Consequently, the history of leadership, even in the early stages of the emerging Islamic empire, reads like a list of warring factions—not only between Shia and Sunni, but in the struggle from one dynasty to another to seize power, both secular and sacred, and the attempt to perpetrate succession within a particular tribe, clan, or family.

Thus, while the sharia (the "path" for Muslims) is not entirely tattered by these incessant struggles, it has come to include the laws of the Qur'án and laws derived from the sunnah (the pattern of conduct discerned from the life of Muhammad as exemplar of His own teachings) and, over time, the variety of interpretations, explications, and applications of often abstruse guidance. As many scholars have elucidated this process, it has become clear that some practices, such as the apparel designated for women, derive from passages that were abused or else interpreted according to the personal proclivities of clerics at a given time in a particular Muslim state (Balyuzi, *Muhammad and the Course of Islam*).

ISLAM IN THE WEST

The history of Islam, as both a religion and as a series of empires, is complex and fascinating. Unfortunately, Islam was little studied by students of Western civilization until the recent revival of pan-Islamic movements aimed at reasserting the confluence of the secular and sacred authority that Islamic theocracies once wielded.

It is only in retrospect that the Western student of Islam can appreciate how much positive influence Islam exerted, especially during the beginnings of what is usually discussed from a Western perspective as the Renaissance—a rebirth of classical studies that could not have occurred without the influence of Islamic scholarship. For this reason, what now seems an aberrant and unexpected resurgence of Islamic influence in global politics is, when understood in the context of a less-biased study of world history, an understandable and natural outcome.

During the seventh century, Islam experienced a fundamental unity in spite of the initial schism between those who followed the elected succession of caliphs (the Sunni) and those who believed in the succession of lineal descendants of the imamate (the Shia). But soon afterward, a series of civil wars developed in the struggle for leadership. The dominance of the Sunni over the Shia minority established the series of caliphates, the list of which effectively outlines the history of Islam to the present day.

Though elected by Muslims, the line of caliphs can be grouped according to the succession of dynasties that successively overthrew one another. Under Muhammad, Islam spread throughout the entire Arabian Peninsula (622–632). Upon His death, a series of internecine struggles for power continued from one dynasty to another, similar in complexity and intensity to the division between the Catholic Church and Protestant denominations in Christianity. The primary divisions of this history focus on the

Umayyad Caliphate in Mecca (661–750), which was overthrown by the Abbasid Caliphate in Mecca (750–1517), and end with the Ottoman Caliphate in Constantinople (1517–1924).

However, this overview is so simplistic as to be virtually useless because it glosses over the wars that occurred as each successive dynasty vied for power, as territories that had converted to Islam became independent of any central authority, and as governance and religious authority became divided. Even the most cursory review of the history of Islam reveals how these intense and relentless struggles for power within the religion, as well as among the territories that had been conquered and converted, diluted immensely the positive worldwide influence that Islam might otherwise have had. The unity of religious principles and governance—as a coherent and inseparable process instigated by the Prophet and continuing for the first few decades after His demise—could not survive intact amid the chaos of relentless and ruthless quests for power.

And yet, while we are witnessing the present-day emergence of what seems to be a pan-Islamic movement, there does not remain within Islam any firmly shared view about how particular laws in the Sharia have been interpreted and applied over time, or from one culture to culture. This diversity of interpretation is particularly relevant to guidance about human rights, the equality of women and men, the tolerance toward people of other faiths, and, perhaps most weighty of all, the idea that Muhammad condoned literal jihad* to spread or secure His religion. Even more crucial than any of these views is the interpretation that there would be

---

* The word jihad means "struggle." It appears no fewer than forty-one times in the Qur'án, often as a reference to individual believers' attempts to strive for spiritual edification or development. In the proper context, the term applies to the spiritual struggle within each believer, the struggle to construct a strong religious community or society, and—in the most misunderstood application— the right or obligation to defend the community physically when necessary, even as the Prophet had to defend Himself and His followers after being attacked by the Quraish in Mecca. Muhammad subsequently fled to Medina and fought these same forces until He had subdued them.

no Manifestations or revelations after Muhammad (Sonn, *Islam: A Brief History*).

REALITY IS WHERE WE ARE

We could attempt to apply sweeping generalizations about how so-called Christian civilization advanced compared to so-called Islamic civilization, but the fact is that no generalizations work very well in portraying what has become a web of infinite complexity regarding the history of civilization throughout the world insofar as the past two thousand years are concerned, especially regarding principles of governance in conjunction with religious belief.

The most useful conclusion we can derive is that by the time Bahá'u'lláh sent His epistles exhorting leaders, both Christian and Muslim, of the world to accept His revelation, it no longer mattered what injustices we had perpetrated against one another. It is only important to appreciate that we are now one people in one global community in dire need of a coordinated and collaborative infrastructure. It is likewise crucial to understand that all religions are sequential, unified, and coordinated expressions of the systematic plan of God to bring about human enlightenment and the advancement of civilization, and that without some confluence of the sacred with the secular, no remedy for our world community is feasible.

THE GOOD CITIZEN VIS-À-VIS THE FAITHFUL BELIEVER

Unfortunately, and unavoidably, what began as an anomaly within Christianity evolved into what we now consider the "Western" view of reality and, to a large extent, a predominant world view—that religion and social order should operate in two entirely separate spheres without any significant interdependence.

Though the issue has a longstanding history in the development of various governments throughout the world, the contemporary— almost universal—acceptance of this concept assumed particular importance in the drafting of the American Constitution. Derived to a certain extent from the opinions of John Locke in his discussion of the "social contract," the statements by both Jefferson and Madison upholding the principle of separation of church and state alluded primarily to the theme of the First Amendment. The overall logic upheld by all supporters of this concept is that the purview of governance should have no influence or authority in the realm of individual conscience.

While the obvious intent of all commentaries on the subject in the early stage in the evolution of American jurisprudence was to prevent any single religion from being imposed as the state religion or dictating how governance should be ordered or maintained, the inevitable outcome, which at the time could not realistically have been foreseen, has been the complete separation of morality from governance. This separation has instigated relentless fiery debates, which have shed very little light on the means for a possible solution. Effectively, the general sensibilities of the vast majority of the population have been subverted to uphold the rights of individuals and discrete minorities, thereby eliminating any hint of religious tradition from most aspects of governance or daily life.

This is an oversimplification, to be sure. Certainly ideas of justice and equality, together with other major spiritual and moral principles, are at the forefront of social law and governmental concern. But the negative effects of this segregation of the social contract from any coherent moral perspective are also readily apparent.

In North America there are two fundamental categories of education: state-funded public education devoted entirely to secular subjects, and private schools, charter schools, and home schooling, which may or may not study philosophy or religious beliefs. The end result is that there is presently little opportunity for students to study in any systematic way the history of ideas and beliefs, which are perhaps the single most important subjects for understanding the foundation of every significant historical movement or civilization. Another unfortunate outcome of this segregation in the system of learning is that we end up with two distinct and often antithetical standards by which to assess human success or failure. There are the secular standards of power and monetary "success" that have come to define the "good citizen" and the "political leader." Less noticed and of less importance in terms of social theories of value are those standards that define the "good person," a metaphysical concept delineated by abstract notions of virtue.

It is against this historical backdrop that we can begin to realize how the word *sin* takes its meaning from the moral or religious context in which it is used. If the society has a shared moral perspective and a coherent and integrated view of reality, there may not be much difference between breaking a civil law and breaking a spiritual law. In such a society, social ordinance finds its origin and basis in a direct or indirect relationship with shared axioms about the material and divine aspects of reality.

As we have already noted, the most coherent, healthy, and happy society is one in which the objectives of the individual citizen uphold and advance the objectives of the collective body politic, where being a "good citizen" is synonymous with being a "good person" or a "valuable person." But as we have also seen—rarely, and never for an extended period of time—is there unity of thought about either aspect of reality, inasmuch as both perspectives are constantly evolving and advancing.

As societal norms might dictate in most countries, we could call a plumber "good" because he is polite, kind, and considerate. Furthermore, he and his wife may have raised really fine children. Together, the plumber and his wife may have helped the community by performing many civic duties and serving in a number of important charities.

Unfortunately, this same plumber has never really become particularly adept at his job. He is just not good with his hands, for one thing. He knows this, and he often apologizes when he has to go back on a job to fix what he has previously done, especially when someone's carpet is sopping wet from a leaky valve or a badly soldered pipe.

Next door to him lives the village dentist. Unlike the plumber, the dentist is amazingly capable. His fees are reasonable, and his work is beyond compare. His root canals are painless, and his patients rave about his work. His reputation is such that people travel long distances to see him. Consequently, his waiting room is always filled.

Unfortunately, this same dentist is lacking in moral values. He cheats on his wife. He drinks much more than he should. He does almost nothing to help his wife with the kids because he is too busy with golf, socializing with his pals, and gambling. And yet he has been nominated for "citizen of the year" by the neighborhood community because of his dentistry practice and the sizeable donations he makes to the city park—though he makes these contributions only because his accountant says he needs the tax deduction and because the city council has agreed to display his name prominently on the dedication plaque.

So, is the plumber sinful because he is incompetent? Is the dentist a good citizen because he serves the dental hygiene of the public, even if he is immoral or amoral? By what standards do we judge these two individuals, or anybody else for that matter? What do we really mean by terms like "good person," "bad person," "immoral behavior," and "sinfulness"?

Clearly, our conclusions about the actions or comportment of someone as being harmful, wrong, sinful, or unlawful derive from the notion of purpose and motive. And purpose and motive obviously concern human objectives as well as the methods by which they should be attained—the purpose of society and the purpose of human existence.

SIN AND REALITY

In the first chapter, we reviewed briefly the fundamental structure of reality from the Bahá'í perspective so that we can gradually attempt to define some of the implications of what we mean by "sin." After all, any notions we might have about immorality or unlawfulness necessarily derive from the definition of how reality is structured, how it originated, what inherent purpose it has, or what purpose it has acquired in a particular cultural or social context.

For example, an individual might describe himself as agnostic and a noble humanitarian. If so, he may still desire to construct a society that benefits human advancement, even if solely in terms of secular concerns such as health, education, and general welfare. Even if he is a staunch materialist, or a self-indulgent hedonist, he still needs to distinguish between the brief ecstatic thrills he enjoys and the order and security of a social contract that will allow him to indulge in his pleasure-seeking pursuits.

The point is that even if we do not accept the existence of a cognitive Divine Being or a Conscious Force Who has created reality with a specific purpose, or if we do not possess a thoroughly examined belief (however derived) in this same Being as a "personal God" Who is ready and able to assist us in our own inherent individual and collective purpose, we are still likely to be well aware of the need to determine as a society how we define concepts of negative action. We cannot arbitrarily ascribe judgmental terms such as "detrimental," "regressive," and "harmful"—or more morally loaded epithets such as "sinful," "wicked," or "evil"—without some logical basis for our assessment. Even if we make judgments based solely on gut reactions, in order to transform these affective notions into legally binding ordinances, we must set forth some logical validity and civil basis for translating emotion into law. In my own youth, for example, one could be arrested for making an obscene gesture. Today, however, while this act might be considered tasteless, it is nevertheless an expression of freedom of speech protected under the First Amendment.

This entire arena of action and attitude in individual and collective social behavior becomes ever more complex as a society grows increasingly more diverse, ever less coherent in its moral perspective, and ever more divided in its views about morality, civil rights, and personal freedoms.

Is an action simply distasteful and personally repugnant, or does it endanger the wellbeing of others? And does the concept of "wellbeing," when employed at the level of society, allude solely to the physical health of its members, or does it not also imply a healthy moral climate? When is an act a breach of the public peace, as opposed to an expression of individual rights? Should it be considered a breach of the social contract to disturb others with loud music or an incessantly barking dog? Are the people next door being abrasively unneighborly? Are they cynical and mean-spirited? At what point should we appeal to the system of social justice instead of simply trying to create an amicable neighborhood by working collaboratively to create an environment that satisfies the needs of everyone to the extent possible?

If the behavior that offends us is not a breach of law but is still considered "immoral" by all accepted norms of human decency, at what point can society draw the line, especially when relativistic standards of moral judgment become ever more lax and exponentially ill-defined?

I am sure the point is sufficiently clear, especially since every reader will have experienced and questioned some part of the conflict I am attempting to portray. But unless society and the individuals in it have some shared view of the social and moral contract entered into by virtue of willingly abiding within a community, then an exponential decay can be expected, whether in law, order, morality, or general neighborliness. In time, a society without a shared sense of some sort of morality will decline until the quality of life becomes intolerable.

It is in this sense that society must determine, through some collective assent or mutual pact, the distinction between individual rights and freedoms and the right of society to create and sustain an environment that is healthy, safe, and generally felicitous. But how does society determine when individual rights encroach on the rights of other individuals or those of the collective? Is there a benchmark or standard that does not change regardless of what changes take place in society?

Again, if everyone has the same values, the same view of the purpose of humanity, and a generally shared sense of what the "good citizen," the "good neighborhood," and the "good community" look like, then consultation among members and their representatives can solve even the most complex problems on an ongoing basis. But without some sort of pact, whether implicit or explicit, ever more virulent and destructive conflicts are inevitable.

My own experience growing up in the 1940s was wonderful. The neighborhood where I grew up was friendly, with one or two exceptions. We all knew each other, knew each other's histories, suffering, and challenges. We were always ready to assist each other in facing tragedy or overcoming difficulties. The safety and security of any child was the collective responsibility of the community as a whole, and though we belonged to diverse religions and cultural heritages, we had a fundamentally shared view of what was and was not acceptable in terms of the implicit moral code and the explicit civic ordinances.

This idyllic period, which seemed to have permanence and durability for me because I had known nothing else, was mostly an anomaly squeezed between wars and other challenges—between the depths of the Great Depression and the onset of the Civil Rights movement, between the slaughter of millions during World War II and the onset of the Cold War. This period and neighborhood were the incubators of my origin.

Of course, this middle-class American neighborhood, though diverse in some regards, was entirely segregated from the African-American population that lived in parts of town I don't even recall seeing. The economy was on the upswing, so anyone desiring a job could find one. Alcoholism, child abuse, and other unspeakable behavior went on behind the scenes, but because these acts were "unspeakable" (literally), they were never discussed—not in the papers, nor around the dinner table.

In retrospect, this brief period was not so much the return of a norm as it was a glitch in the rapid transformation of American society and the American dream. I lived in a dream or an illusion that, though lovely and memorable, was but a brief pause before the American dream quickly began to fall apart as a coherent and secure pursuit, even though the dying waves from this dream of life pulsed out for decades until it crept into the fabric of the world-view of virtually every part of our global community.

Once instant communication began to allow the world to view through the magic portals of TV screens palpable images of the "good life," of the gaudy glare of Western materialism, and of the appearance of happiness writ large in economic sufficiency, few could resist the mantra of "I want that!" or "if I have THAT, I will be happy; I will be satisfied!" No regime, however oppressive and severe, could quash completely the infiltration of this Eden of neon and glitter. But we need not recount the story of how this phenomenon proceeded. We can presently witness that same wave reverberating against the shores of countries worldwide.

4 / REALITY IN RELATION TO MORAL LAW

"I wish I had known all this before," said Pippin. "I had no notion of what I was doing."

"Oh yes, you had," said Gandalf. "You knew you were behaving wrongly and foolishly; and you told yourself so, though you did not listen. . . . No, the burned hand teaches best. After that, advice about fire goes to the heart."

—Tolkien, *The Lord of the Rings: The Two Towers*, p. 260

"Down! Off that sofa, Molly!"

The humbled collie slinks down with ears flat, her "lammy ears," Lucia calls them when our furry four-legged child assumes the submissive lambesque posture of guilt.

Caught in the act once again! How humiliated she feels, as if we had not told her a thousand times about which sofa or bed can be used by her without incurring our scowl and tone of disappointment! It matters not that the good sofa has soft microfiber. Of course it's more comfortable! That's precisely why it's the *good* sofa! Surely she understands this by now!

But temptation almost invariably gets the best of her when she's home alone (or thinks she is) and retribution seems a distant possibility. And who knows, she thinks to herself, perhaps the pet parents won't check for dog hair or touch the fabric to see if it's warm when they arrive. But no, she always gives herself away by being just a little too friendly or a bit guilty-looking when she has violated home rules.

THE VIRTUOUS COLLIE

Has our dog committed a sin? Or how about the curious Pippin in *The Two Towers* as he is sneaking the palantir from under Gandalf's cloak while the wizard is sleeping? Even as Pippin has the magical object in his hands, the hobbit *knows* he is doing something wrong: "'You idiotic fool!' Pippin muttered to himself. 'You're going to get yourself into frightful trouble'" (Tolkien, *LOTR: The Two Towers,* p. 260). Knowingly getting himself into trouble, and "frightful trouble" at that!

Is temptation just too much greater than the collie's resolve to do the "right thing," or has a canine "Satan" undermined Molly's best intentions? Is her fear of getting caught the same as the fear of committing a sin? Is doing something "wrong" precisely the same as committing a "sinful act"? Is Pippin a "sinful" Hobbit? Is Molly a "sinful" dog?

I think not. My dog is a wonder-dog. She helps Lucia get the paper every morning. True, she gets a cookie in return, but she works gratis when she warns us if anyone is even near our gate. She rounds up the cows, whether we want her to or not.

I remember how proud we were at the herding class when the largest ram was obstinate and defiantly refused to budge as Molly circled and barked in her most annoying high-pitched tone—a tone that has caused squirrels to become so rattled that they give up and leap from a tree limb into her mouth rather than endure the auditory pain of her menacing voice. Finally, Molly stopped talking and simply ran full speed at the ram, knocking the stalwart beast onto his back, where he lay senseless for a few moments, his sheep feet wriggling in the air as if he were a dying cockroach.

And when Lucia is deeply troubled about something, Molly tries to get in her lap to protect her from whatever might be causing Lucia to send out negative "vibes." Molly loves Lucia. She went through agility training under Lucia's guidance, and these days she helps Lucia put the chickens in their cages at night. Molly carefully cradles in her mouth the random eggs she finds in the bushes, and then lays them on the kitchen floor with only a mild crack or two, except on those occasions when she is feeling a bit "peckish."

No, Molly may be wilful at times, and she has terrible anxiety attacks when lightning strikes as she tries furiously to dig and crawl into a hole somewhere in our carpet. But having known what panic attacks feel like, I sympathize and go get her "thunder shirt" to calm her, or I turn up some country music or put on the news channel so that the storm sounds are less bothersome. But no, she is definitely *not* a sinful dog!

Come to think of it, can there even be such a thing as a "sinful" dog? Would this designation not imply that the animal has a moral center, that she can conceive in her dog mind the notion of right and wrong, of a good dog versus a bad or evil dog? As a well-trained, intelligent, and faithful pack animal, she knows the "rules of the house." She knows what is acceptable and unacceptable behavior when pack leader Lucia is around.

Her notion of "being good" is ultimately rooted in what she has been trained by us to do. "Good dog!" and "Bad dog!" are, for Molly, inflected sounds with which she associates certain attitudes, actions, and reactions, whether verbalized or detected by her hyper-keen sensitivity to sights, sounds, distant thunder, or the microwaves of human emotion. With the appropriate inflection, we could just as well be saying "Glab Shrug!" or "Block Rock!" and get the same results—except, of course, for the word "cookie." We can't even spell that one without a response.

So is there a difference between Molly's knowing violation of the sofa rules and Pippin's taking the palantir from under Gandalf's cloak? But perhaps we should consider a more obvious example of what might be considered a "sinful" act. After all, Gandalf understands and forgives Pippin for his native "Tookish" curiosity, especially since the force of that inbred propensity is heightened by the mysterious force emanating from the palantir, which has now become a window into the mind of the *inherently* evil Sauron.

But wait! Sauron can't be *inherently* evil! According to Tolkien's world, nothing is. After all, at the Council of Elrond in *The Fellowship of the Ring*, Elrond observes: "Nothing is evil in the beginning. Even Sauron was not so. I fear to take the Ring to hide it. I will not take the Ring to wield it" (Tokien, *LOTR: The Fellowship of the Ring*, p. 351).

In case you are not familiar with Tolkien's work, the ring has no consciousness, though it does possess an inherent instinct to survive. But Tolkien has bestowed upon this symbol the capacity to confer, on whoever wears it, a power over others. This power, or the temptation to have such power, subsequently induces one to become totally self-centered rather than other-centered. The ring seems to be capable of bending the will of whoever wields it to become addicted to selfishness, and paranoid that someone might try to take the ring away, even as Lord Acton famously observed in an 1887 letter, "Power tends to corrupt, and absolute power corrupts absolutely. Great men are almost always bad men" (quoted from Vitullo-Martin and Moskin, *The Executive's Book of Quotations*, p. 225).

Molly does not desire power. Molly does not desire "things," other than food promptly at 11:45 AM. But given a choice, she will go for the microfiber couch, and given the opportunity, she will go for the stinky food. As we eat, she will lie down, nestled among our feet under the table, without bothering us in the least. But this ostensibly mannerly behavior derives not so much from love or the determination to be more refined. In her mind, she knows that some morsel, however minuscule, often falls within reach of her tongue or paw.

And if we are not at home and have left her alone in the house while a thunderstorm emerges within ten or twenty miles, she will go into the trash cans, seize whatever papers are there, and tear them into tiny bits. She leaves them scattered on the floor as a message for us: "Thanks a bunch! You think I don't *know* you left me alone when you are aware how much I *can't stand* thunderstorms!?

Well, here's a little something for you to clean up as recompense for doing the *wrong thing*!"

THE HUMAN CAPACITY FOR REFLECTION
AND OTHER FORMS OF ABSTRACT THOUGHT

Clearly one distinction between Pippin and Molly is that in Pippin's mind there was a moment's hesitation, a point of decision in which he balanced the "badness" of doing something "foolish" or "wrong" (taking something of Gandalf's without asking if it was OK) and satisfying his insatiable curiosity, an inherited character trait perhaps, but one within his power to control.

For Molly there may also have been a momentary pause, but mostly to make sure we were not in the house. For her, there was no reflection about the metaphysical attributes of the decision. This was not a "moral" issue. This was a matter of letting her desire for comfort overpower any residual fear of being discovered by the pack leader and subsequently given punishment in the form of a verbal reprimand.

And because by now she is well aware that the punishment will never be anything more than some harsh inflections, she did not meditate about her spiritual development or the concept of doing "the right thing" or how to become a "better dog." Certainly she has many powers far more accurate and capable than the ones humans possess, but she does not possess a faculty that empowers her to meditate about such abstract concepts as "the good dog" or to recall the scary story about the dog that was eaten by a microfiber sofa (a bedtime yarn I have yet to write).

These facts do not mean Molly is less than an exemplary collie. She can run faster than I. She can still keep up with the garbage truck, and the driver always waves at her and honks his horn to show his admiration. Even at the dog age of seventy-seven, she can detect scents exponentially more acutely than I ever could. She can hear sounds (particularly thunder) that I or any other human would find inaudible. In effect, there is no competition between us because, from the Bahá'í view of reality, we belong to two distinctly different species, regardless of what scientists might have us believe.

Let me explain. From the Bahá'í view of the structure of reality, each category of existence has precisely what it needs to become perfected within the parameters or limitations of its own reality. Thus, within each "kingdom" of material existence—whether mineral, vegetable, animal, or human—there is the possibility of infinite progression or perfectibility: "the perfections of existence are infinite; for it is impossible to find any created thing such that nothing superior to it can be imagined. For example, one cannot find in the mineral kingdom a ruby, or in the vegetable kingdom a rose, or in the animal kingdom a nightingale, such that an even better specimen cannot be imagined" ('Abdu'l-Bahá, *Some Answered Questions*, no. 62.1).

Each being progresses within the category of its own existence; no being can advance or transform into a higher category of reality. But this fact does not imply a limitation or a denigration of any existent being. Every category of existence is complete and sufficient within itself, and every being has all the powers and capacities it requires to function within the "kingdom" to which it belongs. So however cultivated our garden may become, and however exquisite the blossoms may appear, it would be useless to invite them for dinner (even though they might become part of a nice arrangement for a centerpiece at the table).

Likewise, while plants and animals can become cultivated or domesticated by being in our presence—especially if we as gardeners or animal trainers make a concerted effort to have them take on or imitate some human virtues—the flowers will never transition into animals, and the animals will never become human. Molly will never run a business, read a book, or ruminate about the moral of the yet-to-be-written story of "The Sofa that Swallowed the

Dog." Nevertheless, Molly is capable of achieving limitless stages of perfection as an animal, at least theoretically:

> But every created thing has been assigned a degree which it can in no wise overpass. . . . No matter how far a mineral may progress, it can never acquire the power of growth in the mineral kingdom. No matter how far this flower may progress, it can never manifest the power of sensation while it is in the vegetable kingdom. So this silver mineral can never gain sight or hearing; at most it can progress in its own degree and become a perfect mineral, but it cannot acquire the power of growth or sensation and can never become living: It can only progress in its own degree. ('Abdu'l-Bahá, *Some Answered Questions*, no. 62.2)

So it is that however adept, well-trained, and humanlike an animal may become in some of its capacities, it will never desire nor become capable of turning into a human being. The human being, in this sense, is the highest form of material existence because our essential reality, the core of our existence, is a spiritual reality, the human soul, from which we derive all our distinctive human faculties and powers: the memory of ideas, the power to recall and reflect upon these ideas, the power of reason, the conscious awareness of our own existence, a faculty of judgment derived from our power to make choices (our free will), our ability to plan out a course of action based on abstract concepts (such as moral or ideological considerations), and, as we progress, the power to evaluate how we are doing physically, mentally, and spiritually.

And yet, we ourselves are limited, whether in this life or the next, to remaining human souls, even though our capacity to ascend within this category of existence is boundless. We are and will ever remain human beings, whether during our physical stage of existence in which we associate intimately with the intricate physical apparatus that is our body, or in the metaphysical stage in which our powers are freed from the limitations imposed by this indirect association with reality.

In conjunction with this same concept, it is crucial that we appreciate that the Manifestations, those Emissaries sent periodically by God, are Themselves of a distinct and more exalted category of existence than we are. This is why I capitalize pronouns that allude to Them, as a visual device whereby I can acknowledge my understanding and appreciation of Their station.

True, the Manifestations of God do all They can to make themselves accessible to us and to exemplify human virtue for us in everything They do and say. In this sense They are not remote or beyond our comprehension or love. Indeed, They conceal most of Their powers and capacities. But even though we accept them as models of human perfection, we also need to realize that we will never attain Their station, will never ourselves become similarly flawless in our manifestation of divine virtues. In one illuminating statement about this distinction between ourselves and the Manifestations, Bahá'u'lláh states that as we become more fully informed about Their rank and purpose, we will come to realize by degrees precisely how lofty, exalted, and distinct Their station is from our own—that, in fact, They represent the highest expression of divinity we can ever hope to comprehend:

> The essence of belief in Divine unity consisteth in regarding Him Who is the Manifestation of God and Him Who is the invisible, the inaccessible, the unknowable Essence as one and the same. By this is meant that whatever pertaineth to the former, all His acts and doings, whatever He ordaineth or forbiddeth, should be considered, in all their aspects, and under all circumstances, and without any reservation, as identical with the Will of God Himself. This is the loftiest station to which a true believer in the unity of God can ever hope to attain. Blessed is the man that reacheth this station, and is of them that are steadfast in their belief. (Bahá'u'lláh, *Gleanings*, no. 84.4)

In the context of this statement about reality, we can better appreciate why Their appearance among us requires such patience and suffering on Their part. The Manifestations appear among us in the form of ordinary human beings, effectively concealing Their knowledge and powers until such time as it is appropriate for Them to reveal gradually to demonstrate and discuss how we, who have no instincts about how to be better people, might improve ourselves individually and collectively ('Abdu'l-Bahá, *Some Answered Questions*, no. 16.8–10).

Unfortunately, thus far in the history of this systematic teaching of humankind, the Manifestations of God have had to endure the fact that we are not always accepting of what They wish to impart, especially when it goes against our own ideas or habituated customs and traditions.* Consequently, They submit Themselves to our disdain and, more often than not, to our active persecution and rejection.**

Again, each Manifestation establishes an exemplary pattern of behavior, a Sunnah, as the Muslims call it, which we are exhorted to emulate as best we can. But whereas the Manifestations exhibit all human virtues perfectly, we will always be a work in progress because we will never achieve some final point of attainment. Yet never should we perceive this as a limitation or as a failing on our part. It is not within our power or nature to be able to reach a state of perfection, and, furthermore, we still can enjoy eternally becoming ever more spiritually refined so long as we desire to do so and strive accordingly.

From the Bahá'í teachings about the human soul and reality, we learn that because we lack any sort of inherent or instinctive

---

* Since the Bahá'í teachings affirm that the Manifestations are omniscient, They doubtless have foreknowledge of the resistance They will encounter from us.

** For a full discussion of this topic, see Hatcher, *The Face of God among Us: How God Educates Humanity*.

knowledge of how to advance our condition and become more refined human beings, we necessarily require some "outside" source of guidance and instruction. For example, we can appreciate this idea more fully when we raise children. Without our foundational teaching and guidance as parents, children will find it difficult to advance from stage to stage.

So it is with human civilization on planet Earth. We require the enlightenment and encouragement of the Manifestations if we are to progress to a point where we understand our inherent objective as human souls and how we can best pursue that goal through the guidance They provide us in our foundational stage of existence:

> In like manner, the holy Manifestations of God are the focal Centres of the light of truth, the Wellsprings of the hidden mysteries, and the Source of the effusions of divine love. They cast Their effulgence upon the realm of hearts and minds and bestow grace everlasting upon the world of the spirits. They confer spiritual life and shine with the splendour of inner truths and meanings. The enlightenment of the realm of thought proceeds from those Centres of light and Exponents of mysteries. Were it not for the grace of the revelation and instruction of those sanctified Beings, the world of souls and the realm of thought would become darkness upon darkness. Were it not for the sound and true teachings of those Exponents of mysteries, the human world would become the arena of animal characteristics and qualities, all existence would become a vanishing illusion, and true life would be lost. That is why it is said in the Gospel: "In the beginning was the Word"; that is, it was the source of all life. ('Abdu'l-Bahá, *Some Answered Questions*, no. 42.3)

However, this axiom should not be misunderstood to imply that at some stage of development, we humans advance to a point where we no longer need this guidance or where we are totally autonomous in refining our condition. Inasmuch as our advancement can be infinite in degree, though not in state, our need for ever more advanced instruction will never cease.

REALITY AND MORAL LAWS

This is a most important concept to grasp if we wish to understand that moral concepts are ultimately *not* human inventions, nor are they merely attempts to maintain order. Moral law, like physical law, exists independently of our awareness of it or our compliance with it. Moral laws describe reality, both the reality we can perceive and that aspect of reality that is concealed from our five senses. Moral laws thus affect our lives and are operant in all we set out to become or accomplish, precisely because they are not an arbitrary imposition on our behavior; they are not designed to fit some code devised by others to control us or to recreate us in their image of what they think is a good person who can sustain human existence and maintain civil order.

Ultimately, the basis for all valid law, even the most trivial codes governing civil behavior, has at its core a spiritual foundation. The term *valid* here refers to those laws that are not arbitrary but are based on descriptions of metaphysical reality. Perhaps we don't "jaywalk" because we are afraid of being arrested, but the law against jaywalking has a spiritual basis, and on some level we know that the law has been created by well-intended legislators to protect us from our own carelessness. This law is thus for our benefit, as well as for the benefit of drivers whose lives would be deeply impacted were they accidently to cause our death. These are the spiritual principles implicit in the social contract, the covenant between us as citizens who elect and subsequently pay the salaries of those whom we entrust to operate the civil infrastructure on principles of justice, safety, and public welfare.

Regarding the more overt levels of moral considerations, the spiritual laws that concern our personal and private comportment, refinement, and chastity—though part of our individual covenant with God by way of the religions He has revealed to guide us—are no less rationally based. In an important sense, we do not *break* a moral law, nor do we injure God (as Founder of these laws) by our disobedience of, or indifference to, these laws (that may or may not be contained in the social contract). Strictly speaking, we break ourselves upon the reality the law is describing.

To employ a simple analogy, if we liken the path of life we choose for ourselves to navigating a ship, moral laws can be thought of as devices designed to protect us from perils concealed beneath waters that, while appearing tranquil on the surface, are strewn beneath with jagged rocks capable of deterring or even destroying our craft. The laws themselves, in this context, are similar to signs or buoys cautioning us in very straightforward language that these waters are dangerous or even lethal—however calm and gentle they may appear—and that we should follow the signs that outline the safest path if we wish to protect ourselves from harm.

We can choose to ignore the signs or believe that whoever put them there is overcautious and does not appreciate the beauty of these waters, but then experience will be our teacher. And while experience is often said to be the *best* teacher, it is rarely the kindest or wisest teacher. Some lessons are best learned vicariously through stories about those who dared to ignore the signs. Some of these individuals may have gotten by without a scratch, some may have been slightly injured, and others still may not have survived.

Similarly, the laws of every Manifestation indicate the surest path we can take toward our loftiest destination with the least amount of damage, other than the changes and chances that are part of the journey and that no one can completely avoid or control. Some of those laws revealed by a Manifestation may be prescribed for a particular period of time. Others may be universal but refined from dispensation to dispensation. But all describe reality and provide us with the most pragmatic and rewarding methods for us to use for successful living. In this sense, the revealed utterances of the Prophets might well be likened to a handbook, a user's guide for all who abide in the "Day" or dispensation of that Manifestation:

Say: True liberty consisteth in man's submission unto My commandments, little as ye know it. Were men to observe that which We have sent down unto them from the Heaven of Revelation, they would, of a certainty, attain unto perfect liberty. Happy is the man that hath apprehended the Purpose of God in whatever He hath revealed from the Heaven of His Will, that pervadeth all created things. Say: The liberty that profiteth you is to be found nowhere except in complete servitude unto God, the Eternal Truth. Whoso hath tasted of its sweetness will refuse to barter it for all the dominion of earth and heaven. (Bahá'u'lláh, *Gleanings*, no. 159.4)

MORAL LAW AND THE CHAIN OF BEING

While moral law permeates the whole of reality, conscious awareness of moral law and the spiritual relationships that moral law reinforces is confined to human beings, even if what human beings choose to do affects all those beings under their sway. To explain this hierarchal relationship, 'Abdu'l-Bahá has employed an analogy that was also found useful and popular in many medieval and Renaissance philosophies.

This analogy portrays everything in creation as belonging to categories, or what 'Abdu'l-Bahá calls "kingdoms," each of which has a particular position, rank, or degree, and thus can be usefully portrayed as links on a "Great Chain of Being." This analogy is useful in contemporary discussions of value and morality because of two important implications. First, this concept of an ascending chain of kingdoms means that there is a sort of hierarchy of creation, with the human being at the top as the end result of the creative process in physical creation:

Man is in the ultimate degree of materiality and the beginning of spirituality; that is, he is at the end of imperfection and the beginning of perfection. He is at the furthermost degree of darkness and the beginning of the light. That is why the station of man is said to be the end of night and the beginning of day, meaning that he encompasses all the degrees of imperfection and that he potentially possesses all the degrees of perfection. He has both an animal side and an angelic side, and the role of the educator is to so train human souls that the angelic side may overcome the animal. Thus, should the divine powers, which are identical with perfection, overcome in man the satanic powers, which are absolute imperfection, he becomes the noblest of all creatures, but should the converse take place, he becomes the vilest of all beings. That is why he is the end of imperfection and the beginning of perfection.

In no other species in the world of existence can such difference, distinction, contrast, and contradiction be seen as in man. ('Abdu'l-Bahá, *Some Answered Questions*, no. 64.2–3)

This is an incredibly profound insight into the nature of man in relation to the structure of reality. It confirms but also clarifies observations made by some of the most astute minds since the beginnings of philosophical discourse—that we have aspects of our "self" vying for our conscious attention. One, the higher self, consists of those specialized powers that emanate from the soul, such as reason, memory, reflection, will, self-consciousness, and so on. The second is the lower self, which consists of those physical and sensual urges that emanate from the physical apparatus with which we are intimately associated during this life and which we share with the animal kingdom.

The point is that we must somehow coordinate and synthesize both aspects of self into a coherent quest for advancement. To do this, we should not ignore either aspect of the "self," yet we should be constantly vigilant to make sure that the higher or more lofty aspect of self—that capacity that distinguishes us from the animal kingdom—is in control. Thus, like every other "link" on the chain of being, we share the nature of those kingdoms of reality that are below us, and we also share aspects of the powers and capacities that characterize those whose dwelling is the realm of the spirit.

Consequently, like links on a literal chain, we are often pulled in two distinct and often antithetical directions. Responding exclusively to either aspect of "self" could prove disastrous. For example, if we try to ignore our baser self by becoming an ascetic and rejecting all things physical, sensual, or social, we can potentially turn inward and cease to develop or to participate in the construction of a healthy community or society. For this reason, Bahá'u'lláh has forbidden asceticism or monasticism, that all of us might benefit from, and contribute to, the society in which we live. (Bahá'u'lláh, *Tablets of Bahá'u'lláh*, p. 71)

Conversely, to abandon our desire for more subtle forms of metaphysical development—whether purely intellectual matters, or more indirect moral concerns about assisting our community— is to risk becoming totally hedonistic or amoral. Thus, the Bahá'í laws and admonitions about personal behavior and comportment forbid the more obvious forms of self-indulgence. One might say that the "Bahá'í life" or path is a golden mean between the extremes of hedonism and asceticism.

The second relevant bit of wisdom we can derive from the analogy of the Great Chain of Being is the concept of the coherence, or integration, of creation. Humankind may be the fruit of creation, but this does not mean we are independent of the tree that brought us forth: "For all beings are linked together like a chain; and mutual aid, assistance, and interaction are among their intrinsic properties and are the cause of their formation, development, and growth. It is established through numerous proofs and arguments that every single thing has an effect and influence upon every other, either independently or through a causal chain" ('Abdu'l-Bahá, *Some Answered Questions*, no. 46.6).

Of course, this is hardly a new idea. Most contemporary ecological notions of the "circle of life" espouse this same concept, that every part of physical reality is interconnected. But when this view is combined with the Bahá'í concept of human purpose, we can begin to appreciate more directly how the lesser kingdoms of physical reality have important functions in teaching human beings about the specific attributes of spiritual reality, as well as the idea that all creation is a single, organic, everlasting expression of the Creator's desire that His attributes become manifest through every level of existence:

But if ye ask as to the place, know ye that the world of existence is a single world, although its stations are various and distinct. For example, the mineral life occupieth its own plane, but a mineral entity is without any awareness at all of the vegetable kingdom, and indeed, with its inner tongue denieth that there is any such kingdom. In the same way, a vegetable entity knoweth nothing of the animal world, remaining completely heedless and ignorant thereof, for the stage of the animal is higher than that of the vegetable, and the vegetable is veiled from the animal world and inwardly denieth the existence of that world—all this while animal, vegetable and mineral dwell together in the one world. In the same way the animal remaineth totally unaware of that power of the human mind which graspeth universal ideas and layeth bare the secrets of creation—so that a man who liveth in the east can make plans and arrangements for the west; can unravel mysteries; although located on the continent of Europe can discover America; although sited on the earth can lay hold of the inner realities of the stars of heaven. Of this power of discovery which belongeth to the human mind, this power which can grasp abstract and universal ideas, the animal remaineth totally ignorant, and indeed denieth its existence.

In the same way, the denizens of this earth are completely unaware of the world of the Kingdom and deny the existence thereof. They ask, for example: "Where is the Kingdom? Where is the Lord of the Kingdom?" These people are even as the mineral and the vegetable, who know nothing whatever of the animal and the human realm; they see it not; they find it not. Yet the mineral and vegetable, the animal and man, are all living here together in this world of existence. ('Abdu'l-Bahá, *Selections from the Writings of 'Abdu'l-Bahá*, no. 163.2–3)

In another equally informative passage about how we all occupy the same reality but are defined by the nature or capacity of the category of existence into which we are born, 'Abdu'l-Bahá offers the following explanation: "When asked about the individual persistence of the animal's personality after death, 'Abdu'l-Bahá said: 'Even the most developed dog has not the immortal soul of the man; yet the dog is perfect in its own place. You do not quarrel with a rose-tree because it cannot sing!'" ('Abdu'l-Bahá, *'Abdu'l-Bahá in London*, p. 97)

Finally, 'Abdu'l-Bahá observed, "It is evident therefore that man is ruler over nature's sphere and province. Nature is inert, man is progressive. Nature has no consciousness, man is endowed with it. Nature is without volition and acts perforce whereas man possesses a mighty will. Nature is incapable of discovering mysteries or realities whereas man is especially fitted to do so. Nature is not in touch with the realm of God, man is attuned to its evidences. Nature is uninformed of God, man is conscious of Him. Man acquires divine virtues, nature is denied them. Man can voluntarily discontinue vices, nature has no power to modify the influence of its instincts" ('Abdu'l-Bahá, *The Promulgation of Universal Peace*, pp. 247–48).

PART 2: MORAL LAWS AND THE NATURE OF SIN

5 / FREE WILL AND THE POINT OF BALANCE

Should anyone be afflicted by a sin, it behoveth him to repent thereof and
return unto his Lord. He, verily, granteth forgiveness unto whomsoever
He willeth, and none may question that which it pleaseth Him to ordain.
He is, in truth, the Ever-Forgiving, the Almighty, the All-Praised.
— Bahá'u'lláh, The Kitáb-i-Aqdas, ¶49

According to Paul in his letter to the Christians in Rome, "the
wages of sin is death." But Paul is fairly vague about exactly what
"sin" might be, or even what "goodness" might be for that matter.
He does speak about becoming "servants to God," which involves
worshipping, teaching the faith, and accepting whatever Paul
says regarding what Christians should think and do. However, he
focuses primarily on explaining that Christ is the Messiah and possibly God incarnate:

> For when ye were the servants of sin, ye were free from righ-
> teousness. What fruit had ye then in those things whereof ye
> are now ashamed? For the end of those things is death. But
> now being made free from sin, and become servants to God,
> ye have your fruit unto holiness, and the end everlasting life.
> For the wages of sin is death; but the gift of God is eternal life
> through Jesus Christ our Lord. (Romans 6:20–23)

Peter, the presumptive head of the church, takes another approach
to belief. He admonishes the early believers that there is something
more to being a Christian than an ill-defined notion of faith.

He exhorts the converts to Christianity to demonstrate their belief by establishing a pattern of behavior, a path they should follow. He challenges them to be exemplary in their conduct and thereby demonstrate the fruit of their beliefs. He then cautions the believers that the words of Paul are abstruse and that many are led astray by misconstruing his statements to mean whatever they find appealing, particularly regarding which laws to follow among the precepts they have inherited from their prior beliefs as Jews or as Roman polytheists:

> Wherefore, beloved, seeing that ye look for such things, be diligent that ye may be found of him in peace, without spot, and blameless. And account that the longsuffering of our Lord is salvation; even as our beloved brother Paul also according to the wisdom given unto him hath written unto you. As also in all his epistles, speaking in them of these things in which are some things hard to be understood, which they that are unlearned and unstable wrest, as they do also the other scriptures, unto their own destruction. Ye therefore, beloved, seeing ye know these things before, beware lest ye also, being led away with the error of the wicked, fall from your own steadfastness. (II Peter 3:14–17)

Peter does not use the term "sin" in this admonition, employing instead the more general normative terms of "error" and "wickedness." He also says nothing about death being the punishment for disobedience or unbelief. Of course, the Bahá'í authoritative texts affirm that the human soul never dies, regardless of whether or not we are obedient to the law or have allowed ourselves to become "servants to sin": "The soul is not a combination of elements, it is not composed of many atoms, it is of one indivisible substance and therefore eternal. It is entirely out of the order of the physical creation; it is immortal!" ('Abdu'l-Bahá, *Paris Talks*, no. 29.13) Therefore, from the Bahá'í perspective, the concept of death being the consequence of wicked or sinful action is enigmatic if accepted as having a literal meaning.

Since Paul is very erudite and speaks in abstruse terms about very complex spiritual concepts and moral perspectives, we can resolve this enigma first by assuming that he is speaking in symbolic terms, that the "death" to which he alludes is the decline or diminishment of one's spiritual perception, capacity, and state of progress toward the goal of human existence. Of course, the assurance that we have eternal existence may not necessarily be viewed as a good thing; if we believe ourselves to be in a state of sin, confusion, consternation, or bewilderment, then nonexistence might seem preferable to an existence in which we endure an endless condition of despair and regret.

As I have pointed out in discussions of this concept in other books, it is precisely this fear of continued existence that causes Hamlet to withhold himself from self-slaughter. Were he able simply to leap into a condition of nonexistence, of being oblivious to his present despair and depression, he would happily kill himself and "shuffle off this mortal coil." But he considers how much worse his situation would be were he to feel the same anger and despair but have no capacity to respond to exigent conditions or to make a change in his reality:

> . . . and by a sleep, to say we end
> The heart-ache, and the thousand Natural shocks
> That Flesh is heir to? 'Tis a consummation
> Devoutly to be wished. To die to sleep,
> To sleep, perchance to Dream; Ay, there's the rub,
> For in that sleep of death, what dreams may come,
> When we have shuffled off this mortal coil,
> Must give us pause. . . .

> . . . the dread of something after death,
> The undiscovered Country, from whose bourn
> No Traveller returns, Puzzles the will,

And makes us rather bear those ills we have,
Than fly to others that we know not of.

(Shakespeare, Hamlet, III, i, ll 60–81)

FEAR OF ETERNALITY

This realization that our life as a self-aware or conscious soul continues eternally should give all of us pause. It should cause us to reflect about what we intend to do from this point on and also about the fact that we can never escape our "self," that there are no "do-overs," that we are stuck with ourselves forever.

This single axiom should shock us into action more powerfully than possibly any other single consideration. It should immediately evoke in us an impetus to start working immediately to improve our condition. Because the fact is, at least according to Bahá'í belief, that Hamlet was right. We cannot obliterate ourselves or erase the consequence of what we have done.

Even if God is eternally forgiving, the Bahá'í writings, as well as the scriptures of virtually every other religion, make it clear that our performance in this initial physical stage of our eternal reality has important consequences for what we experience in the eternal afterlife. In addition, if we have ever willfully strayed from the right path, we can recall all too well how finding our way back to it is more difficult and requires more willpower and effort than not deviating from it in the first place. The recollection of such experiences also presents us with the empirical evidence that it is possible to become so lost that we might have a great deal of trouble discovering the way back.

As we will discuss later, while we need not fear nonexistence, we would do well to have a healthy respect for the consequences of what we do and who we become in this life (or this initial stage of our eternal life), because while we continue to exist after our passing, our existence in the realm of the spirit, even as it is here, is relative to our personal attainment.

And here I am not merely referring to the fact that all accomplishments are relative to the capacity with which each of us has been created, even as 'Abdu'l-Bahá notes that: "The good deeds of the righteous are the sins of the near ones" ('Abdu'l-Bahá, *Some Answered Questions,* no. 30.12). Neither do I wish to imply that we somehow "earn" salvation or forgiveness. It is through the grace and bounty of God alone that we make any progress, and obviously we rely more heavily on His forgiveness and pardon when we know we have willfully disobeyed the benign guidance revealed to us in His laws.

But here I am also referring to the fact that it may seem conceivable that we could render ourselves so remote, so degraded as to be "relatively" dead or nonexistent, whether in this world or in the world to come. Therefore, to understand this relativity of existence, we need to appreciate several related axioms about reality in terms of the continuity of the human soul.

First, no two souls are alike. Consequently, we can make no valid comparison between any of them. Each individual is endowed with a unique personality and an array of capacities known only to the Creator. Indeed, it is a central goal in this life to explore our talents, faculties, special strengths, and potentialities, and subsequently to develop those powers for the betterment of ourselves and others. After all, as we have already observed, it is only through interaction with others and systematic social practices that we can develop the vast majority of our spiritual powers.

Secondly, and related to this same axiom, is the fact that every soul is born sinless, pure, and undefiled. There is no such thing as "original sin," nor are our powers and challenges (whether physical or mental) the result of some defect in our spiritual essence or some sin committed in a past life. The Bahá'í view of reality explicitly rejects human preexistence or any form of reincarnation. As we noted in the first chapter, according to the Bahá'í teachings about human reality, the human soul has its beginning when it emanates from the spiritual realm during the process of conception, whereupon it associates with the human temple: "Know thou that every soul is fashioned after the nature of God, each being pure and holy at his birth. Afterwards, however, the individuals will vary according to what they acquire of virtues or vices in this world. Although all existent beings are in their very nature created in ranks or degrees, for capacities are various, nevertheless every individual is born holy and pure, and only thereafter may he become defiled" ('Abdu'l-Bahá, *Selections from the Writings of 'Abdu'l-Bahá*, no. 159.2).

Obviously only God has the infinite capacity required to weigh in the balance the variables governing the outcome of any given human life. Only such an infinitely complex Being could determine the degree to which a given soul is utilizing or has utilized appropriately the powers with which it has been endowed. Likewise, only the Creator could judge the extent to which a soul has freely chosen to respond improperly to the divine guidance available to it.

And while every soul is endowed with a different combination of talents and faculties, the Bahá'í texts assert that everyone has sufficient capacity to discern the existence of God and recognize His Manifestation, and possesses the free will needed to heed the guidance provided by the Manifestation: "He hath endowed every soul with the capacity to recognize the signs of God. How could He, otherwise, have fulfilled His testimony unto men, if ye be of them that ponder His Cause in their hearts. He will never deal unjustly with any one, neither will He task a soul beyond its power. He, verily, is the Compassionate, the All-Merciful" (Bahá'u'lláh, *Gleanings*, no. 52.2).

The next related axiom about the continuation of our existence is that while we will have the opportunity to pray for forgiveness and will never be beyond the reach of God's forgiveness, we will begin our afterlife more or less where we leave off in this life, at least in a spiritual sense. Consequently, while we have no need to fear nonexistence, we may fear not having taken sufficient advantage of our opportunity for development in this life:

> The stone and the man both exist, but in relation to man the stone has no existence or being. For when man dies and his body is disintegrated and destroyed, it becomes like the stone, the earth, and the mineral. It is therefore clear that even though the mineral exists, it is non-existent in relation to man.
>
> Likewise, those souls who are veiled from God, although they exist both in this world and in the world to come, are non-existent and forgotten in relation to the sanctified existence of the children of the divine Kingdom. ('Abdu'l-Bahá, *Some Answered Questions*, no. 67.9–10)

Perhaps it is in this sense, then, that Paul speaks of the wages of sin being death. In fact, 'Abdu'l-Bahá seems to confirm such an interpretation in His statement about the relativity of the conditions of human existence in the following statement: "As to thy question, doth every soul without exception achieve life everlasting? Know thou that immortality belongeth to those souls in whom hath been breathed the spirit of life from God. All save these are lifeless—they are the dead, even as Christ hath explained in the Gospel text. He whose eyes the Lord hath opened will see the souls of men in the stations they will occupy after their release from the body. He will find the living ones thriving within the precincts of their Lord, and the dead sunk down in the lowest abyss of perdition" ('Abdu'l-Bahá, *Selections from the Writings of 'Abdu'l-Bahá*, no. 159.1).

TRUE FREEDOM AND DIVINE LAW

In light of these various axioms about the totality of our human experience, it is not entirely comforting that we are assured of the continuation of our "self" or "soul." But we can feel significantly more comforted when we consider the purport of the laws and guidance of the Manifestation in guiding us at every turn. That is, in light of our ultimate destiny and purpose, we should logically regard the laws established by the Manifestation as ceaseless and unvarying sources of critical assistance, rather than as any sort of restriction on our freedom or as sanctions against our opportunity to enjoy and benefit from all the bounties this life has to offer.

From a Bahá'í perspective, every iota of guidance bestowed by the Manifestation for the Day in which we live is carefully calculated to enable us to achieve the maximum fulfillment of our talents and powers. A corollary of this fact is that the path They set forth provides us with the minimum amount of distractions, of needless suffering, or of failure to reach our true potential. Furthermore, since the Manifestation's central purpose as teacher and exemplar is to prepare us for the continuation of our lives in the afterlife, His laws and exhortations are precisely geared to assist us in establishing a sure foundation for our continued progress beyond this brief physical portion of our eternal existence:

> The nature of the soul after death can never be described, nor is it meet and permissible to reveal its whole character to the eyes of men. The Prophets and Messengers of God have been sent down for the sole purpose of guiding mankind to the straight Path of Truth. The purpose underlying Their revelation hath been to educate all men, that they may, at the hour of death, ascend, in the utmost purity and sanctity and with absolute detachment, to the throne of the Most High. (Bahá'u'lláh, *Gleanings*, no. 81.1)

It is in the context of this axiom about the purpose of the Manifestations—to educate us in preparation for the next stage of our existence—that Bahá'u'lláh assures us that all His laws are dedicated to freeing us from distractions and pitfalls; in no way do they constrain our freedom: "True liberty consisteth in man's submission unto My commandments, little as ye know it" (Bahá'u'lláh, *Gleanings*, no. 159.4). In other words, the path delineated by the Manifestation proffers us the greatest amount of true freedom that we can possibly attain (as opposed to the seductive illusion of freedom derived from self-indulgence).

I think that the final part of this statement—which implies that most of us do not or cannot fully appreciate the abiding logic and wisdom underlying His axiomatic statement—is perhaps more relevant now than ever before. This lack of insight on humanity's part is especially true given the present condition of our global community, beset as it is with turmoil and focused entirely on wealth, power, and appearances. However, as Bahá'u'lláh goes on to note, for those able to transcend these temptations and distractions, this understanding of "true liberty" may well assume a central position in guiding them through this present formative stage of life:

> Were men to observe that which We have sent down unto them from the Heaven of Revelation, they would, of a certainty, attain unto perfect liberty. Happy is the man that hath apprehended the Purpose of God in whatever He hath revealed from the Heaven of His Will, that pervadeth all created things. Say: The liberty that profiteth you is to be found nowhere except in complete servitude unto God, the Eternal Truth. Whoso hath tasted of its sweetness will refuse to barter it for all the dominion of earth and heaven. (Bahá'u'lláh, *Gleanings,* no. 159.4)

It is in this sense of the interaction and reciprocal relationship between knowledge and action—spiritual enlightenment as borne out in determined adherence to the laws and guidance of the Manifestation—that the concept of "goodness" can assume a new meaning in our normative discourse. A good person—a kind or just person—need not be seen as a boring or timid soul, withdrawn from the world and fearful of taking a stand or participating in shaping society. On the contrary, this view of what constitutes law and law-abiding creates an entirely distinct and benign connotation—a sign of maturity and a source of security and felicity:

> The ordinances of God have been sent down from the heaven of His most august Revelation. All must diligently observe them. Man's supreme distinction, his real advancement, his final victory, have always depended, and will continue to depend, upon them. Whoso keepeth the commandments of God shall attain everlasting felicity. (Bahá'u'lláh, *Gleanings,* no. 133.1)

From these verities about the reality of the human soul and its destiny, we can infer a view of morality as engendering a thoroughly practical course of action that simultaneously enables us to attain the most exalted happiness we can experience. Indeed, I have often wondered if this clarity of understanding about the nature and destiny of the soul is not some portion of the concealed knowledge to which Bahá'u'lláh alludes when He makes the following observation about ridding ourselves of fear: "In the treasuries of the knowledge of God there lieth concealed a knowledge which, when applied, will largely, though not wholly, eliminate fear. This knowledge, however, should be taught from childhood, as it will greatly aid in its elimination. Whatever decreaseth fear increaseth courage" (Bahá'u'lláh, Epistle to the Son of the Wolf, p. 32).

Related to this verity is Bahá'u'lláh's observation that our deeds should comply with our words, that virtuous words and beliefs based on the correct understanding of a moral principle are powerless unless they are manifested through our actions:

> Say: Beware, O people of Bahá, lest ye walk in the ways of them whose words differ from their deeds. Strive that ye may be enabled to manifest to the peoples of the earth the signs of

God, and to mirror forth His commandments. Let your acts be a guide unto all mankind, for the professions of most men, be they high or low, differ from their conduct. It is through your deeds that ye can distinguish yourselves from others. Through them the brightness of your light can be shed upon the whole earth. Happy is the man that heedeth My counsel, and keepeth the precepts prescribed by Him Who is the All-Knowing, the All-Wise. (Bahá'u'lláh, *Gleanings*, no. 139.8)

Another consideration in understanding the methods and consequences of the moral path is that our steadfastness during this journey is not attained by one decision to do the right thing. The moral path consists of a ceaseless array of unrelenting choices, many made on an almost subconscious or habitual level. And underlying each choice that comes our way is motive. In a very real sense, motive is at the heart of the extent to which our life's journey is successful. And underlying motive is the realization that we have free will in deciding what course of action we will take and *why* we will undertake it.

Here, as in our earlier discussion about the importance of discerning the "end" (goal or outcome) in the "beginning" (strategy or path) as demonstrated in the analogy of the lover seeking the beloved, if we do not establish our own motive for ourselves, other individuals or social forces are usually quite willing and ready to shape it for us. Indeed, this is one implication alluded to by Bahá'u'lláh as a prerequisite for attaining justice—that we become responsible for thinking independently and investigate reality for ourselves:

The best beloved of all things in My sight is Justice; turn not away therefrom if thou desirest Me, and neglect it not that I may confide in thee. By its aid thou shalt see with thine own eyes and not through the eyes of others, and shalt know of thine own knowledge and not through the knowledge of thy neighbor. Ponder this in thy heart; how it behooveth thee to be. Verily justice is My gift to thee and the sign of My loving-kindness. Set it then before thine eyes. (Bahá'u'lláh, The Hidden Words, Arabic, no. 2)

In another passage related to this same responsibility we have for our moral conduct, Bahá'u'lláh remarks that ignorance is no excuse for immorality, that while we all have various combinations of capacities and various degrees of intelligence, everyone is endowed with the ability to recognize the Manifestation and to distinguish between right and wrong:

Unto each one hath been prescribed a pre-ordained measure, as decreed in God's mighty and guarded Tablets. All that which ye potentially possess can, however, be manifested only as a result of your own volition. . . . Men, however, have wittingly broken His law. Is such a behavior to be attributed to God, or to their proper selves? Be fair in your judgment. Every good thing is of God, and every evil thing is from yourselves. (Bahá'u'lláh, *Gleanings*, no. 77.1)

We should obviously take notice that the end of this passage states clearly that God does not ever ordain anything evil for us. What, then, is the source of evil? Should we interpret this passage as implying that nothing evil happens to us unless we bring it upon ourselves?

MAKING EVIL CHOICES

When we employ the term "evil," we should be acutely aware of the context of the usage. We are faced with distinguishing among a wide variety of possible meanings. Are we alluding to unfortunate circumstances beyond our control, such as the "Acts of God" mentioned in insurance policies? Are we referring to actions or events in which what is good or advantageous for one group or one person is unfavorable to someone else? Or are we reserving the term "evil" for those actions where one person is trying to take advantage of another or else using another person as a means for gaining esteem or power?

In discussing the nature of "evil," 'Abdu'l-Bahá explains that some things we might consider "evil" are not inherently so, but only in relation to our perspective toward them: "Scorpions and snakes are poisonous—is this good or evil, for they have a positive existence? Yes, it is true that scorpions and snakes are evil, but only in relation to us and not to themselves, for their venom is their weapon and their sting their means of defence" ('Abdu'l-Bahá, *Some Answered Questions*, no. 74.5).

Clearly, then, the use of the term "evil" in relation to human action, or inaction, revolves around decisions or choices that human beings make and that are in violation of what they know is harmful to their own spiritual well-being or to that of others. If we state the nature of evil in the form of a logical sequence or syllogism, it might read something like this: (A) The laws of God as revealed to us by His Manifestations are designed for our well-being and delineate the most propitious course of action we can employ in our lives; (B) Bestowed upon us are the powers and obligation to think for ourselves and to choose to acquire knowledge of God and of His laws; (C) Evil action, in terms of personal sinfulness or immorality, concerns our malfeasance or nonfeasance in relation to these laws and the various courses of action they make available to us.

DEGREES OF SIN ACCORDING TO OUR PART IN THE PROCESS

As we will discuss later, we need to understand that evil is essentially nonexistent. There is no active source of evil, no evil force operating to undermine the integrity of God's creation, even if some individuals may be out to perpetrate iniquity that will affect us in some personal manner. Thus evil exists in terms of human failure or error, and we employ the term "evil" to describe a wrong choice and its consequence. Or, when such a choice is aggravated by pernicious insistence, "evil" may be a series of wrong choices that bring such harm to the perpetrator and injury to others that the action may correctly be categorized as a "sin."

To a certain extent, Socrates is quite correct—no one does evil in full knowledge. But there are degrees to which we can understand the "end" result of our bad choices in the "beginning" of a process of making them. For example, we may start out by appreciating nothing more than the fact that our actions have consequences, both for ourselves and for others. Then later, as we attain a more comprehensive understanding of the long-term consequences of everything we think and do, we may begin to realize that not only is there continuity to our existence (beyond this physical life) but that our individual journey is inextricably related to and inter-twined with the lives of myriads of other souls on the same kind of journey.

One important end result of this thinking is that we come to grasp another aspect of what Socrates is getting at regarding the social dimension of our personal reality—that, in fact, there can be no such thing as a truly "victimless" crime. We have inherent responsibilities to the society in which we live. Neither practically nor morally can we segregate our lives, our choices, and our well-being from those of our community—a principle that is articulated particularly well by John Donne, one of the masters of English verse and thought:

Meditation XVII
No man is an island entire of itself; every man
is a piece of the continent, a part of the main;
if a clod be washed away by the sea, Europe
is the less, as well as if a promontory were, as
well as any manner of thy friends or of thine
own were; any man's death diminishes me,
because I am involved in mankind.

And therefore never send to know for whom
the bell tolls; it tolls for thee.

(Donne, in *Norton Anthology*, Volume B, p. 1305)

CHOICE AND THE PATTERN OF DECLINE

But whether we harm ourselves or others, there are obviously degrees of knowledge about our negative action and degrees of severity of action that determine what appellation we apply to an act. For example, is what we do inappropriate, negligent, hurtful, immoral, sinful, evil, wicked, unforgivable? Because of the relative implications of these and other such terms, we might find it useful to survey briefly how the interplay among knowledge, motive, will, and effect increases in severity as indicated by the following representative hypothetical reflections by a perpetrator:

I know what I am doing is wrong according to what I have been told by those I have reason to respect, but I think the possible pleasure I will receive is worth the risk.

* * *

I know what I am doing may endanger or degrade my spiritual sense of myself, but if it begins to feel too wrong, I think I will know when to stop.

* * *

I am aware that I have become somewhat addicted to this action that I know is wrong, but I am willing to take the risk now because I know that God is forgiving and I will make up for it later. For now, I am simply going to try to put any guilt out of my mind so that I can enjoy the pleasure of this diversion for just a little while longer.

* * *

I know what I am doing or about to do will hurt another person, if not physically, at least emotionally, but I am tired of the way other people seem to have everything so easy when I have to struggle so hard, so it is only fair that I take advantage of any chance I have at getting ahead.

* * *

I understand the basic concept of justice as demanding from myself what I would think appropriate from others as they interact with me, but I enjoy exalting myself so that I can have a sense of security, power, praise, and the awe of others. I really want to get ahead and become important in the eyes of others, and I will do whatever it takes to achieve this.

* * *

So far, I have not experienced any retribution from God because of the bad things I have done. This makes me wonder if skeptics might be correct about religion being a manmade myth to keep people in their places. I am also beginning to doubt that there is an afterlife where justice will be meted out. Until I feel some consequence, I am going to do whatever I feel is best for me. I have observed how those who succeed in this life are the ones who do whatever is expedient to get what they want—so long as they don't get caught—so I will be careful and not go too far.

* * *

My desire to exalt myself above others, achieve material security, and enjoy sensual pleasure have now become the dominant forces in my life. I am no longer bothered by guilt or ideas about morality, kindness, justice, and all those abstract inventions anymore. Survival is the name of the game, and I am going to be a survivor. Everyone else, including my family, would do well just to stay out of my way.

* * *

I no longer have any sympathy or empathy for any other human beings. I cannot believe that I once had the naïve faith in a metaphysical Being, a personal God who looks after us and makes things right. I guess we believe what we are taught. My drive to excel and succeed is now tinged with such rage and turmoil that I live from moment to moment trying to find some new way of showing others how miserable they really are because I want them to experience what I feel.

* * *

There is no longer any logic to what I do other than planning some short-term way of striking out blindly at life and any semblance of order. I detest order and those who try to impose it on me. I detest those who think that life is good or that people should be nice or kind. The only sense of vitality I experience is when I strike out in anger and see the terror and bewilderment I cause in the eyes of others.

* * *

I eat if they feed me. I hurt them if I can. I run into the wall to feel. . . . .I . . . .I, I, IIIIIIIIIIIIIIIIIIIIIIIIIIIIIIIIIIIIIIIIIIIIIIIIIII. . . . . .

This paradigm of self-wrought personal deterioration could be portrayed a thousand different ways and still leave room for thousands more. But the forces involved, while working in different measures and combinations, are more or less the same. That which assists us in fulfilling our inherent purpose is good. That which deters us in this objective is bad.

Stated more bluntly, that which is detrimental to our inherent purpose is sinful and serves only to debase and degrade our powers and capacities. Other aspects of this process are also apparent in the deterioration of the soul. When we injure others by willingly and wittingly attempting to deter their success, or undermine their development, the degree of severity and harm to ourselves increases proportionately.

The precision of terminology does not matter, whether we categorize increasingly more grievous acts as questionable, unwise, negligent, sinful, evil, wicked, or satanic. Moral terms are always relative to the individual and the context in which any given action is performed. Furthermore, we are unable to judge others because we cannot possibly know all the exigencies at work in their lives, and, in fact, we are forbidden from doing so except in terms of legal obligations—if we are an officer of a court, for example.

We can only judge ourselves, and even that process has to be approached with care and regularity. Bahá'u'lláh thus admonishes His followers, "Bring thyself to account each day ere thou art summoned to a reckoning; for death, unheralded, shall come upon thee and thou shalt be called to give account for thy deeds" (Bahá'u'lláh, The Hidden Words, Arabic, no. 31).

This period of reflection during the day is obviously the best opportunity we have to check out where we are in the process of striving to attain our life's objectives. During this reflection, we can evaluate what we know about our path of choices, choose the next increment of action, and then either continue carrying it out or else initiate a new course of action.

CHOICE AND THE PATTERN OF ASCENT

Naturally, the above schema of an individual in moral or spiritual decline is only a theoretical paradigm of how one might descend into the depths of depravity and inhumanity. Clearly the theme of that decline is an increasing emphasis on the self or the ego together with a mounting addiction to material and sensual goals and rewards. And, of course, we could just as easily devise a paradigm of spiritual ascent. Indeed, in His work The Seven Valleys, Bahá'u'lláh portrays a process that is the opposite of this pattern—the ascent of the human soul with increasing detachment from material acquisition, from sensual delight, and from self-aggrandizement. I have discussed this same process in other works of my own.*

Of course, as we consider the paradigm of decline, we may assume that no conceivable array of circumstances would ever cause us to descend to such depths. And yet we might do well to recall individuals we have known or read about who began as responsible, caring, and moral people, but who, in fact, declined by degrees as they increasingly became obsessed with self-gratification in all its myriad forms. We might also do well to recall how the notion of "being human" is frequently employed as an explanation or excuse for bad behavior: "I'm only human, after all" or "that's just human nature" or "people are all the same!"

I personally believe—and the Bahá'í writings seem to confirm this—that inherent within each of us, so long as it is not destroyed or maimed by ourselves or others, is a vision or concept of "goodness," a panoply of virtues manifested or exemplified in our minds by "the good person," whether that person is someone we have personally known or a character depicted in art. After all, how else would concepts like "nobility" and "justice" become so familiar and important to us? How else would we think ourselves so capable of

---

* See Hatcher, *The Arc of Ascent* and *The Ascent of Society: The Social Imperative in Personal Salvation*, both of which discuss the process of individual spiritual development, as well as the social imperative involved in all individual efforts at improvement.

discerning the "good person" or the "just person" if such ideas were not inherent within our consciousness? Or to extend this sequence of thought to its logical conclusion, where would the good person and his or her good actions originate if not from those Teachers— the Manifestations of God—Who periodically appear to reveal for us a renewed vision of goodness manifested by the pattern of Their actions and creatively articulated by Their utterance?

This synthesis between being and doing is so inextricably interconnected that it is impossible to isolate the two at any given moment, in any given endeavor, precisely because there is an ongoing interplay between these twin elements in everything we do. At the end of an endeavor, we cannot surmise that our intentions were good but our actions were bad, or that our actions were good but our intentions or motives were insincere or evil. We are describing a single process comprised of distinct stages: (1) cognition and decision, (2) willful execution, (3) reflection on performance, (4) then higher expectation for the same process, in a sort of spiraling staircase of spiritual ascent. And yet for any particular part of the ascent, there must be a constant flow back and forth, a persistent oversight on our part between our action and our intent as we monitor our intent in the ongoing process of planning, action, reflection, and further planning.

CLASSICAL SIN: FATE VERSUS FREE WILL

Willful choice and its role and consequences in terms of the ascent or decline of human character is the central concern of classical Greek tragedy. At its best, classical tragedy is good theater; it creates an emotional impact just as effectively today as it did 2,500 years ago when Sophocles wrote some of his greatest work, such as the celebrated *Oedipus* and *Antigone*.

The purpose of this drama was fundamentally religious. These plays were intended to instruct the audience regarding the moral perspectives of Greek philosophy. As such, they can properly be viewed as morality plays. But try teaching them to contemporary students, and they just won't get it. Unless the teacher is fairly knowledgeable about the dual perspective of Greek views about destiny and fate in relation to human choice and free will, the discussion of the play will be pretty drab and murky stuff. The most famous of these plays, *Oedipus the King*, is often the more challenging of the two to have students understand or appreciate.

The problem is that Oedipus' fate seems sealed from the outset. When he consults the Oracle at Delphi, he is told that he is "fated" to kill his father and marry his mother, a nasty fate to be sure and one well worth trying to avoid. Consequently, unaware that he is a foundling, Oedipus does just that—he sets out from Corinth, which he believes to be the home of his parents, and travels toward Thebes.

On the way, he gets into a road-rage argument with the driver of another chariot at a three-way intersection. While the argument is a little trivial—who has the right-of-way—the two begin fighting, and Oedipus wins by killing the other driver. Well, the other charioteer just happens to be King Laius of Thebes, Oedipus' birth father. Unbeknownst to Oedipus, he has just fulfilled the first part of the prophecy.

Oedipus then proceeds on to Thebes, but only after solving the riddle of the Sphinx to free the city from her curse. He thus arrives a hero and champion of the people. Once settled in, he meets Jocasta, widow of King Laius and (unknown to our hero) Oedipus' birth mother. Naturally (or unnaturally), they fall in love, get married, and have kids.

Needless to say, it's all downhill after that. The city has a plague as a result of this unknown "unholy" arrangement. Eventually, Jocasta discovers she is Oedipus' mother and kills herself, whereupon Oedipus discovers the same thing, puts out his eyes with brooches from Jocasta's robe, and leaves the city in exile, disgrace, and ignominy. The end.

So how is Oedipus responsible for anything that has gone wrong with his life or the lives of others? Where is his free will in this?

Why should he be judged culpable for a series of events over which he has no apparent control? Why should he be considered "sinful" according to Greek philosophy if all he has done is try to escape his fate, help the people of Thebes by ridding them of the curse of the Sphinx, and become a good husband, father, and king? Is this fair? Is it just?

During my time as a professor of literature (almost half a century) I've heard some pretty strange interpretations of what Aristotle in the *Poetics* calls Oedipus' *hamartia* or "tragic flaw." Somehow Aristotle manages to blame Oedipus for having the hubris of thinking he can escape (or even considering *trying* to escape) what the "fates" have destined for him. He is just plain stubborn. If he had stayed in Corinth, everything would have been alright. At least that seems to be what Aristotle and my former teachers tried to explain to me, and I didn't believe either Aristotle or them.

And so I decided to think about this for myself and by myself, even as Bahá'u'lláh exhorts me to do, and I came up with the idea that indeed bad things happen to good people, but "sinful" actions must necessarily result from choosing to do what you should not do, even though you have every reason to know better. Without knowledge of the right path, free will has no part to play in our making bad decisions. Furthermore, Aristotle makes it clear that the outcome of the tragic figure is that he or she brings about his or her own downfall. He further observes that this tragic descent does not result merely from *one* bad decision (which could happen to anybody) but from a series of consistently bad decisions, each one of which should serve to remind the tragic figure that he or she has a tendency to respond in a predictably bad manner in certain circumstances. The tragic figure has a "correctable" flaw, a weakness or vulnerability in his or her otherwise relatively noble character.

At some part in considering the sequence of events in the play, I realized that Oedipus does have a problem and that it does concern pride, but it is not the presumption of trying to avoid his fate by attempting to *not* kill his father and *not* marry his mother. To me it would be sinful for him *not* to strive to avoid committing such abominable acts. How could this possibly be blameworthy?

But there is a sense in which he is "guilty" or "wrong"—whatever word best describes his response to his perception of reality. First of all, if we study the religion and philosophy of the Greeks carefully, we come to understand that they believed in two degrees or levels of fate. The loftiest level of fate is destiny—that which is destined is unavoidable. Destined events are beyond human control or intervention. But while destined events cannot be averted, neither can anyone be held directly accountable for their occurrence. We might think of these events in the same way we might view a natural disaster or an "act of God."

The second degree or level of fate is conditional or contingent. For example, something is fated to occur unless some alternative course of action is taken by those involved. Possibly someone with wisdom and foresight can discern the "end" in the "beginning" of those events that will bring about this result, and perhaps intervene, often risking their own lives, by making noble choices to deter what might otherwise have been an inevitable fate.

This secondary or subsidiary level of fate is more akin to a prediction based on a logical extension of ongoing exigencies. If you take drugs, you may become an addict. If you drink alcohol, you may become an alcoholic. If you are not a loving and responsible parent, your children may be injured by your conduct; at the very least, their own relationships would be less of a struggle had you been a dedicated, wise, and loving parent. Sometimes this secondary fate is quite predictable—this *will* happen unless you take action. Sometimes it forecasts a probability—this is *likely* to occur if you do not take action.

'Abdu'l-Bahá presents this same notion of two sorts of fate with some very helpful analogies:

Fate is of two kinds: One is irrevocable and the other is conditional, or, as it is said, impending. Irrevocable fate is that which cannot be changed or altered, while conditional fate is that which may or may not occur. Thus, the irrevocable fate for this lamp is that its oil will be burnt and consumed. Its eventual extinction is therefore certain, and it is impossible to change or alter this outcome, for such is its irrevocable fate. . . . But conditional fate may be likened to this: While some oil yet remains, a strong wind blows and extinguishes the lamp. This fate is conditional. It is expedient to avoid this fate, to guard oneself against it, and to be cautious and prudent. But the irrevocable fate, which is like the depletion of the oil of the lamp, cannot be changed, altered, or delayed. ('Abdu'l-Bahá, *Some Answered Questions*, no. 68.2–3)

So, is there something Oedipus could do to avoid his fate? Is his destiny foreseen, foretold, predetermined, or simply a contingent probability, given the gods' awareness of his personality and quirks?

The obvious answer for me, and one which my students often recognized after a bit of prodding, is that it is not Oedipus' flight from doing the "wrong thing" that drives him to do the "wrong thing." Instead, it is a combination of his persistent irascibility, impulsiveness and pride that brings about his downfall, whether in his behavior at the crossroads, or in his decision to marry Jocasta. He does what he thinks best at the moment, what he *wants* to do. He is adamant about getting his way.

He demonstrates this characteristic, this consistent problem in his personality, throughout the play. And in light of the weighty axiom from Greek philosophy "Know Thyself," he is obliged to recognize this flaw in his response to situations, especially when Tiresias (the blind seer) tries to tell him about it and thereby override Oedipus' knee-jerk decisions with a more considered course of action. In short, Oedipus needs to recognize this tendency to be brash and impulsive, and employ his free will to guard against this flaw in his character as he makes each important decision.

To state the entire mess succinctly, Oedipus is *not* responsible for the circumstances into which he is born—having been left to die, having been adopted, having been told he is going to commit wretched acts. But he definitely *is* responsible for how he reacts during the course of his attempt to avoid the outcome of this prediction. If you are worried about killing your father, it would be best not to kill someone simply because you get into an argument at an intersection. In fact, it would be the better part of wisdom not to kill anyone! In addition (and he should have had this one tattooed on his arm) either don't get married, or really exercise due diligence when it comes to choosing your fiancée.

THE SOUL'S ASCENT

As we have noted earlier, free will does not operate in a vacuum. Our fictional paradigm of descent demonstrated how free will is part of a process that always operates in a context. It is most effectively understood as part of a process of ascent or descent in terms of spirituality or moral character. Furthermore, we cannot really comprehend sin and how it works in our lives until we understand this process.

In my book *The Purpose of Physical Reality*, I explore this theme. To a certain extent, I have been writing variations on this theme ever since because I find it to be an endlessly entrancing motif in the symphony of my intellectual journey. It focuses particularly on why God devised a physical beginning to prepare human souls for a metaphysical reality. After all, for many (including me before I wrote the book), this plan seems strange, possibly even contrary to our inherent purpose of becoming good. The concluding observation I make in this discussion is that physical reality is a carefully (perfectly) constructed training device for our initial understanding and practice of virtue—a sort of drama therapy for the novitiate soul.

'Abdu'l-Bahá alludes to this educational process in a number of discussions, but the one I have always found especially useful in understanding this process is where he observes that the paradigm of "knowledge, volition, and action" can be seen at work in every aspect of our efforts at spiritual development in this dramaturgical exercise that is the brief physical stage of our eternal existence:

> Mere *knowledge* of principles is not sufficient. We all know and admit that justice is good, but there is need of *volition* and *action* to carry out and manifest it. For example, we might think it good to build a church, but simply thinking of it as a good thing will not help its erection. The ways and means must be provided; we must will to build it and then proceed with the construction. All of us know that international peace is good, that it is conducive to human welfare and the glory of man, but volition and action are necessary before it can be established. Action is the essential. Inasmuch as this century is a century of light, capacity for action is assured to mankind. Necessarily the divine principles will be spread among men until the time of action arrives. Surely this has been so, and truly the time and conditions are ripe for action now. ('Abdu'l-Bahá, *The Promulgation of Universal Peace*, pp. 167–68). [italics added]

The knowledge in this paradigm can be complex and multifaceted. Ultimately, this knowledge implies not only becoming aware of the reality of a moral principle at work in the world and the desirability of applying it to our character and our lives, but also our appreciation over time that putting this knowledge into action increases our understanding, in a progressive and reciprocal relationship between knowing and doing. The more profoundly we understand a principle, the more capably, creatively, and expansively we can apply it. But naturally we are not alluding to just any sort of knowledge, but rather what Bahá'u'lláh categorizes as "divine knowledge":

Know verily that Knowledge is of two kinds: Divine and Satanic. The one welleth out from the fountain of divine inspiration; the other is but a reflection of vain and obscure thoughts. The source of the former is God Himself; the motive-force of the latter the whisperings of selfish desire. The one is guided by the principle: "Fear ye God; God will teach you;" the other is but a confirmation of the truth: "Knowledge is the most grievous veil between man and his Creator." The former bringeth forth the fruit of patience, of longing desire, of true understanding, and love; whilst the latter can yield naught but arrogance, vainglory and conceit. (Bahá'u'lláh, The Kitáb-i-Íqán, ¶76)

Of course, merely understanding how the process of knowledge, volition, and action can create a reciprocal upward spiral in our personal refinement does not by itself make anything happen, not until we willfully employ this process. And as we have already mentioned, we are admonished to monitor ourselves on a daily basis. In doing so, our character-building can become somewhat habitual and instinctive but always needful of examination, assessment, and revision or refinement.

Once personal change becomes an integral part of our lives, we can proceed to "incorporate"* ever more lofty and complex expressions of virtue and "goodness." Thus the critical link between knowing and doing is volition, the free will we exert both to decide to apply our knowledge and also to be persistent in establishing habitual patterns and in constantly monitoring our progress. By this means, we are able to take charge of improving our character.

---

* The word "incorporate" comes from the Latin and means, "to become manifest in flesh." Hence, the word has great power in conveying the idea of expressing abstract qualities through physical action.

While this process is without bounds in terms of the number of virtues we can acquire or the extent to which a given virtue can be explored and expressed, this prospect of inexhaustible spiritual development is hardly frustrating simply because it is a ceaseless journey. Each successive stage is incrementally more rewarding and more felicitous than the previous one; we need not wait for some future stage of development to reap the rewards and benefits and joy of our effort.

The virtuous path is thus characterized by increasing joy, exhilaration, and detachment as we proceed along our eternal journey. In addition, from the Bahá'í perspective, we need not hold in abeyance our delight until some final reckoning before we achieve "salvation" because in this continuous process there is no "point" of completion. The very ascent of the soul, this activity of constantly moving forward, means that we are capable of being more satisfied and complete as a human being today than we were yesterday, and if we are persistent in our choice and willpower, we can always be in some degree of existential delight, or at least be confident that such delight is attainable if we are patient.

THE SOUL'S DESCENT

Of course, the process of descent can also occur if we fail to employ sufficient free will to acquire "divine" knowledge or, having acquired it, neglect to express our understanding in action. Even if we appreciate the wisdom and felicity that could be ours were we to incorporate our knowledge into a pattern of virtuous action, unless we *choose* to take this course of action and thence establish a pattern of positive response, our knowledge will have limited value. Indeed, it might be argued that it would be better not to know about the value of attaining virtue than to know its worth and then to reject the implicit obligation for action this process requires. In short, once we understand virtue and the worthiness and reward of acquiring its components, we are accountable for what we do with that knowledge.

Another source of descent worse than nonfeasance, which is also a choice because it involves the active decision to reject virtue, is malfeasance. In this case, we actively pursue that which we know full well is detrimental to ourselves and to others. Of course, from the perspective of the Bahá'í teachings, as well as from Socrates' view about the eternality of the soul, no evil we perpetrate has the same degree of detriment to others as it will ultimately have to ourselves. For whatever riches or fame we might garner in the course of this life, whatever material security we may think we have won, our only enduring reality is our conscious self and its relation to our inherent objective of becoming godly, of coming to understand as much as we can about the attributes of the Creator, and refining our character accordingly.

It is in this context—pursuing a course of action we are aware on some level to be injurious to our own best interest and well-being—that we human beings are enigmatic creatures indeed. Little wonder that Socrates concluded that the only explanation for such behavior is that "sinfulness"—or the perpetration of injustice—is indicative of our insufficient knowledge of our own reality and the outcome of this life. Hence the Greek axiom "Know Thyself" becomes, in the context of Socratic philosophy, particularly profound. How strange, as 'Abdu'l-Bahá observes, it is that we will knowingly act in a manner so detrimental to ourselves:

> How strange then it seems that man, notwithstanding his endowment with this ideal power, will descend to a level beneath him and declare himself no greater than that which is manifestly inferior to his real station. God has created such a conscious spirit within him that he is the most wonderful of all contingent beings. In ignoring these virtues he descends to the material plane, considers matter the ruler of existence and denies that which lies beyond. Is this virtue? In its fullest sense this is animalistic, for the animal realizes nothing more. In fact, from this standpoint the animal is the greater phi-

losopher because it is completely ignorant of the Kingdom of God, possesses no spiritual susceptibilities and is uninformed of the heavenly world. ('Abdu'l-Bahá, *The Promulgation of Universal Peace*, p. 248)

6 / SIN AND REMOTENESS

The body politic should . . . strive night and day, bending every effort to ensure that souls are properly educated, that they progress day by day, that they advance in science and learning, that they acquire praiseworthy virtues and laudable manners, and that they forsake violent behaviour, so that crimes might never occur. . . . the body politic must seek to prevent crimes from being committed in the first place, rather than devise harsh punishments and penalties.

— 'Abdu'l-Bahá, *Some Answered Questions*, no. 77.11–14

In our initial discussions about the structure of reality, we alluded to the Bahá'í view of human purpose as being to know and to worship God. We also discussed that coming to know God really implies coming to know *about* God, because we will never comprehend the "essential nature" or reality of God, though His attributes are apparent everywhere. As we have also observed, we can most accurately learn about God through the overt statements of the Manifestations, and we can learn about God indirectly by the way in which the Manifestations perfectly exemplify divine attributes in all They do and say. Furthermore, we can come to understand and appreciate how everything in nature exhibits the imprint of the Creator and can, if studied astutely, reveal to us a multitude of attributes among the infinitude of all there is to discover.

We have also noted the inseparability and reciprocity of "knowing and doing"—how "doing" is the completion of "knowing" inasmuch as by acting out our understanding of moral principles, we are forced to devise creative expressions of our learning in coordinated and ever more expansive patterns of action or behavior. As we concluded in the previous chapter, it is through this process that we can come to manifest godliness ever more completely in our lives, and in doing so also bring about the spiritual transformation of our essential reality, our individual human soul.

NEARER MY GOD TO THEE

This process of being in forward motion or spiritual ascent is the source of our most enduring and most fulfilling delight, as well as the means by which we gradually acquire and exhibit more and more of the attributes of Him in Whose image we have been fashioned. Or stated metaphorically, by becoming more like God, we gradually emulate our Creator and thus can be said to "enter His presence." Bahá'u'lláh explains this symbolic notion of "proximity" in The Book of Certitude and uses the metaphor of "entering the City of Certitude" (Bahá'u'lláh, The Kitáb-i-Íqán, ¶217) to signify the increased confirmation or certitude that accompanies the process.

One of Bahá'u'lláh's axiomatic expressions of this principle is found in the Arabic Hidden Words, no. 35, where He observes, "O Son of Man! Sorrow not save that thou art far from Us. Rejoice not save that thou art drawing near and returning unto Us." Implicit in this exhortation is that we understand what constitutes these opposing processes of "drawing nearer to God" versus "turning away." Since there is no time or space in the spiritual realm, or even in the physical realm in terms of spiritual development, this admonition assumes that we "get it," that we already know what these metaphors refer to.

And having discussed this process of acquiring divine attributes, we do "get it." We draw near or "return" to God or godliness once we begin the spiritual exercises contained in the process discussed in the previous chapter of knowing, choosing, and acting. That Bahá'u'lláh employs the word "return" would seem to allude to the fact that we emanate from God in the first place, even as the oft-cited passage in the Bahá'í scriptures reminds us: "Verily, we are God's, and unto Him do we return."* But this concept of "return" also works well to comfort virtually all of us when, from time to time, we fail to live up to the expectations we establish for ourselves as we strive to advance our spiritual condition.

As we noted before, this concept of "return" in no way implies preexistence or reincarnation; both of these notions are forthrightly rejected in the Bahá'í texts. Therefore this idea of return or forward motion by virtue of intelligent choices is a fact of our essential reality. Because all souls enter the spiritual realm upon physical death, the continuation of the life of the soul, including the existence of the conscious self, is guaranteed and thus beyond our control. What we *can* control is our spiritual condition at the point of this transition.

For example, will we return in a condition of recognition, joy, and gladness at having understood our purpose, and delight at having done a decent job of fulfilling it? Or will we return after having wasted many opportunities for progress, and in need of forgiveness and assistance to make up for the education we could have received and the progress we could have made during the physical portion of our lives? Or, worse still, will we return totally unaware of the existence or characteristics of spiritual reality and thus completely unprepared for this "rebirth"?

> Blessed is the soul which, at the hour of its separation from the body, is sanctified from the vain imaginings of the peoples of the world. Such a soul liveth and moveth in accordance with the Will of its Creator, and entereth the all-highest Paradise. The Maids of Heaven, inmates of the loftiest mansions, will circle around it, and the Prophets of God and His cho-

---

* For example, see Bahá'u'lláh, Kitáb-i-Íqán, ¶99; *Gleanings*, no. 165.1; and *Gems of Divine Mysteries*, pp. 26, 71.

sen ones will seek its companionship. With them that soul will freely converse, and will recount unto them that which it hath been made to endure in the path of God, the Lord of all worlds. If any man be told that which hath been ordained for such a soul in the worlds of God, the Lord of the throne on high and of earth below, his whole being will instantly blaze out in his great longing to attain that most exalted, that sanctified and resplendent station. . . . (Bahá'u'lláh, *Gleanings*, no. 81.1)

Of course, also implicit in Bahá'u'lláh's comment about "return" may be the idea that no matter how rigorous and well-intentioned we may be in our determination to fulfill our inherent objective as human beings, we are going to falter from time to time, at least in relative terms. In this sense, even the best and most spiritual among us will occasionally fall short of the objectives we have established for ourselves.

Thus, for everyone, there is a periodic sense of "return" because we are persistently trying to improve, or, at the very least, to do as well today as we did yesterday. When we fall short of this goal, we may feel a sense of "remoteness," after which we may rededicate ourselves and, having manifested this determination in action, subsequently experience a sense of "return." This rededication can also bring about immense joy and ease of heart. We have "returned" to a sense of being aligned with our true purpose, of literally feeling "nearer" to our Creator and feeling that once again we have returned to the true path.

But how does this concept of success and failure, of sin and redemption, apply to us as social beings? What is the role of society as a whole, and of us as individual citizens, in applying the concept of a "moral path" to social systems and upholding the common good? As we have already noted, very little of our personal spiritual progress can be achieved in isolation from others.

LAW, SIN, AND PENOLOGY

While maintaining social order requires that we establish a judicial system to assess innocence or guilt regarding criminal behavior, we do not and should not presume—even when this system seems to be working properly—that this judgment is rendering a valid assessment of a person's spiritual condition. Neither does a civil court function as God's proxy to dole out divine retribution. As is stated in the Old Testament, in Deuteronomy 32:35, and repeated by Paul in his letter to the Romans 12:19, it is God's function to render a final assessment of our lives, and it is His to take "vengeance" regarding whatever "sinful" actions we may have committed. This is not the job of a civil court or a social system of jurisprudence and penology.

This does not mean there is no connection between our civil behavior and our spiritual condition. In fact, 'Abdu'l-Bahá states that if a murderer is punished in this life, he will not be punished for the same action in the next: "As to the question regarding the soul of a murderer, and what his punishment would be, the answer given was that the murderer must expiate his crime: that is, if they put the murderer to death, his death is his atonement for his crime, and following the death, God in His justice will impose no second penalty upon him, for divine justice would not allow this" ('Abdu'l-Bahá, *Selections from the Writings of 'Abdu'l-Bahá*, no. 152.1).

In addition to alluding to the relationship between acts carried out in this life and the consequences of these acts in the afterlife—a subject we will cover more fully later—this observation obviously has other important implications. For example, while the Bahá'í teachings state that hell does not exist as a physical place or even as an eternal and irretrievable state of being, Bahá'í texts do affirm that we will experience some sort of consequence in the afterlife for those negative actions ("sinful," "evil," and so on) we have committed in this life.

We can only guess what acts we will become aware of that are instantly forgiven versus those for which we must endure some sort of remedial or educational experience in the spiritual realm. If the Creator has designed this life in such a way that no two souls have exactly the same experience or path of choices, we must also presume that an infinitely just and merciful God is no less capable of providing an equally specific and appropriate response to each and every individual's continuation of life in the next stage of existence.

In the Kitáb-i-Aqdas (The Most Holy Book), Bahá'u'lláh has revealed the laws for this dispensation—both spiritual and social laws. He has also established the foundation for future civil institutions to devise legislation and administer justice. He Himself has ordained only a handful of specific punishments for acts that are, in the Bahá'í context, violations of both civil and moral law, but even in these four instances, Bahá'u'lláh has indicated variable or alternative responses on the part of the judiciary bodies evaluating these acts, responses contingent on the severity and exigent circumstances of the particular violation. Here again, it is worth repeating that this system does not depend on case law.*

The apparent rationale for this flexibility and variability is obvious but worth stating nonetheless. Bahá'u'lláh has established the blueprint for an organic global administrative order that includes institutions that will be responsible in the future for evaluating violations of civil and moral law, as well as assessing appropriate punishment. He has not devised an elaborate code of law, nor has He foreshadowed the creation of case law as such. Instead, the judiciary He creates is exhorted to evaluate every case in the context of the exigencies surrounding a particular violation.

This process is already in effect at the local level in the Bahá'í community to oversee the implementation of Bahá'í law, at least in matters where its violation might have public or community

---

* In the Kitáb-i-Aqdas, Bahá'u'lláh "specifies the punishments for murder, arson, adultery and theft . . ." (Bahá'u'lláh, The Kitáb-i-Aqdas, p. 15). For each of these acts He specifies various degrees of punitive response.

implications. Such instances are adjudged by the annually elected Local Spiritual Assembly, an institution that is a precursor to what in the future will be designated with the appellation of the Local House of Justice.

There are also extremely illuminating and valuable discussions in the authoritative Bahá'í texts about the concept of penology in light of the Bahá'í view of the human personal and social reality. For example, 'Abdu'l-Bahá notes that the Bahá'í concept of response to violation of law, whether civil or moral, is a tool whereby society can create order, deter criminal activity, and progressively construct a supportive and spiritually healthy environment for the education of its citizens. He observes that when such a society is constructed, the concern of each citizen for being thought of as a decent person will do more to ensure obedience to law than the fear of punishment. Or to state the converse of this principle, the fear of being thought of as immoral, untrustworthy, or a law-breaker will be the most effective deterrent to criminal behavior in a society constructed according to spiritual principles.

It might be worthwhile at this point to note that while the purpose of the Bahá'í Faith is to create a peaceful and loving community, the vision of this social construct is not based on naïve idealism. 'Abdu'l-Bahá states that if the community ignores its responsibility to punish the criminal, it is neglecting its obligation to "safeguard the rights of man" ('Abdu'l-Bahá, *Some Answered Questions*, no. 77.10). Nevertheless, even in the context of this observation, 'Abdu'l-Bahá asserts that there must always be a clear distinction between vengeance and chastisement. He notes that vengeance is never appropriate for an individual or a governing body, but chastisement is one means to help secure justice and order.

An individual has no right to seek revenge, but the body politic has the right to punish the criminal. Such punishment is intended to dissuade and deter others from committing similar crimes. It is for the protection of the rights of man and

does not constitute revenge, for revenge is that inner gratification that results from returning like for like. This is not permissible, for no one has been given the right to seek revenge.
('Abdu'l-Bahá, *Some Answered Questions*, no. 77.2)

'Abdu'l-Bahá observes that for the community to fail to punish the
criminal (and thus, in the eyes of some, ostensibly demonstrate
mercy) is to deprive others in the community of that same mercy,
as well as to endanger the right of a citizen to have security: "If,
for example, ye be tender-hearted toward a wolf, this is but tyranny to a sheep, for a wolf will destroy a whole flock of sheep. A
rabid dog, if given the chance, can kill a thousand animals and
men. Therefore, compassion shown to wild and ravening beasts is
cruelty to the peaceful ones—and so the harmful must be dealt
with" ('Abdu'l-Bahá, *Selections from the Writings of 'Abdu'l-Bahá*,
no. 138.5).

Nevertheless, 'Abdu'l-Bahá affirms that the community should
never apply punishment for the purpose of retaliation or for hatred
of the criminal; instead, its objective should always be to bring
about justice, one aspect of which is securing the laws and order of
the community: "But the body politic has the right to preserve and
to protect. It holds no grudge and harbours no enmity towards the
murderer, but chooses to imprison or punish him solely to ensure
the protection of others. The purpose is not revenge but a punishment through which the body politic is protected" ('Abdu'l-Bahá,
Some Answered Questions, no. 77.6). In this same discussion about
the Bahá'í concept of penology, 'Abdu'l-Bahá notes that in an
enlightened and spiritually oriented society, penology will function as a tool for socialization and education. To repeat what we
noted above, when this method is applied appropriately so that
individuals are properly educated, and society assumes spiritual
enlightenment and comportment as its loftiest values, one's desire
not to be regarded a criminal will be the greatest deterrent to crime.

Though 'Abdu'l-Bahá does not explicitly state that penal institutions have an obligation to educate the criminal, He does make one poignant observation about the unfortunate nature of present attitudes about penology: "The body politic should . . . strive night and day, bending every effort to ensure that souls are properly educated, that they progress day by day, that they advance in science and learning, that they acquire praiseworthy virtues and laudable manners, and that they forsake violent behaviour, so that crimes might never occur. . . . the body politic must seek to prevent crimes from being committed in the first place, rather than devise harsh punishments and penalties" ('Abdu'l-Bahá, *Some Answered Questions*, no. 77.11–14).

Obviously no society or social institution is capable of knowing the inmost heart of a citizen. It is unable to determine with complete certainty who is or is not a sinner—that determination is between the individual soul and God alone. Certainly the same principle applies to us as members of the community—we have no ability to assess the spiritual station or progress of another person, nor should we try. We are not privy to their motives or to the countless variables at work in any given choice they make, let alone the confluence of these variables in the outcome of a single course of action.

This fact alone should give us a sense of relief. We must take care of ourselves, our families, and our communities by protecting ourselves against abusive or criminal behavior, but we are relieved of the responsibility of having to render a spiritual judgment or of taking some form of retributive or vengeful action in response to injury suffered at the hands of another. We can only try our best in upholding the laws while manifesting the comportment and character of a "good citizen" and helping to fashion a social environment in which being thought of as decent, law-abiding, and "good" is the greatest reward society can bestow and where being removed from the community would be considered by all as the most grievous of punishments.

Sin, thus, may or may not be distinct from antisocial behavior; there may be some valid reason why one is placed in the position of having to commit what society considers a "criminal" act. But clearly, only assessment by God can determine whether or not an action is "sinful" or whether the perpetrator is in a condition of "drawing near" or "pulling away."

TASTING THE CHOICE WINE

This, then, may be as succinct and lucid a definition of "sin" as we can concoct: the idea that if we willingly and knowingly commit an act that will impede our journey back to God, then such an act is "sinful," even as it is "regressive," "detrimental," or "retarding." And if, like Sophocles' tragic figures, we allow our flaws to become ingrained so that we consistently respond with bad or immoral acts, then our souls will gradually deteriorate, become more "sinful," and become more remote from the presence of God.

But as we noted, this regression does not result solely from committing negative actions; it can also result from stasis, from nonfeasance or negligence. The problem is that if we must evaluate the motive for everything we do, we might end up stumbling through our days while weighing every action in the balance or rethinking every move we make. This is where the wisdom of a divinely devised path or pattern of behavior demonstrates its value for us. However, as we have mentioned, this path is *not* an exacting canon of laws that we are asked to follow mindlessly. Neither does it dictate a series of ritualistic behaviors that would prove frustrating and constraining rather than empowering and liberating.

Instead, Bahá'u'lláh describes His revelation of the spiritual path as unsealing the "choice Wine": "Think not that We have revealed unto you a mere code of laws," He says in His Most Holy Book, "Nay, rather, We have unsealed the choice Wine with the fingers of might and power" (Bahá'u'lláh, The Kitáb-i-Aqdas, ¶5). Imbibing this celestial vintage maximizes individual freedom and enhances our ability to shape our own destiny.

It accomplishes this enigmatic task (empowering us through laws, ordinances, and exhortations) first by freeing us from those avenues that are blatant deterrents or diversions from our inherent objective. If we once again recall the parable of the lover seeking his beloved (see chapter 1), we remember that in addition to urging the lover in the direction he needs to go if he is to discover the object of his quest, the various watchmen "came together, and barred every passage to the weary one."

In this sense, the parable works well to explain how recognition of the wisdom in the laws and guidance of the Manifestation prevents us from becoming distracted from the right path: the watchmen symbolize the laws. Thus while the watchmen at first might have seemed as though they were preventing the lover from escaping or from pursuing a path of freedom, in reality they assisted him to attain his goal. Likewise, the laws and guidance of the Manifestation assist believers to maximize their potential, their freedom, and their ability to develop spiritually.

BARRED PASSAGES

Shoghi Effendi, Guardian of the Bahá'í Faith,* directed that before the Kitáb-i-Aqdas could be translated and published in English, this collection of laws, ordinances, and exhortations that comprise the cornerstone of Bahá'u'lláh's revealed guidance for His followers needed to be codified. Consequently, a logically structured *Codification and Synopsis* of all the specific laws and guidance revealed by Bahá'u'lláh in the Kitáb-i-Aqdas is available for the Bahá'ís, or for any student of the Bahá'í Faith.

Bahá'u'lláh also conferred upon the Supreme Institution, the Universal House of Justice, the authority to make additional laws as needed. Therefore, in time, further authoritative guidance will

---

* Appointed by 'Abdu'l-Bahá as head of the Bahá'í Faith and authorized interpreter of the Bahá'í texts.

become available for our constantly evolving social environment. But one important characteristic of the laws and patterns of behavior set forth in this work is that they keep personal restrictions or constraints to a minimum. Indeed, a significant portion of the Kitáb-i-Aqdas is the abrogation of taboos and prohibitions inherited from prior religious and cultural traditions.

Understandably, in the context of contemporary social mores where there is a dearth of any universally shared perspectives about norms and private behavior, any restriction might be perceived as anathema. But in the context of religious history, the Bahá'í Faith is, as we have said, freed from the bonds of an elaborate canon of law, rituals, or inherited traditions. Bahá'ís are prohibited solely from those actions or behaviors that would weaken or damage the very faculties of reason and judgment that are absolutely critical in enabling them to discern the right path and to sustain the willpower to follow it.

For example, Bahá'u'lláh prohibits the use of alcohol, drugs, gambling, companionate marriage, and sex outside marriage. Not coincidentally in the nearly one and a half centuries since the revelation of this work, we as a world community can now appreciate how destructive many of these indulgences are on a societal level.

Of course not everyone has a predisposition to become overwhelmed by these urges or indulgences. It is certainly conceivable that one could be a "moderate" or "social" drinker, a drug user who confines his "habit" to less destructive chemicals, a gambler who sets strict limits on how much of the family savings he or she will risk, or a sexually active individual who does not become totally promiscuous or obsessed. The problem is that we usually discover the dramatically negative effects of these practices only after they have consumed much of our will so that, once we realize the dilatory and overpowering effects of these behaviors, we end up devoting a major portion of our free will trying to avoid negative behavior rather than working to spiritually advance ourselves and the communities in which we live.

It is worth repeating (because it cannot be overemphasized), that the "true liberty" Bahá'u'lláh asserts following His guidance will provide involves neither needless, arbitrary constraints nor mindless obedience. Rather, there is a discernible logic underlying every prohibition or exhortation, a logic that results in the maximization of our loftiest powers and the attainment of our most rewarding and felicitous mode of living.

EXHORTATIONS FOR GROWTH

At least as important as the "watchmen" that bar diverting but dangerous passageways are those that chase us toward the object of our desire. Symbolically, these forces that urge us to undertake an active role in our journey might be the laws and exhortations of Bahá'u'lláh that delineate affirmative exercises capable of enhancing our powers of body, mind, and spirit. This pattern of living, sometimes alluded to by believers as the "Bahá'í life," consists of a daily regimen of specific actions geared to keep us spiritually "nourished" and to help us monitor how we are doing in relation to our avowed objectives as declared followers of Bahá'u'lláh.

Principal among the practices that characterize this way of life is obligatory daily prayer. While prayer is beneficial at any time, the rationale for the obligatory nature of certain prayers is obvious but well worth articulating. If we are to maintain a lifelong journey of attempting to acquire divine attributes, it is essential to maintain an ongoing dialogue with the source of those attributes. For while God is unknowable in His essence, we have immediate and continuous access to those powers and attributes that emanate from Him like rays of light radiating from the sun.

If we were left solely to our own emotional inclinations about when to have this dialogue with our Creator, we would probably pray on two prominent occasions—when we are experiencing great suffering and when we are experiencing extreme felicity and gratitude. But just as the physical aspect of "self" is best maintained by regular daily material nourishment, our essential spiritual reality also requires regular daily spiritual nutrition. Therefore, as a minimum adequate nourishment for the daily reinvigoration of our spiritual powers, Bahá'u'lláh has revealed three specific prayers, from which the believer should choose one to recite each day to partake of this spiritual sustenance.

Allied to this affirmative law is the requirement that each believer read from the revealed works of Bahá'u'lláh in the morning and in the evening. No set amount of reading is established, nor are any specific materials designated from among the more than one hundred works revealed by Him. Here again, the wisdom is that the new revelation from God is the source of all transformation for humankind, whether individually or collectively. Similar to the nourishment received from our prayerful conversations with God, the access to the knowledge of God comes directly through those works specifying the remedies prescribed by the "All-Knowing Physician" for the contemporary ills that afflict us:

> The All-Knowing Physician hath His finger on the pulse of mankind. He perceiveth the disease, and prescribeth, in His unerring wisdom, the remedy. Every age hath its own problem, and every soul its particular aspiration. The remedy the world needeth in its present-day afflictions can never be the same as that which a subsequent age may require. Be anxiously concerned with the needs of the age ye live in, and center your deliberations on its exigencies and requirements. (Bahá'u'lláh, *Gleanings*, no. 106.1)

In addition to these and other spiritual exercises that constitute part of the daily routine or spiritual regimen of a Bahá'í, Bahá'u'lláh also delineates in detail that personal hygiene and public comportment should give outward expression to inner harmony and chastity. As mentioned already, this guidance is intertwined within the overall Bahá'í view of reality as a perpetual reciprocity between our inner perception and our outward or physical habituation of progressive enlightenment.

Without attempting here to rehearse all the exhortations dealing with such matters as bathing, perfuming the body, or wearing clean clothes, suffice it to say that Bahá'u'lláh both abrogates many needless inherited taboos and traditions regarding apparel, diet, and other customs, while simultaneously upholding the overall concern for cleanliness and refinement of every sort—even manners and etiquette.

Many of the works of Bahá'u'lláh revealed after the Kitáb-i-Aqdas (1873) are collections of beautiful and succinct lists of attributes one should aspire to possess. Adorned with such poetic titles as the "Ornaments," the "Effulgences," and the "Splendors," these works contain definitions and elucidations of those attributes that should characterize and distinguish a Bahá'í. Likewise, 'Abdu'l-Bahá, in a great many of the letters written to believers throughout the world, explicates what it means to "live the Bahá'í life":

> "O army of God!" writes 'Abdu'l-Bahá, "Through the protection and help vouchsafed by the Blessed Beauty [Bahá'u'lláh]—may my life be a sacrifice to His loved ones—ye must conduct yourselves in such a manner that ye may stand out distinguished and brilliant as the sun among other souls. Should any one of you enter a city, he should become a center of attraction by reason of his sincerity, his faithfulness and love, his honesty and fidelity, his truthfulness and loving-kindness towards all the peoples of the world, so that the people of that city may cry out and say: 'This man is unquestionably a Bahá'í, for his manners, his behavior, his conduct, his morals, his nature, and disposition reflect the attributes of the Bahá'ís.' Not until ye attain this station can ye be said to have been faithful to the Covenant and Testament of God."
>
> "The most vital duty, in this day," He, moreover, has writ-

ten, "is to purify your characters, to correct your manners, and improve your conduct." (quoted in Shoghi Effendi, *The Advent of Divine Justice*, ¶40)

Finally, we cannot leave this subject without referring to one of the most memorable and powerful of Shoghi Effendi's many discourses about the critical importance of developing nobility of character as a prerequisite to any other objective. In a lengthy exegesis on the importance and implications of the concept of "chastity," he says that this crowning jewel of attributes must be evident in every aspect of the life of the Bahá'í:

> Such a chaste and holy life, with its implications of modesty, purity, temperance, decency, and clean-mindedness, involves no less than the exercise of moderation in all that pertains to dress, language, amusements, and all artistic and literary avocations. It demands daily vigilance in the control of one's carnal desires and corrupt inclinations. It calls for the abandonment of a frivolous conduct, with its excessive attachment to trivial and often misdirected pleasures. It requires total abstinence from all alcoholic drinks, from opium, and from similar habit-forming drugs. It condemns the prostitution of art and of literature, the practices of nudism and of companionate marriage, infidelity in marital relationships, and all manner of promiscuity, of easy familiarity, and of sexual vices. It can tolerate no compromise with the theories, the standards, the habits, and the excesses of a decadent age. Nay rather it seeks to demonstrate, through the dynamic force of its example, the pernicious character of such theories, the falsity of such standards, the hollowness of such claims, the perversity of such habits, and the sacrilegious character of such excesses. (Shoghi Effendi, *The Advent of Divine Justice*, no. 47)

7 / THE CONTAGION OF NONFEASANCE AND COLLECTIVE SIN

The fundamental principle underlying this solemn Pact should be so fixed that if any government later violate any one of its provisions, all the governments on earth should arise to reduce it to utter submission, nay the human race as a whole should resolve, with every power at its disposal, to destroy that government. Should this greatest of all remedies be applied to the sick body of the world, it will assuredly recover from its ills and will remain eternally safe and secure.

—'Abdu'l-Bahá, *The Secret of Divine Civilization*, ¶120

It is a commonly held axiom that all that is necessary for the triumph of evil is for good men to do nothing. Are lethargy, ambivalence, and apathy sins? We have thus far described sinful acts as stemming from the active pursuit of self-interest, even though this broad brush paints a wide variety of actions as possibly detrimental to ourselves or to others. But what about inaction? Of course, we did mention that according to Catholic doctrine, sloth is one of the seven deadly sins. But what about refusing to follow those positive activities that characterize Bahá'í life, or, for those who are not Bahá'ís, failing to respond in ordinary situations where justice, morality, and courage are required? Is it sinful simply to refuse to strive to attain some degree of moral or spiritual advancement? Is stasis evil? Is stasis even possible?

THE SUBTLETY OF NONFEASANCE

Since this book is focused on the reality of the soul in relation to its progress, we might think this topic better suited for an entirely different sort of discussion. But after we review a few salient points about this inaction, we may come to appreciate that various forms of "nonfeasance" are quite as conducive to a state of spiritual decline as malfeasance, the active pursuit of regressive or perverse paths of degradation.

So let's begin with Hitler, who is possibly the most useful and readily accessible historical example of malfeasance. What, we might ask, does Hitler have to do with understanding the sin of nonfeasance? After all, there have been countless villainous tyrants in the history of human civilization. Every culture contains real-life icons of evil. But in this present time of crucial change and transformation from our former view of Earth as a conglomeration of nation states to our present appreciation of global interdependence, Hitler provides us with a mythic figure to caution us about the pitfalls of allowing one of us to employ modern technology to subdue the world, to terrify masses of people into submission, to make manifest the fictive horror of Orwell's and Huxley's visions of a systematized global tyranny of body, mind, and spirit.

These days, virtually every movie that is centered on themes of good versus evil is not about the fight against one or two villains whom the local sheriff must heroically defeat in a small Western town. No, to grab our attention in the context of our contemporary world, the threat must be global. We just aren't interested unless the conflict involves the survival of humankind, which usually devolves upon one or two particularly savvy, athletic, and fearless men (assisted now and again by a very attractive woman, who, more often than not, is simply the equivalent of a cheerleader at a football game).

Now, you may well wonder what this scenario has to do with the usefulness of Hitler. And the answer is that whenever we need an example of the depths of depravity to which a human being can decline, or of how the influence and contagion of one evil individual can afflict and infect great masses of people, we always have at hand the example of Hitler. He may not have been the most evil person who ever wielded power, and he may not even have won the mantle of being statistically the most effective mass murderer in history. But he is out there for all to see, concealing nothing, masterfully articulating a program of hatred, genocide, and venomous and cynical rage against the light, like a mad scientist gathering together enthralled students in a perverse scheme to scatter a virulent toxin.

No, Hitler is not in the background like Stalin, with his thick moustache and nice hair. He is not very imposing or commanding—we would not buy a used car from this man. We cringe as we watch, through the accurate lens German technology wrought, this wimpy-looking lunatic atop a podium. We wince at the sight of the generals and soldiers and smiling blond masses saluting, paying homage, not to God or country, but to this almost comical-looking figure—the *Führer*. We watch incredulously as the vile man smiles, cradling the chin of a young girl. We gag as we see him dance gaily when he learns Paris has fallen.

We see him flanked by handsome men, intelligent men, all so sharp in their smartly tailored uniforms, watching in awe as the little painter points on a map to the next country he will conquer and obliterate. We watch this film, slightly in disbelief that less than a lifetime ago this drama really happened, though it seems so overdone, so sappy and maudlin, as if this were Charlton Heston playing Moses for Cecil B. DeMille. Surely this craziness could not really have happened, not in the modern world among such a sagacious and cultured people. But that's no actor mimicking a tyrant. That really is Hitler. He really did exist, and people, most uncoerced, adored this man, cheered at his presence, and did whatever he commanded.

"How could it have happened?" we all asked after the war, when Allied troops discovered the massive and methodical machines of genocide as they came upon the death camps, each more ghastly than the other. And so . . . and so we held the Nuremberg trials to ask those who actively orchestrated the horror, "Did you not know?

Do you not see what you did in these films? Do you not have some explanation to justify this grotesque massacre of actual human beings? See there the mass graves and starved bodies shoved into pits by bulldozers? You who claim to be advanced, you who touted a global civilization, a third kingdom, please tell us something, anything, to explain how this could happen!"

The reactions of the accused varied widely. One member of Hitler's entourage sat in court babbling to himself because he apparently had been driven insane from the ordeal or was already deranged from the start. Two managed to take their own lives in the honorable style of the Germanic mythic heroes. Others were led in a queue to the gallows, where their necks were snapped as if such easy recompense could suffice for the millions who had been abused in concentration camps and in countless other places, who had suffered hour after hour and day after grisly day, dreaming of justice, aching for peace.

But no one gave us the answers we wanted. None said forthrightly, "I had allowed myself to become thoroughly corrupted and evil! I allowed my desire for power to overcome my sense of my own humanity. I descended to the depths of baseness. I became worse than the beasts of the fields. What I did and ordered others to do was sinful and grotesque, and I feel such guilt and shame that it will require an eternity to redeem myself, if redemption is even an option for one so monstrous as I. Please, do with me as you think best, for I have lost my way! Like Faust, I sold my soul and deserve whatever hideous chastisement you can devise, and the harsher the better—something excruciatingly painful, slow, and unrelenting until I melt away in pure agony. Only then will there be some feasible hope for my immortal soul!"

That's what we wanted to hear. Naively, that's what we actually expected to hear! Surely they knew that what they did was transparently and overtly evil, vile, and beyond the grasp of virtuous minds to conceive. Surely they knew these were human beings that they treated as though slaughtering the basest of animals for some satanic feast. We wanted to understand how their coldly rational minds could actually countenance such lunacy.

So you see, Hitler is useful for us because we have documents, pictures, films, and a trial. We can watch it all through those finely crafted German camera lenses and hear him, with unmistakable clarity, spew his insane rhetoric to tens of thousands of smiling Germans waving their broken crosses. We can trace the entire debacle in our collective history from its meager inception in a beer hall to its fiery demise, every step carefully documented by meticulous records from a methodical mentality. We can never again question the limitless depths to which the human soul can descend.

Had Hitler also been tried at Nuremberg, a good defense attorney could possibly have made a case that Hitler was not responsible for his actions. After all, we seem to agree that he was quite insane. "The problem was," the attorney would argue after parading a team of psychiatrists applying polysyllabic terms to portray this particular personality disorder, "Hitler was a small man, a meek man, an artist! He would never have done the horrible things he did if those around him had not encouraged him. He was just carrying out the will of the people as their elected leader!"

The attorney would then show films of Hitler speaking to the vast crowds who concurred with everything he was saying, who raised their arms in unison as they shouted "Heil Hitler!" or "Hail, My Leader!" or "Hail Victory!" The attorney would remark, "Who among us would not be coaxed deeper and deeper into the contagion of such a mob mentality, with these happy cheering voices shouting in unison, urging us to conquer the world on behalf of the fatherland!

"I ask you, ladies and gentlemen of the jury," the attorney might say in his closing, "who really is to blame—this unfortunate, deluded man who so desperately and obviously needed affection and psychiatric help—and, sadly, in the very country where psychiatry was born? No! I say those to blame are all those cheering crowds surrounding him and encouraging him, instead of getting him the help he needed. It was *they* who took advantage of this infirm and deluded man to pursue their own perverse obsession with conquering the world. It was they who convinced him that he was really not a very good painter and that his lunatic ideas were sound!

"No, do not blame this sick, sick individual who quite obviously could not discern right from wrong! Blame instead all those who had reason to know better, those around him who were not insane, those who sought only to use him as their catalyst, the means to vault themselves into power, by isolating him from those who might have guided him aright, who could have gotten him the help he so desperately needed.

"Let me conclude, ladies and gentlemen, with a familiar statement about those days when Hitler's fantasy world was becoming all-too-real and when only a few good people dared to speak out. They are the words of German pastor Martin Niemöller, who, you must remember, was attracted to Hitler in the beginning, though in time he came to realize how dangerously deluded this man was, and what great damage, if allowed to proceed unchecked, he would do to himself and to Germany:

> First they came for the Jews and I did not speak out because
>   I was not a Jew.
> Then they came for the Communists and I did not speak
>   out because I was not a Communist.
> Then they came for the trade unionists and I did not speak
>   out because I was not a trade unionist.
> Then they came for me and there was no one left to speak
>   out for me.*

---

* Niemöller, cited in the online *Holocaust Encyclopedia*, an online work published by United States Holocaust Memorial Museum. http://www.ushmm.org/learn/holocaust-encyclopedia.)

"In these succinct and ironic lines of verse, this fine and heroic pastor admits his own sin, his own guilt in allowing this poor man to be urged into power by his so-called friends, some of them quite as disturbed as he. Here Niemöller is confessing that once the people had reason to know better but remained complacent out of fear or self-interest, they themselves were to blame for all that followed."

Hitler then looks down and slumps in the defendant's chair. He is thin. His ill-fitted suit is wrinkled. His head sways a bit from side to side as he stares down. His iconic moustache is gone, and he seems unaware of what is transpiring. He looks diminished and bewildered by the crowded courtroom, as if he had wandered in from the street to ask for directions or a handout. If some soul were to enter looking for a grotesque and heinous villain, he surely would be the last person they would suspect. No, only a being with divine powers would be able to assay the depravity and guilt of the man. In short, only God could adjudicate this case.

We can hope that in our hypothetical reflection, the prosecution was allowed to show some footage of Auschwitz or Dachau or Buchenwald. Probably Hitler would still have been convicted, but most likely the judge would not have allowed it since Hitler himself did not physically do these things. Such footage would have been adjudged as prejudicial to the jury, and Hitler would have been placed in some institution for the criminally insane, as was one of his surviving cohorts, Rudolf Hess.

It doesn't matter. What we have from this history lesson is so valuable (for those who still bother to study history) that from the seeds scattered out of the gruesomeness of it all germinated the tree of a present-day universal awareness of genocide and of the need to have worldwide oversight for our emerging global community.

But there also came to light the sense of collective shame and guilt of a people universally recognized for their intelligence, ingenuity, and rich culture. Painfully, the people of this and every other land began to realize ever more excruciatingly how differently history might have played out had only a few acted differently or in a more timely fashion. For example, on 20 July 1944 (by the time Germany had clearly lost the war), Claus von Stauffenberg and other like-minded conspirators tried to assassinate Hitler so that the war could be ended and peace with the Western Allies could be made before the not-so-peace-minded Russian troops swarmed in from the eastern front.*

But this sin of nonfeasance was not Germany's alone. Had England acted more quickly, or had America overcome its understandable isolationism, the price of action—when it finally was taken—might not have been so exorbitant.

But here and now, both on the personal level and collectively, we have plentiful evidence that this pathology of nonfeasance still abounds. On the one hand, there are quite legitimate reasons for avoiding getting actively involved in physical confrontations or stepping into the middle of a fray to restrain combatants. The epidemic of "bullying" among young children demonstrates the contagion of this response. But apathy in terms of our obligation to speak out against bullying, racism, or other overt forms of injustice would certainly seem to constitute immoral or sinful behavior. Stated as a verity, inaction that helps facilitate or encourage injustice makes us complicit in injustice. We may not be the perpetrators per se, but we empower the perpetrators by failing to acquire and exercise the virtue of courage.

Thus we can easily distinguish between the nonfeasance or inaction on the part of those who are truly unaware that there is a need for action and that of those who restrain themselves from expressing an opinion or taking action because they are afraid of

---

* In fairness to the German people, not only have they collectively learned important lessons about tolerance from their experience, they erected a memorial to the heroism of the conspirators in the very courtyard where they were hanged. Furthermore, there were other earlier attempts to assassinate Hitler.

endangering their social standing. Surely, as soon as we become aware that action is needed in order to establish or uphold justice, yet refuse to act, we are committing injustice ourselves.

We have tacitly defined sin (or the source of sin within ourselves) as the promptings of the lower self—what 'Abdu'l-Bahá calls the "insistent self." But we might understandably wonder how this definition applies to the sin of nonfeasance. How do the promptings of our baser instincts urge inaction? In the document *Century of Light*, commissioned by the Universal House of Justice, we find the observations that throughout human history, most people were content to pay obeisance to the whims and selfish desires of political and religious leaders, and that Bahá'u'lláh has come to free humankind from this bondage. This freedom necessarily includes the responsibility of all to participate in bringing about justice for the whole of humankind:

> Throughout history, the masses of humanity have been, at best, spectators at the advance of civilization. Their role has been to serve the designs of whatever elite had temporarily assumed control of the process. Even the successive Revelations of the Divine, whose objective was the liberation of the human spirit, were, in time, taken captive by "the insistent self," were frozen into man-made dogma, ritual, clerical privilege and sectarian quarrels, and reached their end with their ultimate purpose frustrated.
>
> Bahá'u'lláh has come to free humanity from this long bondage, and the closing decades of the twentieth century were devoted by the community of His followers to creative experimentation with the means by which His objective can be realized. (*Century of Light*, 9.33–34)

Our conscious decision not to assist the downtrodden in our midst or to refrain from speaking out against injustice in all its myriad forms is usually not merely the result of lethargy or distraction, though these could contribute to negligence on our part. Most often our failure to act, to uphold justice, or to promulgate social responsibility results from fear of endangering our reputation among those we wish to impress, or else fear of retaliation— concern that by upholding righteousness, we too might become subjected to the same injustice being perpetrated on those whom we should assist.

Cowardice, like darkness, can thus be portrayed as the absence of a positive force—most often the courage to respond to our social responsibility. Nevertheless, this failure to respond results from a willful and conscious decision *not* to be courageous. In other words, we know that courage would be available to us if only we exerted the effort, but we actively choose not to employ this virtue latent within us. Importantly, then, courage need not be understood as the process of becoming fearless—being afraid is not in itself a vice. Rather, true courage derives from developing the habit of acting righteously in spite of any initial fear we experience. As we nurture this habit over the course of time, our fears about acting will probably abate, and our courage will increase.

As with most forms of sin or evil at the level of personal conduct, nonfeasance is contagious, as are cowardice and social inaction. As we have previously noted, perhaps the best analogy to understand how evil works within us individually and collectively is by comparing it to a contagious disease. Cynicism, for example, can infect us so quickly, so insidiously, and so subtly that before we are aware that it is even working on us, it has destroyed our love, our faith, our determination, and even our courage.

Evil is thus infectious because it creates an environment that poisons virtues. In such an atmosphere, cynicism spreads—invisible but lethal. The dominance of the contemporary attitude of not wanting to get involved in other people's dilemmas but rather to look after ourselves or possibly our immediate family has shaped us into a collection of individuals rather than a collaborative or coherent community. And ironically, the exponential increase in social technology enabling us to communicate instantly with anyone in the world has entrenched this isolation rather than help reducing or overcoming it.

We have virtual friendships, and we might even theorize that we have virtual communities of friends with whom we maintain constant conversations. But these virtual communities and electronic exchanges of thought have no impact on transforming literal society unless some tangible form of action results from it. Certainly this technology is not inherently evil. Like any innovative tool, these devices and the social networks they foster and enable can be used to unite us in common causes and can empower us to strategize methods of fostering real change. However, they can also give us the illusion of actual collaboration when, in fact, we may have merely focused our energy on words translated into electronic signals bouncing off satellites. If electricity were suddenly unavailable, these friends would no longer be accessible, this community would instantly evaporate, and we would immediately appreciate our need for face-to-face interaction with our friends and neighbors.

But let us continue with our point regarding the extent to which nonfeasance, or the decision not to exercise a virtue, is a sin. Is nonfeasance as sinful as actively perpetrating injustice and cruelty? If we simply want to live our lives safely in a society where security is hard to sustain, or if we wish to protect ourselves and our family from the pernicious and toxic environment that seems to have become endemic in contemporary culture, then why should we be blamed for holding back? Who could blame us for not stepping into a fray that seems unstoppable and hopelessly out of control? Or, stated another way, is it possible that in some situations apathy might be a sane and logical response to reality? If we sincerely believe, for example, that the political system is irreparably dysfunctional, then why should we spend time, money, and energy trying to express an opinion knowing that the political infrastructure in most countries is determined by power derived from moneyed interests and only negligibly from the collective opinions of ordinary citizens?

Here we need to distinguish between the nonfeasance of the individual operating within a local environment, and the citizen deciding how to respond to a broken body politic. For example, let us consider how a young boy used his camera to capture a ten-minute video of a grandmother who was serving as a monitor on a school bus for middle-school students. Without provocation, the students start mocking the woman, teasing her about her weight, relentlessly chiding and berating her, even as she tries her best to sit still and pay no heed.

This incident functions almost as a scientific experiment inasmuch as the bus was, for all intents and purposes, a closed environment where the children had to make their own choices about how to respond. Even the boy filming this did not do so in order to document the injustice of this thoroughly disgusting, immoral, and hurtful behavior. Rather, his purpose was to post this video on a website where such outlandish and "humorous" incidents are commonly displayed for the world to admire. It was his wish that the piece would "go viral" and that he might become a fifteen-minute hero or even make a buck or two.

But once people viewed what had taken place out of the context of the peer-group environment—this closed bus community—all began to realize how abominable this mob mentality had been. The video immediately went viral, to be sure, but even to a society largely apathetic about the plight of its members, this vivid portrayal of how American progeny from a "respectable" middle-class neighborhood act when not under the scrutiny and oversight of people in authority had an overpowering emotional impact.

The parents involved visited the home of the grandmother to apologize in person. A fundraising site was established to provide her with the money she was trying to raise with her job so that she might, at long last, travel abroad. That's the bright side. More than seven hundred thousand dollars was raised. Even more heartening, this sixty-eight-year-old lady used one hundred thousand dollars of that money to start a foundation, the Karen Klein Anti-Bullying Foundation. More than thirty-two thousand people soon contributed. The four students who taunted her were suspended for a year.

And yet, the good that derived from this unfortunate episode does not really outweigh what this incident demonstrated about the moral tenor of our society. For while these four students came from good homes and were not lowlife miscreants from disenfranchised communities, so were all the other students who did nothing to deter this action. Not a single voice on the video was heard speaking out against the bullying that transpired. Not one young person came to the grandmother's defense.

More than the ostensibly felicitous outcome of people coming to the financial aid of the victim—something that can be comfortably done from a safe distance—this incident demonstrates that possibly the segregation of state and religion in terms of public education has taken a heavier toll than we yet fully appreciate.

THE CONTAGION OF VIRTUE

If we wish to change this collective attitude of apathy and social nonfeasance, we cannot wait until someone figures out how to reintroduce morality into education without challenging the "sacred" doctrine separating church and state.* As we have been aware for ages, morality cannot be legislated or coerced. But morality can be modeled. It can be instigated at the local level, encouraged, and facilitated. Indeed, that is precisely where the transformation of

---

* In the United States Constitution, this doctrine is considered implicit in the First Amendment, but subsequent rulings based on this amendment have taken to extreme the notion that no religion has the right to express or impose itself in the public domain, including education, to the exclusion of all other religions. Furthermore, the concept of what constitutes a "religion" has become so obscured and muddled as to have no important relationship to beliefs in God, the soul, or any sort of metaphysical reality.

society must begin, at the so-called grassroots level. At the local level, a model of the "good" community can be created with sufficient efficacy and appeal that its medicinal properties will be welcomed, emulated, and, paradoxically, spread as quickly as the plague.

This local modeling can happen! In fact, it has happened and is happening. For similar to the contagion of cynicism and apathy, health itself can have the same sort of attraction and exponential organic evolution. For example, if, on this bus, one or two students had spoken up, the results would have been different. If, when this ordeal began, one child had sat down next to the woman to show sympathy or to provide some degree of moral protection, we could reimagine the video as demonstrating the contagion of virtue. Certainly the parents demonstrated some degree of such an effort. Even though powerless to change in one collective response the lethal atmosphere of society as a whole, their modeling of a caring and collaborative community "went viral" and, no doubt, influenced the opinion of those who saw the video.

This phenomenon of the spread of virtue is well documented with the appearance of successive Manifestations, each of Whom brings about a new civilization, though beginning with just a handful of followers. Prior to teaching others, these followers first demonstrate the power of virtue by creating a loving and moral model—a microcosm of what society could be. The rest of the process, as they say, is history, and well-documented history at that. I recently read an essay about the early expansion of Christianity in which the bewildered author was puzzling about how this religion spread so rapidly throughout the Mediterranean when it had little pragmatic benefit other than the joy of the belief itself.

Creating vital and collaborative neighborhoods based on a common desire for living in a spiritually imbued environment is a major focus of the Bahá'í Faith. Through a succession of carefully devised plans and strategies, the Bahá'í community worldwide is engaged in establishing neighborhoods that model the foundation of a caring and proactive community life through a core of activities—devotional gatherings, children's classes, study circles, and junior youth empowerment programs—centered in and around the homes of the people who live in the neighborhood.

Of course, each of us is tested individually throughout our lives to overcome our inertia—to acquire virtues and put them into action. This type of vigilance is especially important in those moments when tests come unexpectedly. But nothing proves more empowering than exercising these attributes and developing spiritual capacities in a supportive environment, in a community—however large or small—where virtue is the norm. Therefore, no endeavor can be more weighty at this time than collaborating to create such an environment at the local level, though clearly each individual must decide how he or she can best participate by determining what practices he or she is best suited to carry out:

> Neither the local nor national representatives of the community, no matter how elaborate their plans, or persistent their appeals, or sagacious their counsels, nor even the Guardian himself, however much he may yearn for this consummation, can decide where the duty of the individual lies, or supplant him in the discharge of that task. The individual alone must assess its character, consult his conscience, prayerfully consider all its aspects, manfully struggle against the natural inertia that weighs him down in his effort to arise, shed, heroically and irrevocably, the trivial and superfluous attachments which hold him back, empty himself of every thought that may tend to obstruct his path, mix, in obedience to the counsels of the Author of His Faith, and in imitation of the One Who is its true Exemplar, with men and women, in all walks of life, seek to touch their hearts, through the distinction which characterizes his thoughts, his words and his acts,

and win them over tactfully, lovingly, prayerfully and persistently, to the Faith he himself has espoused. (Shoghi Effendi,
Citadel of Faith, p. 148)

THE INSISTENT SELF AND NONFEASANCE

But if we maintain our original premise—that the principal
cause of sin within us is the "insistent self," or, rather, our willful
negligence in controlling our baser instincts and urges—how do
we account for the evil of nonfeasance? What does our "self" have
to gain by doing nothing, by remaining passive or inert?

One response to this mostly rhetorical question has already been
noted. We want to be liked. We want the approval of our peers and
associates. To acquire or sustain that approval, we are willing to set
aside whatever noble instincts we have in order to be accepted, in
order to "fit in" with the crowd, even if what we are being called
upon to do involves some degree of insanity or depravity. For the
fact is that we are inherently social beings, and our inherent longing for a social support is not a sign of weakness but a distinctly
human necessity.

True, lesser species seem to have family and group forms of
social structure, but this is instinctive and oriented almost entirely
toward survival and prosperity on a physical level. Human beings
are necessarily social because they cannot develop, survive, and
prosper without a support system, whether within the family or,
more broadly, within a community where most often our noble
behaviors are sustained and refined. However, this same support
system, if allowed to become dysfunctional and corrupt, has as
much power to thwart those same noble behaviors to which we
should aspire.

Because of this inherent need for interaction in order to be
healthy socially and psychologically, our "self" can become
extremely malleable and pliant when we risk depriving ourselves of
these resources. Our "self"—unless trained otherwise—may well
urge us to conform to whatever standards of behavior or thought

will allow us to become accepted, appreciated, and befriended. And if we are conflicted as to the virtue or wisdom of a course of action that is prevalent within our immediate social environment (even a virtual one), we may well find it extremely difficult to stand alone, to reject group mentality, to take a stand and resist the insistence of the "self" to seek praise and approval.

As we have noted, this aspect of the insistent self may cause us to participate in malicious actions or to refrain from intervening to prevent injustice from occurring. Therefore, while it is understandable that we initially think of an "insistent" part of our selves as being active, raucous, and annoying, it can also assert its influence in an equally destructive form by "insisting" that we do nothing, that we not trouble the waters or that we not become the cause of disunity—even when the "unity" in question represents the collaboration of people bent on an unwise, unwarranted, or unjust course of action.

THE POINT OF ACTION

Our history and literature are filled with heroes and heroines who changed the course of human society by simple, virtuous actions or by their refusals to be complicit in socially acceptable forms of blatant injustice. One of the sparks that ignited the modern civil rights movement was the now-famous refusal of Rosa Parks to change her seat in obeisance to a white man. Countless examples exist of how powerful a single action can be when a human being refuses to submit to the unrelenting voice of the insistent self.

This brings us to what I find to be the most vital part in this process of responding to the Satanic voice within us, the Evil Whisperer, this temptation to short-circuit and thereby pervert what could and should be empowering forces and heroic actions. I call this the moment of decision—the point in the process of knowledge, volition, and action when the choice between action and inaction sits in the balance. We may calmly or carelessly stride right through such moments, but if we are attentive to the desire for spiritual refinement, if we have become determined to strive to be a good person and a noble citizen, then when we encounter these critical points, our world should pause and our internal clock should stop because we have arrived again at one of those moments when we can alter the course of our lives and, possibly, the lives of others.

Upon reflecting on our own decisions, we will probably realize that at the moment when we thought we were at the crucial point of decision, the decision had already been made. As we have noted throughout our discussions, most of what seem to be "points" of change are really processes in disguise. True, some processes occur so rapidly that we recall them as an instant in time, a moment when we exerted our will, or *should* have exerted it—a point when we resisted temptation or instead chose to give in!

At times such as these, we might expect or desire some sort of explicit indication that the point of decision has arrived—perhaps a drum roll or the crash of cymbals (or symbols). Should we not have some unmistakable sensation that the moment of truth has arrived, that we are in the spotlight, that the celestial audience is holding its breath waiting to see what we will choose to do? Some small voice should whisper in our ears, "This is it! This is a point of no return!"

But, alas, rarely do such overt cautions occur, a fact that may give us the feeling that no one is watching, that this is really an entirely private matter, that somehow even the omniscience of God is veiled from this private space. Indeed, we may well question whether or not this truly *is* a moment of choice, because it feels so very much like the moment before it or the one that occurred five minutes ago when this process started.

Do I make a decision now? How about now? Possibly in a few minutes, if temptation becomes more intense? After all I wouldn't be having this internal conversation if I weren't still in control, unless it is possible that my neurotransmitters are making me feel so tempted that my better judgment has already been usurped.

Of course, the truth is that once we are at such a point in the process of making a moral decision, we probably lost the battle ten minutes ago when we sensed on some level that a perverse course of action was upon us, or else pretty close. When we allow ourselves to arrive at what we believe to be the point of balance (where the decision could go either way), more than likely we have deceived ourselves into thinking that so long as we are consciously consider- ing the matter, we are still in control of our will. Or we may think we can test ourselves by seeing how close to danger we can get before we can no longer escape unscathed, like a child passing his hand over a flame and getting ever closer to see if all he has heard about the danger of this magical brightness is factual. And like that child, we will often not be satisfied until personal negative results have proven the cautionary words of the laws and exhortations of the Manifestation to be so profoundly true. Then we are faced with untangling our lives and finding our way back onto the moral path through the accompanying emotional waves of guilt and remorse.

When we willingly and wittingly allow ourselves to test the wisdom of a law about reality, when we sense within us a more rational part of "self" whispering "I know I probably shouldn't be doing this, but let's just see . . ." then there may not be a further "point" of decision because we are already acting unwisely. We are already in the midst of risking the loss of control of our lives. It is precisely in this context that free will is not all that free. The earlier it is exercised, the more powerful it becomes in matters of moral decision and self-guidance.

This, then, is the wisdom of following the path of true freedom the Manifestation has entrusted to us, a path that maximizes our powers and freedoms, as opposed to that path toward the foxfire of a freedom that, once tested, is understood to be but license and enslavement. Once we have studied and accepted the reality of the Manifestation, once we have come to *know* there is no ulterior motive, no caprice, no unwarranted constraint in the path and plan He has laid out for us, once we have subsequently accepted

His guidance as naught but loving wisdom, we eliminate from our daily pursuit of excellence the need to respond to the thousands of daily choices that would serve only to restrain our progress, retard our growth, and plunder our felicity: "Were man to appreciate the greatness of his station and the loftiness of his destiny he would manifest naught save goodly character, pure deeds, and a seemly and praiseworthy conduct. If the learned and wise men of goodwill were to impart guidance unto the people, the whole earth would be regarded as one country. Verily this is the undoubted truth" (Bahá'u'lláh, *Tablets of Bahá'u'lláh*, p. 171).

PART 3: THE AWFUL TRUTH ABOUT SATAN

8 / THE SOURCE OF EVIL

It follows therefore that there is no evil in existence: Whatsoever God has created, He has created good. Evil consists merely in non-existence. For example, death is the absence of life: When man is no longer sustained by the power of life, he dies. Darkness is the absence of light: When light is no more, darkness reigns. Light is a positively existing thing, but darkness has no positive existence; it is merely its absence. Likewise, wealth is a positively existing thing but poverty is merely its absence.

It is thus evident that all evil is mere nonexistence. Good has a positive existence; evil is merely its absence.

—'Abdu'l-Bahá, *Some Answered Questions*, no. 74.6–7

At this point we have delineated some fundamental aspects of what constitutes goodness and what constitutes sin. Goodness is following the affirmative actions that Bahá'u'lláh and previous Manifestations have articulated as being characteristics or attributes of the "good" or "godly" person. Sin is the negation, neglect, or abandonment of those virtues we are exhorted to uphold. Sin is also the active pursuit of, or indulgence in, those forbidden behaviors that deter the understanding and exercise of these virtues. Perhaps at its worst, sin is the willful attempt to deter others from pursuing freely these same noble objectives. In other words, there is obviously an infinite variety of forms and degrees of sin.

We have not yet dealt explicitly with another major objective in our study, a straightforward, detailed discussion concerning reality and the source of sin, whether in the cosmos at large or within our own selves. We have discussed at some length the notion of the "insistent self" as a source of perversity at work in our daily striving to be selfless and noble, but what is the source of this "darkness" within?

Are there such things as perverse powers? What is that source that influences our self, seems to countermand our noble intentions, or usurp our spiritual attributes and virtuous powers? Is there an evil spirit that can tempt us or weaken our spirituality against our will? Is there an actual being, a Satan, such as the perverse figure portrayed in the Bible and in other religious scripture? If there is such a being, is this the fallen angel Lucifer, as portrayed in Revelation? Or is this "evil whisperer" a jinn, similar to Iblis as portrayed in the Qur'án?

The rampant success of sinful acts and evil people throughout history and in our own contemporary global community would seem to indicate that there must be some evil force at work. We can hardly believe that these pernicious actions and antisocial behaviors somehow appear without a cause. Something cannot come from nothing. And the fact that we allude to these horrible and ghastly acts as being "inhuman" would seem to indicate that we instinctively believe that the abuse of others—whether physical, emotional, or spiritual—goes against our collective standard as human beings, against our very nature!

We have discussed the origin of concepts of virtue as well as the guidance from the Manifestations of God that would assist us in becoming noble, free, and refined. But asserting that sin or evil is merely the failure to recognize or follow this assistance does not feel adequate. The absence of goodness does not seem a sufficient explanation to account for what we have witnessed in our collective past or present history, nor does such a notion adequately explain our daily individual experience. It would not seem to explain what we have viewed in films of concentration camps or in a YouTube video showing heartless bullying on a school bus.

THE ORIGIN OF EVIL

As we have noted, the Bahá'í teachings assert that there is nothing in creation that is inherently evil, neither a person nor a force.

154

There are natural phenomena, such as earthquakes, floods, and plagues that, from our human perspective, are fraught with untold tragedy. Nevertheless, we usually regard these as logical, geophysical processes that have no motive or malevolent intent. We do not believe them to be perpetrated by God to punish or harm humankind. These "acts of God" may cause great harm, and because God is omnipotent we may be tempted to blame Him. If He has the power to prevent catastrophes, then why doesn't He?

In our calmer and more reflective moments, we may tend to lean more toward designating such disasters as simply unfortunate—as grievous and tragic, but the result of happenstance. We usually do not designate these phenomena as "sinful" or "evil" per se. But we may well still find our belief in an omnipotent and benign God tested or stretched when we behold such tragedies. If God has ordained certain interventions, such as the appearance of a Manifestation, why does He not also demonstrate His love and concern by intervening to prevent such tragic events from affecting the lives of innocent people?

Some may interpret these events in history as being part of a carefully devised plot to teach humankind progressively how to form a spiritually centered civilization. But does that mean we are to look upon major upheavals as part of God's design, or as lessons we must learn from our own heedlessness and inattention to our inherent purpose as emanations from God? Is it possible that we could accomplish our part in God's plan without manmade disasters so often perpetrated by a mere handful of depraved individuals?

From a Bahá'í perspective, the answers seem to be made clear in the beginning of *The Promised Day is Come*, where Shoghi Effendi quotes Bahá'u'lláh as stating that all the turmoil we have endured and will undergo prior to establishing a global accord is the result of our own collective malfeasance, and of the refusal to heed the divine guidance outlined in the instructions He revealed to the world leaders in His letters: "The promised day is come, the day when tormenting trials will have surged above your heads, and beneath your feet, saying: 'Taste ye what your hands have wrought!'" (Bahá'u'lláh, cited in Shoghi Effendi, *The Promised Day is Come*, p. 3).

Is human frailty sufficient cause for all the calamities we have experienced or will experience in the future? Is everything we view as evil and wicked the end result of our own actions and inactions, and not at all from an evil force, from some perpetrator, a Prince of Darkness? Are we that blind to our failures, so permissive as to allow such massive injury to ourselves and our fellow human beings?

HELPFUL ANALOGIES

Any number of analogies could work well to illustrate how evil can exist, can devastate our lives, and yet still be *essentially* non-existent. Here, of course, we are using the term "essential" quite literally to designate the "essential reality" of what we experience as a force, but which, in fact, is the diminishment or complete deterrence of a force—the force of the Holy Spirit, of "good" and "godliness" in all their manifest forms.

One obvious and frequently used analogy to explain this process is the operation of heat in relation to cold. Without heat, there could be no life; therefore, cold (relatively speaking) could be perceived as a lethal force, as a source of death. But of course cold is not a force—there is no such thing as a source of "cold energy" because cold is the *essential* nonexistence of one particular form of energy. It is the absence of the power of heat or, more generally, the slowing down of molecular activity. Nevertheless, the absence of energy to bring about molecular activity engenders tangible results that we need to describe. And when we describe this process from the perspective of suffering its consequences, we find it more powerful to portray them in terms of their capacity to do us harm, to cause hypothermia or death. Thus we are well aware we should not wander into the Arctic wastes in a bathing suit simply because we refuse to be intimidated by an essentially nonexistent force.

We could employ many other equally useful images, but the point is that just because evil does not result from a source, nor is a power unto itself, it does not mean that it does not occur, even as cold occurs once heat diminishes. But before we proceed, it would be helpful to employ one more important comparison, perhaps the most frequently used analogy in scripture to represent the difference between good and evil—the opposition between knowledge and ignorance, which itself is most often explained by comparing spiritual knowledge and insight to the power of light.

Darkness, rather than being a force in itself, is the absence of the force of light. It is a particularly useful symbol of evil because it often renders us unable to find our way, and thus is usefully portrayed as an obstacle to progress. It has all the properties of an active force in our lives because it can have such a dramatic effect. And, naturally, we presume that any effect must necessarily have an active cause, which, of course, darkness does—the absence of light.

The point is thus clear that while darkness is not a force per se, it would be absolutely ludicrous to assert that darkness does not exist or that its effects are not severely detrimental. Shoghi Effendi states the entire axiom about evil succinctly by employing this analogy: "We know absence of light is darkness, but no one would assert darkness was not a fact. It exists even though it is only the absence of something else. So evil exists too, and we cannot close our eyes to it, even though it is a negative existence. We must seek to supplant it by good, and if we see an evil person is not influenceable by us, then we should shun his company for it is unhealthy" (Shoghi Effendi, in *Lights of Guidance*, p. 512).

To restate our conclusion, nowhere in the Bahá'í texts is there the proposition that evil itself does not exist or that evil does not cause devastating consequences. Instead, the Bahá'í writings make it clear that there is no essential reality that is "evil," no evil force or evil being that exists independently and thus has power to influence our character against our will or operate independently in either the material or metaphysical aspects of reality.

This point is crucial but subtle. To assert that evil is *essentially* nonexistent is precisely correct, even if the statement feels unsatisfying or possibly similar to a semantic ploy that causes us to ignore reality. Clearly people can become evil, and when they do, they can bring about injustice and other horrible consequences. This they do largely through their own free will. But to repeat, there are no metaphysical sources of evil, no evil spirits causing people to become devoid of character or humanity. There are no evil demigods. There is no evil force permeating our atmosphere that one might be able to channel or appropriate for some malicious purpose to assault us or usurp our free will or overtake consciousness for its devious ends. Neither is there a Satan, a Devil, a Beelzebub. True, an evil person can attempt to lead others astray, can tempt them to indulge in pernicious or evil acts, but the decision to respond and follow such a path is still left to one's own conscience and volition.

Clearly, then, this simple but no less profound sequence of thought should not be glossed over as if it were nothing more than a philosophical or theological discourse of little import to our daily experience. If we must deal with evil, both individually and collectively, we have to understand what it is, where it comes from, and what powers it possesses.

For example, if evil were indeed the result of some satanic demigod warring against the Creator, then our approach to protecting ourselves from this influence or ridding ourselves of it would be quite different. Our struggle might be more akin to the strategies of horror movie heroes who struggle against the forces of evil for the sake of human survival, possibly against some hulking marauder in a hockey mask who is super strong and who simply refuses to stay dead.

On the other hand, if evil derives from our collective rejection of guidance from God as revealed through His successive Manifestations, then an entirely different course of action should be undertaken. The fight should be waged individually and collectively and should be focused on establishing an environment where our individual efforts at rejecting inappropriate, unseemly, or blatantly pernicious behavior should be encouraged and nurtured in every way possible. And, difficult as such a campaign would be—and is for those presently dedicated to the reformation of human society—it does not necessarily follow that we must become superheroes in the sense of contemporary fiction, nor that we invent destructive machinery to assist us in wiping out some mega-morphed insect, or huge, malevolent, extraterrestrial humanoids!

SOME LOGICAL RESPONSES TO EVIL

If evil is logically comparable to the absence of energy, it would seem equally logical that we could combat evil in a manner similar to the two basic options we would employ if fighting cold (the absence of heat) or darkness (the absence of light). In the case of cold, we could travel toward a warmer clime or else clothe ourselves sufficiently to ward off its detrimental effects, even though this clothing might encumber us and reduce the efficiency with which we move about and accomplish our daily tasks.

In the case of darkness, we could maneuver toward the source of light or else enkindle some sort of light ourselves. Again, the more effective response would be to travel toward some durable source of light, because if we must provide our own, then we must have available materials essential for producing illumination—flint, matches, or more complex materials that may not always be close at hand.

THE COLLECTIVE RESPONSE

As analogies about how we should respond to evil, these two examples work well to explain how we counteract evil, whether individually or collectively. Collectively, as citizens of a small planet, we can try to gather aid for those peoples in dire need who, without outside assistance, would have to devote so much of their lives trying to scrape together the basic necessities for survival that they become unable to advance themselves intellectually or spiritually.

But even as we come to their assistance, we can also institute measures so that these same suffering masses can acquire the education and materials needed to develop a viable economy and a stable infrastructure. The people themselves would then have all they need to become self-sustaining.

If proffered with justice and wisdom, these measures would be introduced as a graduated process whereby there would be short-term, medium-term, and long-term plans to bring about desired solutions for equitable assistance for the whole of humankind. Here again, the response would be twofold—to provide temporary sustenance for those in need, and to create an environment in which jobs are created so that everyone could become a contributing member of the common good. By analogy, the short-term response would provide for protection against the loss of light and heat, while the long-term response would represent the gradual but systematic movement toward an environment of warmth and enlightenment.

Extending this same analogy, we can appreciate that the insistent self may take many forms, as we have seen, even as the term can apply equally to individual and to collective action or inaction. In our present world condition with instant communication and with access to the most intricate matters of state within almost every country and territory, we have no trouble determining what peoples may be deprived of the bare necessities of nutrition, medical assistance, education, shelter, and freedom from oppression.

On the short term, agencies such as Doctors without Borders, UNICEF, the Red Cross, and other humanitarian organizations are nobly attempting to respond to the immediate needs of peoples who are suffering. In any number of instances, of course, the governments overseeing these peoples in such dire need are themselves the oppressors, or else have some vested interest in preventing humanitarian relief from reaching their citizens. The most obvious motive for such governmental malfeasance is the desire to prevent the populace from instituting just governance.

In these cases, we can observe quite correctly that the "insistent self," when operating at the levels of governance and power, can poison the social environment and forestall remedial relief as well as prevent the instigation of the first stages of long-term solutions such as raising a stable infrastructure, building medical facilities, instituting agricultural reforms, setting up a viable educational system, and providing decent housing, sanitary systems, and universal access to power and potable water.

While the United Nations and other alliances try all they presently can by way of overcoming the oppression of pernicious governance in order to assist the suffering masses in our global community, the need for a systematic solution worldwide clearly requires some global pact whereby every nation is a willing and enthusiastic partner in a federated world commonwealth—a planetary body politic that has sufficient support and power to enforce the collective decisions of an elected world parliament or legislature.

Until such a solution is forthcoming, the response to evil on a worldwide basis will necessarily take place in a piecemeal fashion through the relentless courage and humanitarian efforts of those individuals and organizations that have managed to overcome exclusive concern for self-interest in order to improve the lives of their fellow-citizens of the world community.

THE INDIVIDUAL RESPONSE

The responsibility of the individual to make an effort to combat evil follows a somewhat analogous course of action: identifying symptoms of evil at the local level of family or neighborhood; fostering collective and collaborative awareness and concern; and constructing attitudes, activities, and patterns of behavior that provide alternatives to the present condition. The initial stages of response must deal with immediate relief from a condition of spiritual deprivation or moral decline. But as we have noted, such a response must be precluded by knowledge coupled with desire or will. For unless we realize that we are in need spiritually—that we are operating without our moral compass, regardless of what tempted us to wander from the path of true felicity—we are hardly going to know that we are "freezing" to death or that we have become wayward and are wandering about in the darkness. We need eyes to see and ears to hear, even as Christ reminded His followers about the prophecy from Isaiah:

> Therefore speak I to them in parables: because they seeing see not; and hearing they hear not, neither do they understand. And in them is fulfilled the prophecy of Esaias, which saith, By hearing ye shall hear, and shall not understand; and seeing ye shall see, and shall not perceive: For this people's heart is waxed gross, and *their* ears are dull of hearing, and their eyes they have closed; lest at any time they should see with *their* eyes and hear with *their* ears, and should understand with *their* heart, and should be converted, and I should heal them. (Matthew 13:13–15)

A thousand different chances or changes may come our way to awaken us to the reality of our condition. But it is solely through our own will that we can seize upon these instances, these glimpses of light, to exert the effort to extricate ourselves from the dark and withering cold of remoteness so that we might strive for renewal and reformation. Furthermore, prior to glimpsing this light of hope and subsequently restructuring our lives systematically to follow a path conducive to spiritual development, it is critical that we come to appreciate that we ourselves have caused our condition, that whether by acceding to personal weakness or by falling prey to the temptations or promptings of others, our moral choices result from our own willful action or inaction.

And while we are always capable of using our willpower to suppress negative tendencies and channel our energies into useful purposes, in this life we never completely escape from the temptation of the self because it is the single most unrelenting, pernicious, and dangerous force we must confront, combat, and conquer.

Selfishness or self-centeredness (as opposed to being "other-centered") can be overt and obvious. We have examples in literature of characters who were notoriously greedy and stingy, such as the fictional character of Scrooge in Dickens' *Christmas Carol*, or King Midas from Greek legend. But we can turn to current events to discover, for example, the equally amazing stories of individuals whose financial corruption led them to defraud others of their life savings under the pretense of assisting them through some fictional lucrative enterprise. Amazingly, after being caught, virtually all of these charismatic figures—intent solely on amassing limitless personal fortunes—seem utterly devoid of any sense of guilt or regret when revealing how they methodically destroyed the lives of those whose trust they won through guile and dissimulation.

THE PERSONIFICATION OF EVIL AND THE SOCIAL AND PSYCHOLOGICAL MOTIVE OF SATAN

Of course, exalting the self over others need not be manifest so literally and overtly in the form of financial greed. Moreover, a significant factor in evaluating the extent to which we are focused on our "self" rather than on the welfare of others is motive. The importance of motive is easily demonstrated when we acknowledge that the same action undertaken by the same individual on two different occasions could have precisely opposite meaning and value if the motives for the two acts are antithetical.

Performed with a pure motive, an action might be selfless and noble. The same action undertaken to obtain favor or personal advancement might appropriately be considered ignoble, underhanded, or at least disingenuous. It is for this reason that images of the self or self-interest as being "Satanic," "serpentine," or the "whispering tempter" are all very apt metaphors for a quality that can so subtly insinuate itself, often without our immediate conscious awareness, into the motive of virtually anything we attempt. Doubtless this is one important reason that Bahá'u'lláh exhorts His followers to bring themselves to account on a daily basis.

Even those of us striving sincerely to dedicate our lives to noble causes are susceptible to the insistent self, especially when we are exhorted to comport ourselves with dignity and refinement. There can be a fine balance between that pride in ourselves as beings fashioned in the image of God and that overweening conceit we might have in what we imagine we have accomplished or attained. Bahá'u'lláh, in the Kitáb-i-Aqdas, His Most Holy Book, cautions that we must be ever wary of our motives, and He explains the subtlety of this process by alluding to one who, while seating himself at the back of the room, does so with the spurious motive of trying to impress others with his humility and piety: "Amongst the people is he who seateth himself amid the sandals by the door whilst coveting in his heart the seat of honour. Say: What manner of man art thou, O vain and heedless one, who wouldst appear as other than thou art?" (Bahá'u'lláh, The Kitáb-i-Aqdas, ¶36).

We can conclude, correctly I think, that the various forms of this "serpent" in the garden of our heart are the sources of virtually every human misdeed, whether it be a vicious, unkind remark about a friend, or else an intricate, malicious scheme to amass a vast fortune through the domination and control of others. Whether one be a mere mischief-maker or a ruthless tyrant, the motive is generally the same, even though it may assume an infinite variety of forms and degrees of severity. In short, the "serpent" of self is best deterred by preventing its entrance at the outset: "O Friend! In the garden of thy heart plant naught but the rose of love, and from the nightingale of affection and desire loosen not thy hold. Treasure the companionship of the righteous and eschew all fellowship with the ungodly" (Bahá'u'lláh, The Hidden Words, Persian, no. 3).

9 / THE ESSENTIAL NATURE OF SATAN

God has never created an evil spirit; all such ideas and nomenclature are symbols expressing the mere human or earthly nature of man. It is an essential condition of the soil of earth that thorns, weeds and fruitless trees may grow from it. Relatively speaking, this is evil; it is simply the lower state and baser product of nature.

—'Abdu'l-Bahá, *The Promulgation of Universal Peace*, p. 411

The importance of the idea of Satan derives directly and logically from the axioms about sin we have been trying to assemble, as well as from the concept of trying to shape our own "ends" by fine-tuning the relationship between our expectations and our actions. We begin such a process by learning to distinguish between those urges within us that emanate from the physical temple—through which our true self, our "essential self" (the human soul), operates, and with which it intimately associates—and those lofty aspirations we acquire when we reflect on the guidance the Manifestation bequeaths us and implement the daily practices He mandates for our spiritual enlightenment and transformation.

We thus continue our discourse by examining the age-old dichotomy between the higher self and the lower self, between the angelic or rational self and the animal or physical self. Unlike the medieval Christian response of the ascetic and monastic movements who attempted to avoid the lower self by practicing various forms of denial, deprivation, and social isolation withdrawing from the world—the Bahá'í view is akin to the more humanistic orientations that surfaced in the Renaissance. According to the Bahá'í approach, there should be a synthesis of both aspects or expressions of self in which the higher or loftier "self" coordinates the integration between the two.

In fact, similar to Milton's concept of "right reason,"* or the concept of the "Great Chain of Being" we discussed earlier, the Bahá'í teachings stress the need to achieve integration between the spiritual and physical aspects of "self" rather than enduring some inner conflict or ceaseless internal warfare. And yet, because attaining this homeostasis requires constant monitoring, maintaining such a critical balance and internal order requires continued vigilance.

WHY THE LOWER SELF IS SO "INSISTENT"

"Can't we both just get along?" we might well ask our two aspects of self. And the answer, obviously, is that we can, but only so long as the two expressions of our reality agree about what we are trying to accomplish and how we are going to get the job done. Problems arise when the lesser self—our desires and temptations—stimulate those neurotransmitters so much that our passionate emotions override our good judgment. In fact, the lower self, like an unruly child, is not always content to function within the confines of its "proper place," unless reason constantly reminds it of the objectives of the higher self. The implied acknowledgment that the higher self is the one in charge of the operation is something the lower self is often reticent to admit.

Usually the lower self tries to take charge at fairly obvious and predictable times. For example, we sense its urging when we are tempted by others to do something that is sensually appealing but morally abhorrent. Other times this serpent of the "insistent self" can slither up and take us by surprise. And because these moments

---

* "The philosophic conscience, the power, implanted by God in all men, to apprehend truth and moral law" (from the glossary of *The Complete Poetical Works of John Milton*, p. 566).

sometimes occur when we are least prepared, they are precisely the most opportune moments for the "insistent self" to exert its greatest influence.

Obviously this tension need not be a ceaseless battle, nor need it endure very long at a fever pitch. We can manage extended periods of détente and decorum wherein we maintain a sense of orderliness, an internal peaceable kingdom. But like a brush fire that always leaves behind a few scattered embers here and there, at some point the flames may once again ignite, and yet again we must fight the good fight and douse the flames of passion and egotism with the redemptive waters of reflection, reason, rededication, and self-discipline.

WHAT'S IN A NAME?

It is to this human frailty that scriptures allude with such powerfully dramatic symbols and personifications. The insistent self is alluded to with epithets such as "the Devil," "Satan," "the Evil One," "the Tempter," or "the Deceiver," but the meaning is always the same—the urgings of our lower or base nature:

> . . . the evil spirit, Satan or whatever is interpreted as evil, refers to the lower nature in man. This baser nature is symbolized in various ways. . . . God *has never created an evil spirit*; all such ideas and nomenclature are symbols expressing the mere human or earthly nature of man. It is an essential condition of the soil of earth that thorns, weeds and fruitless trees may grow from it. Relatively speaking, this is evil; it is simply the lower state and baser product of nature. ('Abdu'l-Bahá, *The Promulgation of Universal Peace*, p. 411) [italics added]

And yet, though only symbols and allusions, these vivid terms, together with the attendant mythology surrounding the origin and modus operandi of these "tempters," are sufficiently useful and evocative that we find them employed with equally powerful metaphors in the Bahá'í texts as we do in the scriptures of previous religions. Thus, in the Bahá'í writings, this inherent part of our nature is sometimes referred to as "the Evil Whisperer," "Satan," or "the Evil One." But the meaning and intent underlying the use of these terms is ever the same. These dramatic epithets convey a sense of how the promptings of selfish intentions are invariably at war with all our virtuous intentions to become good people—to be selfless, loving, and helpful. Applied collectively, these terms speak of those forces that would deter society from establishing a peaceful and cooperative social environment, whether in our individual homes or in the world at large.

Clearly, the above passage about the symbolic or metaphorical nature of all terminology attributing evil in humankind to allegorical forces should not be taken to mean that there is nothing to worry about—that sin, explained as the absence of goodness, is less formidable and threatening. As Shoghi Effendi states in the passage we have already cited, "no one can deny that evil exists"! And even as it is capable of usurping all our good intentions, so does it possess the infectious contagion of a virulent disease capable of corrupting an entire household, community, nation, or empire. Certainly any cursory glance at history demonstrates the power this affliction can wield.

In this context of the capability of evil to spread like a plague upon a land, we discover that sacred scripture often employs military terms in portraying our attempt to combat it. Our struggle is often described as a "battle" or "campaign" in which we nobly set out to "win victories." Similarly, the use of the mythic personifications of the Devil or Satan as some powerful or alien "other" alludes to a complex offensive against our lower self that we must wage in order to attain our potential and fulfill those capacities with which we have been endowed. The imagery of our baser instincts as a wicked tempter is thus an entirely useful and accurate portrayal of our need to stand guard against the devious means by which our insistent self can dissuade us from following our most righteous and felicitous path and thereby render us susceptible to the infectious disease of "self."

THE BATTLE WITHIN

Is our resistance "unnatural"? Is it not strange that we attribute our creation to God and yet are urged by this same Creator (through the words of His Manifestations) to guard ourselves against perfectly normal urges that are not inherently evil or ruinous? After all, they are promptings of hormones, neurotransmitters, and other natural processes taking place in our bodies.

But until we pass from this realm to the next, the dangers inherent to the insistent self never fully abate. Ironically, we are especially vulnerable in moments of vanity when we think we have finally got it conquered—perhaps precisely when we are tempted to take pride in having overcome pride itself!

According to a story I have heard from a number of sources, when Taraz'u'lláh Samandarí—a well-known Bahá'í—was on his deathbed, he asked those at his bedside to say a prayer for constancy, what is sometimes called "firmness in the Covenant." But since he had lived a life entirely dedicated to serving the Bahá'í Faith and its followers, he was asked why he, of all people, should feel the need for such a prayer. His answer was, "There is *still* time."

We might infer from this account that he was aware of how, even though his life on this plane of existence could be counted in mere hours or minutes, there was still sufficient time for him to become overconfident, to succumb to pride. But I think we can also suppose that had such an unlikely turn occurred, a loving and forgiving God most certainly would have readily pardoned his transgression and would have assisted him through these birth pangs by welcoming him into the next stage of his life.

In this sense, the story should probably not be taken to indicate that we can make some unforeseen false step, thereby undoing all the good we have struggled a lifetime to achieve, and stumble into hell (which, after all, does not exist in any physical sense). It does reflect the axiom that our vigilance regarding the insistent self is not a casual or occasional exercise. The insistent self, like an unconscionable thief dwelling within us, constantly attempting to find a means of gaining entrance into our inmost thoughts and willful control, is always lurking somewhere nearby during this physical stage of our life's journey.

In addition, there is the oft-cited and perplexing passage from a section of the Kitáb-i-Íqán that is often referred to as "the Tablet of the True Seeker" in which Bahá'u'lláh cites those virtues and practices that characterize one who is persistent in discovering the truth about reality and, having come upon that truth, dedicates himself or herself entirely to being a tireless servant of God:

> He should forgive the sinful, and never despise his low estate, for none knoweth what his own end shall be. How often hath a sinner, at the hour of death, attained to the essence of faith, and, quaffing the immortal draught, hath taken his flight unto the celestial Concourse. And how often hath a devout believer, at the hour of his soul's ascension, been so changed as to fall into the nethermost fire. Our purpose in revealing these convincing and weighty utterances is to impress upon the seeker that he should regard all else beside God as transient, and count all things save Him, Who is the Object of all adoration, as utter nothingness. (Bahá'u'lláh, The Kitáb-i-Íqán, ¶214)

Taken at face value, this passage would seem to portray a patently unjust or inappropriate action on the part of a loving and ever-forgiving God—why would a "devout believer" be subject to the "nethermost fire" on the basis of a last-minute doubt or fear? Conversely, how could someone who has lived a life of sin be instantly transformed into a true believer, or, at the very least, saved from that same fire? Surely a life of service would count to offset a last-second panic attack, just as the lifelong sinner would, in the after-life, be held accountable for the harm he or she had done to others.

And that's the point, isn't it? We expect God to be by nature just, reasonable, forgiving, loving, but also logically consistent in His assessment of our inmost motives and lifetime of struggle. Surely this Being, though essentially unknowable, would never act out of caprice or, stated more informally, "out of character." And His character, unlike His essence, is well-known and consistently predictable in love and logic. Therefore, whatever the emotional turmoil of the suddenly frightened devout believer or the flash of joyous belief of the suddenly insightful sinner, the end result of this process of fleeting emotions will be in accord with what is appropriate, just, and helpful to these two souls.

In other words, however frightened, fearful, and overwhelmed with doubt the dying believer may be, we can also presume with confidence that a loving, forgiving, and helpful God will assist this servant in finding a restoration of faith and confidence, provid-ing ease of heart as the transition is completed and the continual progress of the soul is assisted. The point is that this awareness that at any moment we are subject to being overconfident, prideful, or disdainful should keep us wary of our own spiritual status and ever watchful against the assumption that we are somehow beyond failure or superior to someone who appears to have failed.

Likewise, however redeemed and joyful the sinner may feel at this sudden influx of power with the resurrection of the long-neglected life of the spirit, there is no indication in this passage that there will not follow a more lengthy and considered reflection on lost opportunities as he or she reviews a largely wasted life.

Put simply, the point of Bahá'u'lláh's perplexing observation here is not to portray some eternal condition, but rather a tem-porary—if powerful—change of heart with the attendant and equally powerful emotional effects. The moral of this passage is that we should never think of our spiritual progress as secure or finished, nor should we ever think of our success as founded on how much better we think we are doing than someone else. We should be constantly vigilant of our dependence on the assistance we receive from God and His Manifestation.

But naturally this same cautionary advice is valuable in the present, not merely at the moment of our transition to the next stage of our lives. For this temptation or susceptibility to doubt, to fall victim to the cynicism that permeates contemporary society, is as apt to us now as it will be later. And as we confront the baser desires or the temptation to doubt, we also must be heedful that we not allow ourselves to attribute to these desires or conditions a power or will of their own. Such an attribution would be an egregious flaw in our thinking and in our response to our need to be vigilant about our entire self—the integration of all our parts into one organic being from which our cognition and willpower emanate. But just as we can have an internal dialogue as we reflect on a given situation or course of action, so too can we become aware of our capacity to consciously control where we allow our thoughts to wander or, at the very least, what we do with them once they get there.

It is in this context that although we may not be responsible for evil or inappropriate thoughts and images that might enter our mind, we are responsible for any action based on them. That is, however pure we try to keep our focus and thoughts, there are times when, through accidental exposure to tawdry images, or licentious behavior, or unseemly language, we are vulnerable to corrupt desires that may evoke base instincts in us by appealing to our lower self.

Not that the aspect of self that seeks sensual delight or material diversion or self-aggrandizement is always so subtle. If we allow ourselves to toy with some course of action that we know full well borders on the breach of explicit spiritual guidance, we should also be fully aware that we are, at our own peril, venturing into dangerous territory. As we have already noted in chapter 6, we may feel no immediate negative effects. In fact, the closer we are to transferring control of ourselves from our rational will to our vain desires and passions, the more our sense of comfort shifts by degrees from being repulsed by to being attracted to some expression of self-indulgence.

This is a most prized trick of the insistent self and its tactics. It entices us to deceive ourselves. Self-indulgence, whether experienced as the orgasmic triggering of a flood of neurotransmitters, or the more subtle enticement of attaining the approval of peers or approbation of the crowd, is not experienced as a dramatic point when bells sound and flashing signs appear to warn us, "Hold on! The crucial moment of choice has arrived! The time to decide is . . . NOW!"

The fact is that these "delights" are actually delightful. Were it otherwise, they would not be so enticing and, once experienced, so addictive. There is no sense trying to deny that drugs make one feel good or that sex does the same. In fact, with modern technology we can now view this ecstatic pleasure in colorful PET scan images of the brain. That is why it is senseless to tell someone addicted to a self-destructive activity to "Just Say No!" After all, the willpower to reject addiction is precisely the internal power that is compromised by the addictive behavior.

True, there may be initial stages of various degrees of guilt. In the long run there may be intense moments of regret. Over the long haul, we may have moments of reflection when we are completely shocked by what we have become, by our pronounced deviation from our avowed path. But in the short run, in the midst of the moment in which we suddenly find ourselves immersed, there is no time to reflect and very little desire to make time.

And because we may wish to delay as long as possible the onset of guilt and disappointment in ourselves, we may find it appealing to immerse ourselves further, to enjoy this "vacation" from our moral perspective for as long as we can. And obviously, the longer the vacation and the more we deviate from our path of good intentions, the more arduous, perilous, and rigorous will be the trek back. Or else, if the path seems beyond our capacity, we may decide to lower our expectations to befit the descent of our personal reality.

GRAPHING SPIRITUAL ASCENT

As we have already noted, we are not in competition with any other soul—only with our own potential. Consequently, we might find it useful to envision some objective assessment of our life's journey in terms of what we accept as the appropriate level of our performance versus our expectations at any given moment or over an extended period of time.

Here we are referring to the fact that emotional feedback is a valuable tool in our personal assessment. For example, unlike what some psychologists may affirm regarding guilt that may arise from one's religious beliefs, negative feelings about ourselves or our performance are neither good nor bad. Emotions provide feedback about how we are performing in relation to our expectations about ourselves. And these emotions in relation to performance may derive from our progress as students, athletes, professionals, or—in this case—people aspiring to become spiritual or "good."

Clearly, our emotions tell us how well we are performing in relation to our expectations, whether these expectations come from our own well-considered goals—and, of course, whether the goals are valid, or else derive from misguided sources, such as unwise parents, oppressive coaches, or tyrannical bosses. Valid emotions are, in this context, those feelings that give us measured feedback about how we are doing in relation to the carefully considered goals we wish to attain. We feel guilt when we think we could do better, and we feel good when we are keeping up with our valid expectations. If we feel guilt, we examine whether to raise our performance or adjust our objectives.

But we will deal with this subject in more detail later. For now, let us examine the following chart to understand what an ideal paradigm might look like if we attempt to plot our progress with some degree of objectivity. In this chart we can observe that we are always performing relatively well in relation to our expectations. In addition, this chart demonstrates graphically (and perhaps unrealistically for most of us) the gradual and willful elevation of what we expect from ourselves:

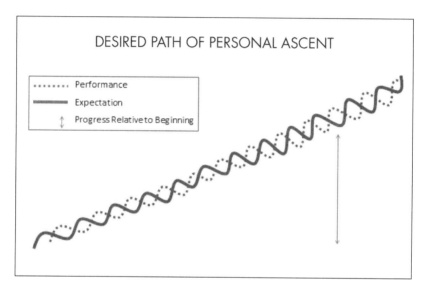

DESIRED PATH OF PERSONAL ASCENT

.... Performance

———— Expectation

↕ Progress Relative to Beginning

Here we see variable responses to expectations. Some days we are doing better than we planned, whereas on other days we are falling a bit short of what we aspire to. But the overall progress is steady, predictable, and confirming so that our success begets further ascent and our ascent encourages us to raise our expectations regarding what we can accomplish.

What this illustration does not reveal—assuming it accurately reflects the "self" in relation to reality rather than someone's distorted interpretation of reality—is that the plotting of this ascent might include periods where, to outward seeming, we are falling precipitously into despair, dismay, suffering, or chaos. If we are afflicted by trials and tribulations, by crisis and even by physical suffering, we might assume we would experience a perceptible decline.

But we are not plotting physical comfort or success in ordinary terms! Rather we are holistically assessing the spiritual progress of the essential "self" as the ascent of our soul. We are observing this life from an admittedly lofty and divine perspective, rather than according to the standards with which most mortals would evaluate it. In considering this ostensible conflict in perception of ascent, we do well to turn to the words and example of 'Abdu'l-Bahá.

In one particular message to a believer, 'Abdu'l-Bahá offers a series of paradoxes that demonstrate vividly the reversal of perspective that occurs as one becomes confirmed in viewing reality from the lofty perspective of its inherent spiritual purpose. Tests and suffering, rather than representing decline in personal wellbeing and achievement, are the means by which the soul can become confirmed, most especially when these tests are endured in the path of service for the ultimate good of humanity:

> O thou servant of God! Do not grieve at the afflictions and calamities that have befallen thee. All calamities and afflictions have been created for man so that he may spurn this mortal world—a world to which he is much attached. When he experienceth severe trials and hardships, then his nature will recoil and he will desire the eternal realm—a realm which is sanctified from all afflictions and calamities. Such is the case with the man who is wise. He shall never drink from a cup which is at the end distasteful, but, on the contrary, he will seek the cup of pure and limpid water. He will not taste of the honey that is mixed with poison.
>
> Praise thou God, that thou hast been tried and hast experienced such a test. Be patient and grateful. Turn thy face to the divine Kingdom and strive that thou mayest acquire merciful characteristics, mayest become illumined and acquire the

attributes of the Kingdom and of the Lord. Endeavour to become indifferent to the pleasures of this world and to its comfort, to remain firm and steadfast in the Covenant and to promulgate the Cause of God. ('Abdu'l-Bahá, *Selections from the Writings of 'Abdu'l-Bahá*, no. 197.1–2)

And yet, by no means does 'Abdu'l-Bahá imply that one should abandon concern for the world and its peoples or take no part in assisting the betterment of society and the human condition. 'Abdu'l-Bahá interprets the meaning of this very same letter with the following:

The intent of what I wrote to thee in my previous letter was this, that when exalting the Word of God, there are trials to be met with, and calamities; and that in loving Him, at every moment there are hardships, torments, afflictions.

It behooveth the individual first to value these ordeals, willingly accept them, and eagerly welcome them; only then should he proceed with teaching the Faith and exalting the Word of God.

In such a state, no matter what may befall him in his love for God—harassment, reproach, vilification, curses, beatings, imprisonment, death—he will never be cast down, and his passion for the Divine Beauty will but gain in strength. This was what I meant.

Otherwise, woe and misery to the soul that seeketh after comforts, riches, and earthly delights while neglecting to call God to mind! ('Abdu'l-Bahá, *Selections from the Writings of 'Abdu'l-Bahá*, no. 198.2–5)

Similarly, 'Abdu'l-Bahá offers this poignant insight into how he views his own grievous persecution at the hands of those who had vilified him in hopes that they might cause him to be imprisoned or executed:

Rejoice in my bondage, O ye friends of God, for it soweth the seeds of freedom; rejoice at my imprisonment, for it is the well-spring of salvation; be ye glad on account of my travail, for it leadeth to eternal ease. By the Lord God! I would not exchange this prison for the throne of the whole world, nor give up this confinement for pleasures and pastimes in all the fair gardens on earth. My hope is that out of the Lord's abundant grace, His munificence and loving-kindness, I may, in His pathway, be hanged against the sky, that my heart may become the target for a thousand bullets, or that I may be cast into the depths of the sea, or be left to perish on desert sands. This is what I long for most; this is my supreme desire; it refresheth my soul, it is balm for my breast, it is the very solace of mine eyes. ('Abdu'l-Bahá, *Selections from the Writings of 'Abdu'l-Bahá*, no. 199.5)

GRAPHING THE "COMFORTABLE" LIFE

In the next graph of the spiritual progress of a soul or "self" in this world, we can view the portrayal of a life in which the individual is fairly healthy in the sense of being in constant touch with his or her performance in relation to expectations, but where the overall progress from the standpoint of spiritual development is negligible.

Thus, we might say that, psychologically, this person may be fairly stable and healthy and perhaps relatively content with life. But again, such a conclusion is predicated on the assumption that the individual is not evaluating life from a divine perspective, which would take into account all the variables—the struggles, trials, afflictions, tests, opportunities, and deprivations—that a person faces.

Not that we can make such an assessment of the life of another; clearly we cannot. We have enough trouble evaluating how we ourselves are doing. After all, if the authentic standard for our spiritual assessment can be accurately discerned only after we are detached from this life, all we can do is guess whether we are better, purer, more enlightened, and more altruistic now than we were at some previous time in our lives.

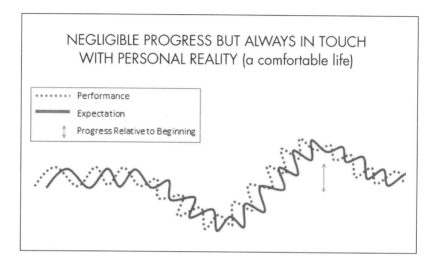

GRAPHING THE LONG TREK HOME

Next we take a look at a scenario in which one does well in both respects for a considerable length of time. This person is reflective, responsive to challenges, accustomed to regular self-evaluation and to planning and action in his or her attempt to become aligned with lofty aspirations. This individual is also making some progress over time by elevating expectations according to a daily practice of increasing the number of virtues and manifesting them in an ever more refined or intensive pattern of action.

As Shoghi Effendi notes, this pattern of "living the life"—rather than simply talking about it—is what ultimately produces substantive proof to others that the Bahá'í Faith might be worth investigating: "One thing and only one thing will unfailingly and alone secure the undoubted triumph of this sacred Cause, namely, the extent to which our own inner life and private character mirror forth in their manifold aspects the splendor of those eternal principles proclaimed by Bahá'u'lláh" (Shoghi Effendi, *Bahá'í Administration*, p. 66).

This axiom echoes Bahá'u'lláh's own observation that merely telling others about the Bahá'í teachings will have no appreciable effect unless and until the teacher has first taught himself or herself: "Whoso ariseth among you to teach the Cause of his Lord, let him, before all else, teach his own self, that his speech may attract the hearts of them that hear him. Unless he teacheth his own self, the words of his mouth will not influence the heart of the seeker. Take heed, O people, lest ye be of them that give good counsel to others but forget to follow it themselves" (Bahá'u'lláh, *Gleanings*, no. 128.6).

In the following paradigm, there has come a period of time in the life of this person where suddenly he or she has lapsed significantly from being able to meet his or her expectations. Perhaps this person experienced some tragedy and was unable to cope. Perhaps there was some affliction that tested his or her faith, or some unexpected addictive behavior that sidetracked this individual from the path of dedication and spiritual conduct.

Whatever the cause, the individual has fallen away from personally established expectations, but rather than relinquish hold on the standard of attainment by which self-evaluation is gauged, this same person has determined to engage in a noble struggle to regain a pattern of life that is no less valid or desirable simply because one has temporarily experienced failure or inability to maintain it:

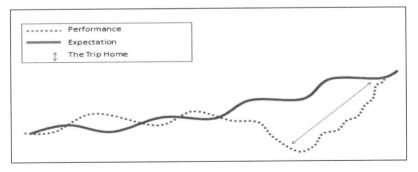

In other words, as we observe that the progress in this life features an apparent fall from the desired pattern of action, we can also discern a remarkable application of will and determination to achieve recovery—a story made all the more noble because the person refused to adjust expectations to befit a self in decline. We might thus conclude that for this individual, the knowledge of reality was never lacking, nor did this person determine to alter the goals for a well-lived life.

We might try to guess what finally helped this person reverse the decline. Was it "hitting bottom" that produced a shock of sufficient severity that determination to change was instigated? Was it the assistance of a friend? The impetus might have been the confluence of a myriad influences—possibly the prayers of others or the grace and assistance of other heavenly resources.

But the point of reversal is only the beginning. The greatest effort and the most severe test of faith in the story this graph reflects is that the "happy ending" was most probably the first part of the soul's ascent from the dark abyss of remoteness. After the arduous task of changing unhealthy patterns of behavior, the soul probably sensed the joy of moving nearer. Soon the upward motion became its own reward so that in the course of time, the ascent attained the heights of felicity, and the individual acquired the virtues of self-confidence and certitude.

Another important realization this plot reveals is the meaning underlying the metaphorical term "resurrection," at least as the term is most often employed by the Manifestations. Resurrection implies a spiritual awakening or reawakening. And while we are not able to see how the rest of the "graph" of this life proceeds, we would hope that this individual, having learned from painful experience, will never again allow such a dramatic and precipitous decline to occur and produce another schism between the studied path of expectation and the daily expression of that aspiration in ever more exalted patterns of action. Indeed, we would hope this individual has had thoroughly ingrained in his or her conscious self the simple but utterly encompassing exhortation we have previously cited as the abiding axiom regarding our progress through life: "Sorrow not save that thou art far from Us. Rejoice not save that thou art drawing near and returning unto Us" (Bahá'u'lláh, The Hidden Words, Arabic, no. 35).

10 / SATAN AS CREATIVE MYTH

Thou hast surely witnessed how they that have confessed their faith in
Him and they that rejected Him have warred against each other, and
sought one another's property. How many fathers have turned away from
their sons; how many lovers have shunned their beloved! So mercilessly
trenchant was this wondrous sword of God that it cleft asunder every relationship! On the other hand, consider the welding power of His Word.
Observe, how those in whose midst the Satan of self had for years sown
the seeds of malice and hate became so fused and blended through their
allegiance to this wondrous and transcendent Revelation that it seemed as
if they had sprung from the same loins.

—Bahá'u'lláh, The Kitáb-Íqán, ¶118

What Bahá'u'lláh observes about the usefulness of symbolic
myths regarding portrayals of spiritual concepts—particularly
allusions to Heaven, Hell, and Satan—relates to the translation
of reality into an accessible narrative, an allegorical story that a
believer of any age or level of enlightenment can grasp: "Even the
materialists have testified in their writings to the wisdom of these
divinely-appointed Messengers, and have regarded the references
made by the Prophets to Paradise, to hell fire, to future reward
and punishment, to have been actuated by a desire to educate and
uplift the souls of men" (Bahá'u'lláh, *Gleanings*, no. 81.1).

While these mythical or symbolic allusions were never intended
to be literal representations of reality, they have, through the ages,
served as useful and powerful translations of abstract realities and
relationships into vivid and accessible narratives. In these myths,
concepts of virtues, vices, spiritual conditions, and spiritual relationships can be expressed and discussed in the form of parables—

allegorical stories. By employing this technique, the Manifestation enables us to comprehend and articulate complex theological and metaphysical matters, whether or not we immediately recognize the ineffable abstractions underlying this benign fiction.

The efficacy of this methodology is so useful that, even while explaining these terms and myths as purely symbolic, both the Báb and Bahá'u'lláh still employ them in Their own writings. In my book *The Face of God Among Us,* I discuss how Christ employs the parable as His principal teaching device. He likewise explains His own station in symbolic or metaphorical terms, using figurative images that were sometimes plain to the ordinary believers but baffling to the literalists, the Pharisaic clerics, and the divines in His audience.

Christ thus portrays Himself as the "Son" of God, the "Father"—a wonderfully useful poetic rendering of the relationship between the Manifestations as Vicegerents of the essentially unknowable Creator. The literal interpretation of this figurative appellation evoked a stringent rebuke by Muhammad, Who six centuries later in the Qur'án, disproved such conclusions. He observed that God is single, unique, and alone. God is infinite, timeless, without beginning or end. Thus, God is neither begotten, nor does He beget literal offsprings: "Say: He is Allah, the One and Only, Allah, the Eternal, Absolute. He begetteth not, nor is He begotten, And there is none like unto Him" (Surah 112:1–4).

This statement of fact serves as an effective axiom to refute the idea of a literal Trinitarian doctrine—that Christ and God are the same or that They are of the same essence: "Christ Jesus, the son of Mary, was (no more than) a Messenger of Allah, and His Word, which He bestowed on Mary, and a Spirit proceeding from Him, so believe in Allah and His Messengers. Say not 'Trinity'! Desist! It will be better for you, for Allah is One Allah. Glory be to Him, (for Exalted is He) above having a son. To Him belong all things in the heavens and on earth. And Allah is sufficient to dispose of (all) matters" (Surah 4:171).

In other words, when Christ alludes to God as the "Father" and to Himself as the "Son," He is employing symbolic or poetic language to explain both the exalted station of God, a station infinitely beyond Christ's own station, and the loving relationship that exists between God and His Creation, including Christ's mission to discuss and portray that love. He is thus the "offshoot" or creation of God designed to manifest godliness completely and perfectly in terms that ordinary believers can comprehend.

CHRIST VERSUS SATAN

As I also explain in *The Face of God Among Us*, in addition to the wonderfully creative parables with which He explains complex theological doctrine, Christ also employs a parable or a mythological presentation of what He Himself endured before He began His ministry. After being anointed and thereby fulfilling the prophecy of His becoming the Messiah (the Anointed One), the Gospels describe how He journeys into the wilderness where, for forty days, He fasts and faces temptations by Satan.

Obviously this story could only have come from Christ Himself. If He was alone, no one else was there to observe the tempting or testing. Likewise, if Satan is truly a mythical representation of temptations of the flesh or various attractions of the lower aspect of self, no actual being was there to test Christ. In other words, if we cannot accept that there is literally an evil spirit or demigod who is allowed by God to tempt Christ—or, if one believes Christ *is* God, that God would allow a being to tempt Him—then this story must necessarily be a parable or symbolic method whereby Christ explains to His followers how He now possesses a loftier station than He had previously revealed. And one aspect of this station is that He is sinless and has rejected all temptations for worldly ascendancy, delights of the flesh, or employing His powers for personal gain. Instead, His sole purpose is now to become a means by which God can make Himself known and understood to these people. Accordingly, He has become "the way, the truth, and the life; no man cometh unto the Father, but by me" (John 14:5).

One indication of the importance Christ attributes to this allegorical narrative of what Satan represents (the temptation to use power for self-interest) is that we find it prominently in all three synoptic gospels of Matthew, Mark, and Luke.* Furthermore, the story itself is worth repeating for our present purposes because it serves as a wonderfully lucid symbolic presentation of the internal struggle that on some level each of us must undergo. And inasmuch as the Bahá'í writings attest that everything the Manifestations do and say is for the purpose of teaching us something about ourselves, the story demonstrates how we should respond to the same type of temptations that inevitably emanate from both our lower "insistent" self and from the world at large:

> And Jesus being full of the Holy Ghost, returned from Jordan and was led by the Spirit** into the wilderness, being forty days tempted by the devil. And in those days he did eat nothing, and when they were ended, he afterward hungered. And the devil said unto him, "If thou be the Son of God, command this stone that it be made bread."
>
> And Jesus answered him, saying, "It is written, That man shall not live by bread alone, but by every word of God."
>
> And the devil, taking Him up into an high mountain, showed unto him all the kingdoms of the world in a moment of time. And the devil said unto Him, "All this power will I give thee, and the glory of them: for that is delivered unto me, and to whomsoever I will I give it. If thou therefore wilt worship me, all shall be thine!"

---

* The episode appears in Matthew 4:1–11, in Mark 1:12–13, and in Luke 4:1–13.

** We presume this to be the Holy Spirit.

And Jesus answered and said unto him, "Get thee behind Me, Satan: for it is written, 'Thou shalt worship the Lord thy God, and him only shalt thou serve.'"

And he brought him to Jerusalem, and set him on a pinnacle of the temple, and said unto him, "If thou be the Son of God, cast thyself down from hence: For it is written, 'He shall give his angels charge over thee, to keep thee, and in *their* hands they shall bear thee up, lest at any time thou dash thy foot against a stone.'"

And Jesus answering said unto him, "It is said, 'Thou shalt not tempt the Lord thy God.'" And when the devil had ended all the temptation, he departed from him for a season. (Luke 4:1–13)

From a literalist perspective, this story might seem to vindicate a belief that Satan is an actual being, some form of demigod identified in the Book of Revelation as the devil, perhaps the same source of evil that appears as the serpent in the Genesis myth of Adam and Eve.

Because the Christian myth or fable of Satan is told only in the Book of Revelation (also known as the Revelation of St. John the Divine), composed about seventy years after Christ's crucifixion, it is valuable to repeat at least two of the allusions in this account that explain the origin and motive of Satan. It is from this work, and not from anything in the utterances or teachings of Moses or Christ, that the figure of Satan emerges. It is likewise from the following account that English author John Milton created his influential fictional epic *Paradise Lost*, a work that, since its composition in 1667, has served as a virtual canonical source for the image of Satan in Western art and thought:

And there was war in heaven. Michael and his angels fought against the dragon, and the dragon fought and his angels, and prevailed not; neither was their place found any more in heaven. And the great dragon was cast out, that old serpent called "the Devil" and "Satan" which deceiveth the whole world. He was cast out into the earth, and his angels were cast out with him.

And I heard a loud voice saying in heaven, "Now is come salvation, and strength, and the kingdom of our God, and the power of his Christ for the accuser of our brethren is cast down which accused them before our God day and night." And they overcame him by the blood of the Lamb, and by the word of their testimony, and they loved not their lives unto the death. (Revelation 12:7–11)*

This narrative from Revelation is the ultimate source for Christian beliefs about the mythical figure of Satan. In the Old Testament, Satan is seldom mentioned, and when he is, he is portrayed mostly as an agent of God whose task it is to test or assess virtue.

The testing of Job is the most obvious example of this Old Testament use of the myth. In the story of Job, Satan is not an adversary of God; rather, it is his mission to test and tempt people of faith. The outcome of this testing is that those who are tested become stronger and thus more or less impervious to trials and tribulations of life, or else they falter or fail altogether.

But with the Christian allusion to the myth, Satan specifically transforms into the Devil, the fallen angel Lucifer, who wars against God and who is exiled from Heaven to dwell eternally in Hell. The motive of the Devil henceforth is to lure the souls of vulnerable believers into sin and damnation. He has no power over their will, however, and they must freely accede to his machinations.

In this sense, Milton's depiction of Satan is an accurate rendering of the figure who, upon realizing he cannot defeat God, sets out on the lesser mission of trying to force Him into condemning

---

* See Milton, *Paradise Lost*, Book 6 regarding his narrative of the war in heaven.

or rejecting the very same human beings He has lovingly created innocent and uncorrupted.

IBLIS AND SATAN IN THE QUR'ÁN

In the Qur'án, we find a portrayal of the jinn Iblis, a mythic figure who functions in much the same capacity as the fallen angel Lucifer in Revelation. But the differences between the two portrayals are important to note.

First, in the Qur'án, a jinn is not an angel. It is a common belief in Islamic teaching that God created at least three distinct categories of conscious beings—humans, angels, and jinn. Where the angels are created inherently benign, both the jinn and the human beings have free will. It is in this context that God announces He will create a "Perfect Man," Adam, to dwell among the humans to teach them. But He also admonishes all who dwell in the realm of the spirit that even they must bow down before Adam because of His lofty station as a Representative from God fashioned to manifest perfectly all the divine attributes.

Like the angel Lucifer in Revelation, Iblis is incensed that he—a being of spirit, fire, and free will—should have to pay obeisance to a being created from water and clay, a creature taking on the lowly form of an ordinary human being. He thus rejects God's command and is punished by being exiled from heaven.

However, in the Qur'ánic narrative, Iblis beseeches God to let him test human beings by becoming the tempter who "whispers" temptations in their ears as they traverse the path of life. He thus has basically the same function as Satan the Tempter in the Old Testament: "He [Iblis] said, 'Because Thou hast thrown me out of the way, lo! I will lie in wait for them on Thy straight way. Then will I assault them from before them and behind them from their right and their left: nor wilt Thou find, in most of them, gratitude (for Thy mercies)'" (Surah 7:16–17).

Though God allows Iblis to "serve" in this capacity, He testifies in another Surah that Iblis and his companions will not have any power over the faithful. Naturally, we infer from this statement that it is precisely through exercising their free will and rejecting the tempting of the "Evil Whisperer" that the faithful will demonstrate their certitude and fidelity.

Of special interest to Bahá'ís in regard to Iblis' description of how he will "assault them from before them and behind them" is a particular prayer for protection revealed by the Báb. In this prayer, the Báb alludes to this threat by Iblis as a symbol of the urgings of the insistent self:

> Say: God sufficeth unto me; He is the One Who holdeth in His grasp the kingdom of all things. Through the power of His hosts of heaven and earth and whatever lieth between them, He protecteth whomsoever among His servants He willeth. God, in truth, keepeth watch over all things.
>
> Immeasurably exalted art Thou, O Lord! *Protect us from what lieth in front of us and behind us, above our heads, on our right, on our left, below our feet and every other side to which we are exposed.* Verily, Thy protection over all things is unfailing. (The Báb, in *Bahá'í Prayers*, p. 133) [italics added]

Regarding this prayer, there are two other noteworthy allusion to the temptations of the self as expressed in the story of Iblis in the Qur'án. First of all, the original version of this prayer was written in the Báb's own hand, and He configured the calligraphy into the shape of a pentangle, even as Bahá'u'lláh would later do with the Súriy-i-Haykal, the Surah of the Temple. This symbolic arrangement is significant because the pentangle or pentacle in the context of Bahá'í symbolism represents the human temple or body.

The most obvious meaning of this symbolic arrangement of the prayer is that the pentacle has five points, which represent the head, the two arms, and the two legs of the human body. Furthermore, in the context of the Bahá'í teachings, the human temple is the device by which the soul in this life is able to manifest the attributes of God. And as we have noted, it is from the physical or bodily aspect of our "self" that our greatest temptations in this life emerge, whether they be literal temptations of the flesh or, indirectly, temptations to exalt ourselves over others through physical or social ascendancy.

As with the two images of the Devil or Satan in the Bible, two similar accounts exist in the Qur'án. We have noted the figure and the role of the mythic Iblis as Tempter or Evil Whisperer, but there is also an account of Satan's tempting of Adam and Eve. In Surah 7:18–27, we find an allusion to the myth of the Garden of Eden, followed by the admonition to the "children of Adam" to be wary of Satan's temptations and machinations and not fall prey to his deceit even as their parents did:

> So by deceit he brought about their fall: when they tasted of the tree, their shame became manifest to them, and they began to sew together the leaves of the garden over their bodies. And their Lord called unto them: "Did I not forbid you that tree, and tell you that Satan was an avowed enemy unto you?"
>
> They said: "Our Lord! we have wronged our own souls: if Thou forgive us not and bestow not upon us Thy mercy, we shall certainly be lost."
>
> (Allah) said: "Get ye down, with enmity between yourselves. On earth will be your dwelling-place and your means of livelihood, for a time." He said: "Therein shall ye live, and therein shall ye die; but from it shall ye be taken out (at last)."
>
> O ye children of Adam! We have bestowed raiment upon you to cover your shame, as well as to be an adornment to you, but the raiment of righteousness, that is the best. Such are among the signs of Allah, that they may receive admonition!
>
> O ye children of Adam! let not Satan seduce you, in the same manner as he got your parents out of the garden, strip-

ping them of their raiment, to expose their shame: for he and his tribe watch you from a position where ye cannot see them: We made the evil ones friends (only) to those without faith. (Surah 7:20–27)

UNDERLYING MEANING OF THE MYTH

Again, "myth," in the sense we are employing the term, is not a fabrication of reality but rather reality creatively or poetically translated into narrative art. But merely because myth takes the form of a parable or allegory does not mean that it is less valid in the perceptions and conclusions it conveys than any attempt to portray reality directly or literally. Myth, when constructed creatively as a teaching device, is thus capable of providing us with a presentation of truth in parallel terms—whether as symbol, metaphor, parable, fable, or allegory. Through artistic renderings, abstract notions of truth, virtue, and spiritual relationships are outfitted in the garb of ordinary life, and by this method, abstruse ideas about both physical and metaphysical aspects of reality are made accessible to everyone, from the most untutored to the most erudite among us.

In this sense, myth is not the literal truth, but neither is it a lie or deception. As the audience—in this case humankind as a whole—becomes more experienced and better informed about the fundamental principles governing our origin and purpose, the Manifestation is gradually able to teach us in a more direct manner those concepts that formerly could be explained *only* in mythical terms. And yet, as we will discover in the following chapter, included among the straightforward interpretations by the Báb and Bahá'u'lláh of myths, parables, and symbols is Their own use of poetic language, including vivid personifications of the temptations of the lower self as "satanic fancy," "the Evil Whisperer," "the Evil One," and various other equally evocative appellations.

11 / THE POWER OF CONCEITS

We know absence of light is darkness, but no one would assert darkness was not a fact. It exists even though it is only the absence of something else. So evil exists too, and we cannot close our eyes to it, even though it is a negative existence. We must seek to supplant it by good, and if we see an evil person is not influenceable by us, then we should shun his company for it is unhealthy.

—Shoghi Effendi, in *Lights of Guidance*, p. 512

As we have repeatedly noted, the Bahá'í teachings assert that religion is a logical process devised by the Creator to direct human affairs. We have also noted that the concepts of sin and evil can be logically understood in terms of turning away from the light of life-giving powers from the Holy Spirit, a force emanating from God and made available to humankind as it becomes channeled through the sequential revelations of the Manifestations or Prophets of God.

As we have further discussed, all notions of an evil force or of an essentially evil being are symbolic or metaphorical ways to express a complex process in accessible terms. Thus, when we feel the desire to do something we know to be harmful to ourselves or to others, it often feels as though there were another consciousness within us warring with our nobler and more rational self. Consequently, the Manifestations have found it helpful to employ metaphors and symbols to portray this palpable sensation of an inner tension or conflict between our higher self and some evil force trying to usurp our allegiance to God and to goodness. The Manifestations also use these same conceits to articulate how we can become aware of these conflicting attitudes within us and, more to the point, how we can best come to terms with them by combating that negative or self-serving "satanic" voice within.

THE PROTECTION OF HUMILITY AND WISDOM

One of the more straightforward cautionary exhortations about the best means of guarding ourselves against the temptations of the insistent self can be found in a letter of Bahíyyíh Khánum, daughter of Bahá'u'lláh, in which she discusses the central function of the complementary qualities of submission and wisdom:

It is irrevocably decreed that whatsoever has been revealed and written down by the Supreme Pen and the holy hand of 'Abdu'l-Bahá will come to pass and be fully realized in this world, wherefore does it behove the people of Bahá, the souls attracted to His Splendour, to become all eyes and ears, and to be in body and soul and limbs and members all sagacity and prudence. Addressing the believers, Christ tells them: "Be ye harmless as the submissive dove, and wise as the serpent" (cf. Matthew 10:16).

In this momentous matter there must be no laxity, no inattention, for a whisper might become an axe laid to the root of the Tree of the Faith—a word from an ambitious soul could be a spark tossed into the harvest of the people of Bahá. We take refuge with God! May He guard us ever, from the recklessness of the insistent self.

For the harbouring of an evil purpose is a disease which shuts out the individual from all the blessings of Heaven, and casts him deep into the pit of perdition, of utter ruin. The point to make is that anyone, high or low, rich or poor, learned or unlettered, although to all appearances he may be a jewel among men, and the fine flower of all that is best—if he gives utterance to some pronouncement or speaks some word from which can be detected the scent of self-worship, or a malicious and evil purpose, his aim is to disintegrate the Word of God and disperse the gathering of the people of Bahá. From such individuals it is a solemn obligation to turn away; it is an inescapable duty to pay no heed whatever to their claims.

The clear promises of God, both His tidings of joy and His warnings, are being fulfilled, and it is inevitable that just as the sweet musk-laden winds of the Abhá Paradise are beginning to blow, and the flames of God's love to spread, so too must wintry blasts and icy breaths begin to fill the air. You must therefore exert superhuman powers to guard the Cause of God, and beg humbly and with a contrite heart for help from the Kingdom on High. (Bahíyyíh Khánum, *Bahíyyíh Khánum: The Greatest Holy Leaf*, pp. 212–13)

While this savvy advice places a great deal of responsibility on the believer to ward off the temptations of the self, logic might seem to dictate that there is not much to worry about. In light of all we have discussed regarding the underlying logic of Bahá'í concepts of sin and Satan, we could understandably conclude that we have nothing to fear except fear itself, at least on a personal level.

Surely we would never knowingly work against our own best interest or do that which we know to be detrimental to our happiness and wellbeing, especially given a belief in the eternity of our existence. Indeed, we might presume it to be an easy task at the first sign of trouble, or the first indication that we might be losing our self-control, to heed rigorously these signs of danger and jump into the warm embrace of God's grace as we delight in His redeeming love and protection.

However, the reality is that these poetic images about the power of the satanic temptations have endured because they accurately portray the subtlety and relentlessness of self-gratification and aggrandizement. Therefore, though the Bahá'í writings effectively decode and demystify these fictive images as poetic license employed by the Manifestations to impress upon us the seriousness of this internal tension, Bahá'u'lláh Himself still employs some of these same epithets with the same affective language that characterizes the utterances of prior Manifestations.

When Bahá'u'lláh uses these conceits to convey the seductive power and impact of sin and the effects of negligence on our efforts to achieve and maintain spiritual development, the poetic allusions impress upon us the extremely subtle and serious nature of what might seem, especially to the unwary and naïve, a simple, easy, and relatively mindless process. But from the tenor of His terminology and from His vivid depiction of this dialectic, it becomes apparent that the dangers we confront are no less perilous merely because we now appreciate the logical reality represented by the poetic epithets. In other words, since we know these menacing terms are symbolic, we might understandably conclude that we no longer need to employ these images, that they were created for an unsophisticated and unlearned people who required such mythic images to "keep them in line."

And yet quite the opposite is the case. Bahá'u'lláh observes that these poetic descriptions of evil are useful teaching devices: "Know verily that the purpose underlying all these symbolic terms and abstruse allusions, which emanate from the Revealers of God's holy Cause, hath been to test and prove the peoples of the world; that thereby the earth of the pure and illuminated hearts may be known from the perishable and barren soil. From time immemorial such hath been the way of God amidst His creatures, and to this testify the records of the sacred books" (Bahá'u'lláh, The Kitáb-i-Íqán, ¶53).

THE NAMES OF SATAN

Among the most frequently employed epithets used in the Bahá'í writings to represent what seems to be an evil being at war with our noble intentions are "Satan," "the Evil Whisperer," "the Evil One," and the less imagistic but extremely descriptive "insistent self."

What is obvious from the way these epithets are used is that the temptation of "sin" and "self" are no less powerful, dangerous, or enticing simply because we now understand that they do not emanate from an evil being or an active force but from an aspect of our own reality. Even as Shoghi Effendi observes in this chapter's epigraph, "We know absence of light is darkness, but no one would assert darkness was not a fact" (Shoghi Effendi, in *Lights of Guidance*, p. 512). By the same token, while sinful action results solely from our turning away from the light of God's guidance, we would be utterly foolish to deny that such a rejection can happen or, when it does, to deny that the results are destructive and devastating. The damage is no less real because we comprehend the logic underlying the process.

As we have noted before, 'Abdu'l-Bahá explains that "the evil spirit, Satan or whatever is interpreted as evil, refers to the lower nature in man" ('Abdu'l-Bahá, *The Promulgation of Universal Peace*, p. 411). At the same time, we are aware of another, more lofty force inherent within us and emanating from our essential reality, our soul, which, as we have noted, is fashioned in "the image or likeness of God" ('Abdu'l-Bahá, *The Promulgation of Universal Peace*, p. 654).

In this life, we thus endure a sort of tension within us between these two forces, both of which are quite real. In this same discussion of these two distinct aspects of the human reality, 'Abdu'l-Bahá presents a wonderfully insightful observation about how we can become aware of the dialogical process at work in coming to terms with these influences that are constantly and unremittingly vying for our attention, regardless of how spiritually refined we may think we have become:

The human reality stands between these two—the divine and the satanic. It is manifest that beyond this material body, man is endowed with another reality which is the world of exemplars constituting the heavenly body of man. In speaking, man says, "I saw," "I spoke," "I went." Who is this *I*?

It is obvious that this *I* is different from this body. It is clear that when man is thinking, it is as though he were consulting with some other person. With whom is he consulting? It is evident that it is another reality or one aside from this body with whom he enters into consultation when he thinks, "Shall I do this work or not?" "What will be the result of my doing this?" Or when he questions the other reality, "What is the objection to this work if I do it?" And then that reality in man communicates its opinion to him concerning the point at issue. Therefore that reality in man is clearly and obviously other than his body, an ego with which man enters into consultation and whose opinion man seeks. ('Abdu'l-Bahá, *The Promulgation of Universal Peace*, p. 654)

It is extremely important to appreciate, in reviewing the analysis of this process, that 'Abdu'l-Bahá is not speaking about a dialogue between our spiritual self and our lower or satanic nature. The dialogue he portrays takes place while the individual is in a state of meditation and reflection, a discursive process that, 'Abdu'l-Bahá explains, is a constant internal dialogue in the form of consultation between the rational mind and the human spirit, as opposed to the communion of prayer in which our own spirit supplicates the Holy Spirit for guidance:

Bahá'u'lláh says there is a sign (from God) in every phenomenon: the sign of the intellect is contemplation and the sign of contemplation is silence, because it is impossible for a man to do two things at one time—he cannot both speak and meditate.

It is an axiomatic fact that while you meditate you are speaking with your own spirit. In that state of mind you put certain questions to your spirit and the spirit answers: the light breaks forth and the reality is revealed.

You cannot apply the name "man" to any being void of this faculty of meditation; without it he would be a mere animal, lower than the beasts.

Through the faculty of meditation man attains to eternal life; through it he receives the breath of the Holy Spirit—the bestowal of the Spirit is given in reflection and meditation.

The spirit of man is itself informed and strengthened during meditation; through it affairs of which man knew nothing are unfolded before his view. Through it he receives Divine inspiration, through it he receives heavenly food.

Meditation is the key for opening the doors of mysteries. In that state man abstracts himself: in that state man withdraws himself from all outside objects; in that subjective mood he is immersed in the ocean of spiritual life and can unfold the secrets of things-in-themselves. To illustrate this, think of man as endowed with two kinds of sight; when the power of insight is being used the outward power of vision does not see.

This faculty of meditation frees man from the animal nature, discerns the reality of things, puts man in touch with God. ('Abdu'l-Bahá, *Paris Talks*, no. 54.8–14)

Dialogue with the insistent self, then, is not really a conversation with a distinct and separate voice or source, but merely our own internal debate about thoughts or actions that derive from our desire for sensual pleasure or vanity.

It is in this sense of the dual aspect of our reality during the earthly stage of our life that we are being pulled in two mostly antithetical directions—the desire to satisfy our desires as a physical edifice of "water and clay" and the aspiration to fulfill our higher reality as a spiritual essence, or soul.

The concept of the "Satanic" in the Bahá'í writings thus represents varying degrees of the persistence of ego and the internal dialogue in which we attend to the details of our life by struggling to manifest simple virtues, such as trustworthiness, kindness, politeness, good manners, and sincere interest in and concern for those whom we meet, even on a casual basis. At the other extreme, this dialogue can at times become a pitched battle waged with such vehemence that it can threaten our overall spiritual wellbeing.

It is in this latter context that Bahá'u'lláh most often employs the term "Satan" to allude to the conduct of those individuals who, at the time of the appearance of the new Manifestation, are so caught up in traditional thought and vested interest in maintaining the status quo that they war against the light of the new Revelation. In one tablet, Bahá'u'lláh characterizes such conduct as turning "unto the manifestation of Satan":

> He, however, who denied God in His Truth, who turned his back upon Him and rebelled, who disbelieved and made mischief, the verdict of "impiety," "blasphemy," "death," and "fire" was passed upon him. For, what blasphemy is greater than to turn unto the *manifestations of Satan,* to follow the doctors of oblivion and the people of rebellion? What impiety is more grievous than to deny the Lord on the day when faith itself is renewed and regenerated by God, the Almighty, the Beneficent? What death is more wretched than to flee from the Source of everlasting life? What fire is fiercer on the Day of Reckoning than that of remoteness from the divine Beauty and the celestial Glory? (Bahá'u'lláh, *Gems of Divine Mysteries,* p. 45) [italics added]

Today a sizeable portion of the human race is almost entirely bereft of any awareness of spiritual reality and has become distracted from heeding their inherent need to attend to spiritual enlightenment and edification. When large numbers of people become thus afflicted, then the world might well be characterized as "the metropolis of Satan": "A world in which naught can be perceived save strife, quarrels and corruption is bound to become the seat of the throne, the very metropolis, of Satan" (Bahá'u'lláh, *Tablets of Bahá'u'lláh*, p. 177).

In His most important doctrinal work, The Kitáb-i-Íqán (The Book of Certitude), Bahá'u'lláh sets forth many arguments dedicated to explaining how and why the generality of people, including religious authorities and clerics, fail to recognize and accept the new Manifestation and the Revelation He brings. Here again Bahá'u'lláh uses the term "Satan," as well as the more ominous term "Prince of Darkness," to portray the atmosphere created by these self-absorbed souls:

> Thou dost witness today how, notwithstanding the radiant splendor of the Sun of divine knowledge, all the people, whether high or low, have clung to the ways of those abject manifestations of the *Prince of Darkness*. They continually appeal to them for aid in unraveling the intricacies of their Faith, and, owing to lack of knowledge, they make such replies as can in no wise damage their fame and fortune. It is evident that these souls, vile and miserable as the beetle itself, have had no portion of the musk-laden breeze of eternity, and have never entered the Ridván of heavenly delight. How, therefore, can they impart unto others the imperishable fragrance of holiness? Such is their way, and such will it remain forever. Only those will attain to the knowledge of the Word of God that have turned unto Him, and repudiated the manifestations of *Satan*. (Bahá'u'lláh, The Kitáb-i-Íqán, ¶130) [italics added]

THE EVIL WHISPERER

The use of the epithet "Evil Whisperer" would be particularly important to Bahá'u'lláh's Muslim audience because Muhammad uses similar terms, referring to the Devil or to Satan: "Say: I seek refuge in the Lord of mankind, the King of mankind, the God of mankind, from the evil of the sneaking whisperer, who whispereth in the hearts of mankind . . ." (Surah 114:1–5).

This is the same figure alluded to in Muhammad's retelling of the Adamic myth in which the jinn Iblis refuses to bow down before Adam when God ordains Adam to be a Manifestation of God among men:

> When We said to the angels, "Prostrate yourselves to Adam," they prostrated themselves, but not Iblis. He refused. Then We said: "O Adam! verily, this is an enemy to thee and thy wife: so let him not get you both out of the Garden so that thou art landed in misery. There is therein (enough provision) for thee not to go hungry nor to go naked, nor to suffer from thirst, nor from the sun's heat."
>
> But Satan whispered evil to him: he said, "O Adam! shall I lead thee to the Tree of Eternity and to a kingdom that never decays?" In the result, they both ate of the tree, and so their nakedness appeared to them: they began to sew together, for their covering, leaves from the Garden: thus did Adam disobey His Lord, and allow himself to be seduced. (Surah 20:116–21)

I think this image of a sly voice whispering in our ears to tempt us to be selfish, or to ignore those laws revealed to restrain us from addictive or inappropriate behavior, or to take advantage of a situation or of someone else to advance our own condition, is a wonderfully rich conceit for the purposes of conveying the internal struggle of trying to become a good person or to maintain compliance with what we know to be the right path. As the Bahá'í writings note, the more we can establish a habit of keeping our thoughts and motives pure, the less sway this voice will have. Indeed, we might hope to achieve a state where our thoughts are consistently focused on our spiritual advancement and we need to devote but little attention to being wary about the assault of the insistent self: "Follow not that which the Evil One whispereth in your hearts, for he, verily, doth prompt you to walk after your lusts and covetous desires, and hindereth you from treading the straight Path which this all-embracing and all-compelling Cause hath opened" (Bahá'u'lláh, "Súriy-i-Haykal," *The Summons of the Lord of Hosts*, ¶98).

THE CONTAGION OF CYNICISM

Of course, the fact is that in this life we never attain a state where we are completely safeguarded from or immune to the temptations that may emerge from the self within or from the infectious cynicism that can afflict us from without. From religious history in general, and from particular figures in Bahá'í history, we learn that in this life we are never immune to this infection that 'Abdu'l-Bahá has characterized as having the same properties as the pathology of a physical disease, such as leprosy.

Of course, this is symbolic language and by no means a condemnation of those who, through no fault of their own, have literally contracted this dreaded disease: "Leprosy may be interpreted as any veil that interveneth between man and the recognition of the Lord, his God" (Bahá'u'lláh, *Gleanings*, no. 36.3). Therefore in using this disease to symbolize such a veil, 'Abdu'l-Bahá applies this analogy to portray both those who fail to recognize the Manifestation and heed His laws, and those who, having recognized and accepted His station, actively attempt to deter the Prophet, to harm Him, and to destroy His religion and its teachings.

Similar to other grievous sins, such as child abuse or other sorts of horrific actions that impede the spiritual development of others, this sin is not merely a personal failure. This virulent infection can incite one to seduce others to the same kind of cynical and pernicious contempt for the Manifestation and His teachings.

Possibly because "misery loves company," or else out of jealousy for those who are able to sustain their belief, one who has lost faith or has become cynical about spiritual beliefs can develop the harmful practice of challenging or undermining the faith of others. Curiously, this infection or affliction can metastasize, even when the victim of this disease is fully aware of the station of the Manifestation and knowledgeable about the altruistic aims of His revelation.

But the cynicism resulting from personal abhorrence of the light can cause one who is thus obsessed to spiral rapidly beyond the reach of remedial assistance. It is a pathology that might be well illustrated by comparing it to the effect of reversing one of two attracting magnets so that the unseen forces that were formerly drawing and binding these objects together now quickly produce the opposite effect.

Like the fictional Lucifer, such individuals may become repelled by the light that formerly attracted them, because in order to become reconciled, they must become subservient to the same beliefs and authority which they may have publicly denounced or rejected. This is a severe test of pride for one whose pride is the very source of what has caused the breach of faith and allegiance in the first place.

But while we may understand how and why this pathology happens—even as it is likewise understandable why those who are in more lofty positions of "nearness" may sometimes be the most susceptible to such vanity—the logical appreciation of the process does not render the disease any less contagious or its effects any less severe. The fact is that a logical understanding of a pathology is of meager assistance to one afflicted by a malady that induces irrational behavior and that abhors the logical conclusion that only through submission can restoration of faith and nearness to the presence of the divine be attained.

Obviously the cause of this spiritual affliction will differ from individual to individual, but the one warning 'Abdu'l-Bahá repeatedly gives regarding this spiritual condition is that we should not be so foolhardy as to think we have immunity when associating with individuals who have contracted this detestation of the light.

Nor should we allow ourselves to be so vain as to imagine we can reason with someone whose very actions are based entirely on passions, vain imagination, and the outright rejection of the reasonable solution.

In his last telegram to the American believers before he passed, 'Abdu'l-Bahá responded to a question they had asked him regarding how to treat individuals who were out to destroy their beliefs. He wrote back succinctly, "He who sitteth with a leper catcheth *leprosy*" (quoted in *Directives from the Guardian*, no. 44) [italics added]. Shoghi Effendi, using the same conceit, cautioned believers with the following: "Covenant Breaking* is truly a Spiritual disease, and the whole view-point and attitude of a Covenant Breaker is so poisonous that the Master likened it to *leprosy*, and warned the friends to breathe the same air was dangerous. This should not be taken literally; He meant when you are close enough to breathe the same air you are close enough to contact their corrupting influence" (Shoghi Effendi, in *Lights of Guidance*, p. 183) [italics added].

THE EVIL ONE

In addition to 'Abdu'l-Bahá's wonderfully descriptive phrase "the insistent self," Bahá'u'lláh employs another powerful epithet for the temptations of the "self"—"the Evil One"—portraying the attention we should pay to this subtle attraction to those pernicious desires to which we are exposed in this life. He uses this epithet more than any other for this purpose, and given the reliance on logical discourse that permeates all of the Bahá'í authoritative

---

* One who publicly denies the line of succession (i.e. Bahá'u'lláh, 'Abdu'l-Bahá, Shoghi Effendi, the Universal House of Justice) or who rebels against the Center of the Covenant ['Abdu'l-Bahá] and actively works to undermine the Covenant (*A Basic Bahá'í Dictionary*, p. 62).

texts, the unambiguous and evocative tenor of this phrase is liable to stun those encountering it for the first time.

For one thing, the phrase is capitalized, as if this were indeed the title of an actual being. However, the capitalization is not a matter of respect but rather the result of a rule in the mechanics of writing in English—we capitalize the personification of a force. And with this term, "the Evil One," we are personifying the force that might coax us or tempt us to ignore the light, to turn away from it, or possibly to join forces with others who have become similarly cynical in their despair.

For example, in the following passage, Bahá'u'lláh describes the machinations of those divines who spread lies in an effort to undermine belief in the new Manifestation, but He is careful not to attribute their actions to any inherently evil character, but rather to the influence of the insistent self working within them as "the Evil One": "Their eyes are drunken; they are indeed a blind people. Their proofs are the calumnies they uttered; condemned are their calumnies by God, the Help in Peril, the Self-Subsisting. The Evil One hath stirred up mischief in their hearts, and they are afflicted with a torment that none can avert" (Bahá'u'lláh, *Gleanings*, no. 17.3).

In a more encompassing and optimistic yet totally frank statement about the new Revelation and the care with which the peoples of the world must embrace and guard this new guidance from God, Bahá'u'lláh cautions:

> How high the reward of him that hath not deprived himself of so great a bounty, nor failed to recognize the beauty of his Best-Beloved in this, His new attire. Watch over yourselves, for *the Evil One is lying in wait*, ready to entrap you. Gird yourselves against his wicked devices, and, led by the light of the name of the All-Seeing God, make your escape from the darkness that surroundeth you. Let your vision be world-embracing, rather than confined to your own self. *The Evil*

One is he that hindereth the rise and obstructeth the spiritual progress of the children of men. (Bahá'u'lláh, *Gleanings*, no. 43.5)[italics added]

Two other passages give useful insight into how Bahá'u'lláh uses this epithet creatively to describe succinctly what would otherwise require an elaborate exposition of the abstract concepts involved. In several instances Bahá'u'lláh states that no external force can afflict or harm Him: "My imprisonment doeth Me no harm, neither the tribulations I suffer, nor the things that have befallen Me at the hands of My oppressors. That which harmeth Me is the conduct of those who, though they bear My name, yet commit that which maketh My heart and My pen to lament" (Bahá'u'lláh, Epistle to the Son of the Wolf, p. 23). Using the symbolic epithet "the Evil One" to represent inclinations to commit such deeds, Bahá'u'lláh states, "My captivity can bring on Me no shame. Nay, by My life, it conferreth on Me glory. That which can make Me ashamed is the conduct of such of My followers as profess to love Me, yet in fact follow *the Evil One*. They, indeed, are of the lost" (Bahá'u'lláh, *Gleanings*, no. 60.1) [italics added].

In other words, Bahá'u'lláh seems to be saying that simply declaring one's belief in Him and giving lip service to the Bahá'í Faith do not by themselves ensure a follower that he or she is necessarily protected from spiritual failure or susceptibility to the temptation to commit "evil" acts. It is for this reason that Bahá'u'lláh cautions each believer that before he or she attempts to teach someone else about the Bahá'í Faith, the teacher must first teach himself. Otherwise, the words will be hollow and have no enduring effect. In this context, it is well worth repeating a passage previously cited: "Whoso ariseth among you to teach the Cause of his Lord, let him, before all else, teach his own self, that his speech may attract the hearts of them that hear him. Unless he teacheth his own self, the words of his mouth will not influence the heart of the seeker" (Bahá'u'lláh, *Gleanings*, no. 128.6).

Finally, Bahá'u'lláh emphasizes the verity that anyone desiring to be a follower must show forth belief in action, and not words alone: "Say: Doth it beseem a man while claiming to be a follower of his Lord, the All-Merciful, he should yet in his heart do the very deeds *of the Evil One?* Nay, it ill beseemeth him, and to this He Who is the Beauty of the All-Glorious will bear Me witness. Would that ye could comprehend it!" (Bahá'u'lláh, *Gleanings*, no. 128.1) [italics added].

PART 4: EXPLORING THE DEPTHS OF HELL

CHAPTER 12 / HELL IS A VERY SCARY PLACE

In the heavenly Books, mention is made of the immortality of the spirit, which is the very foundation of the divine religions. For rewards and punishments are said to be of two kinds—one being existential rewards and punishments and the other, ultimate rewards and punishments. Existential paradise and hell are to be found in all the worlds of God, whether in this world or in the heavenly realms of the spirit, and to gain these rewards is to attain life eternal.

—'Abdu'l-Bahá, *Some Answered Questions,* no. 60.2

If all allusions to Satan are merely symbolic portrayals of the "insistent self," or the temptation to reject pursuing the life of the spirit in exchange for indulging in material and sensual delights, then are the allusions to Hell likewise entirely symbolic? Is it not feasible that Satan could symbolize our own distraction from doing the right thing but that Hell could still exist as a real place, or at least as an actual state of being?

TRADITIONAL LOCATIONS OF HELL

During the latter part of the fifth century when the "Apostles' Creed" was devised as a testimony of Christian belief, the non-scriptural statement that Christ "descended into hell," where He freed all those souls who were confined there, was added.* Derived from various interpretations of Greek and Anglo-Saxon terms, the doctrine came from the classical notion of Hell (Hades) as being located in an underworld considered to be the abode of the dead.

---

* "Apostles' Creed," http://www.vatican.va/archive/ccc_css/archive/catechism/credo.htm

For several hundred years, this myth of hell as an abode of eternal fire and damnation gained popularity in Christian art and iconography and culminated in Dante's early fourteenth-century epic *The Divine Comedy*. A complex allegorical work in which the narrative persona Dante successively tours Hell, Purgatory, and Heaven, this masterpiece of world literature provided a vivid portrayal of the three possible abodes to which one might be relegated after death.

Giving artistic expression to theological beliefs that had evolved in western Christendom by this time, the first part, *The Inferno*, portrays Hell as funnel-shaped, with circles at each level, as if the Guggenheim Museum were shaped like an ice-cream cone and were extremely hot and noisy from all the screaming and torture going on inside. Dante's vision of this netherworld of eternal damnation has three divisions: Upper Hell, Lower Hell, and Lowest Hell, with each successive level containing increasingly more fiendish and perverse sinners.*

The vindication of the heliocentric concept of our solar system had a major effect on belief concerning the location of hell. Copernicus' theory that the sun is the center of our planetary system (*Concerning the Revolutions of the Celestial Spheres*, 1547) became generally accepted more than a century later, with Newton's publication of *Principia* (*Mathematical Principles of Natural Philosophy*, 1687) being a significant influence in changing popular opinion. For if the Earth is not the center of the universe, then Hell has to be located someplace else (other than the center of the Earth). Furthermore, Christian theology was having a difficult time keeping pace with the rapid advances in other scientific discoveries about reality, as well as the application of the scientific method to everyday life.

---

* Michelangelo portrayed a version of the same concept in his painting of the Last Judgment on the altar wall of the Sistine Chapel.

It was one thing to believe that there could be an afterlife in which we endure and undergo experiences appropriate to what we have done in this life. But since only aberrant twists in Christian theology allowed for a physical body to undergo physical punishment (reincarnation or bodily ascent to some physical abode), then hell had to be some sort of "placeless" place, and the punishment had to be more internal or psychological/emotional than physical.

In his influential epic *Paradise Lost* (1667), John Milton devises a theoretical universe to account for an alternative placement of hell, though in spite of the general acceptance of the Copernican heliocentric model of the universe, Milton retains the Ptolemaic geocentric model, thereby conveniently avoiding having to contest the suddenly archaic Christian view that Earth is the center of God's creation.

Accordingly, Milton places Hell outside of the "created universe" of the Ptolemaic geocentric order. Hell is described as being part of the region of Chaos, or uncreated matter, and Milton portrays it as extremely unpleasant. Milton's famous description of Hell is first glimpsed as the defeated fallen angels—following their expulsion from heaven after losing the all-out war with God—gradually become conscious. They look around to discover themselves in "A Dungeon horrible, on all sides round / As one great Furnace flam'd, yet from those flames / No light, but rather darkness visible" (Milton, "Paradise Lost," Bk. I, ll. 61–63, in *The Complete Poetical Works of John Milton*).

Milton's description continues, but this single oxymoronic phrase of a "darkness visible" came to be an evocative symbol for William Styron,* who employed this conceit to represent the most

---

* Styron wrote *Darkness Visible: A Memoir of Madness*, a chronicle of his devastating clinical depression. He is one of the few writers to convey the ineffable and inescapable terror that becomes the "hell" of someone suffering from this disease, though he also delineates a path to hope and recovery.

dismal throes of clinical depression, an internal state so dire as to cause so many to end their lives rather than continue to endure this emotional/mental state of utter despair and hopelessness. Milton obviously understood this fact, that physical torture, however dire, could not compare to the torment of a tortured mind or soul.

Whether or not Milton himself in his own blindness had to struggle against this affliction—what the depressive Winston Churchill referred to as "the Black Dog"—Milton has his most complex character, Satan himself, describe the true reality of hell not as physical deprivation or torture, but as a state of mind: "The mind is its own place, and in itself / Can make a Heaven of Hell, a Hell of Heaven" (Bk. 1, ll. 254–55). Or stated as an abiding principal about the soul's reality, the internal sense of self supersedes any external exigencies affecting our well-being.

All the great thinkers and artists long ago realized this fact, even if some of the theologians had entrapped themselves into literalist views of scripture and the need to exercise the "rod" more than the "staff" to frighten their flock into being obedient and thereby avoid the bramble of sin.

BUT ISN'T HELL A SCARY PLACE?

Here again it bears repeating that motive is everything in the journey of the soul, whether we are referring to the process as a whole or to the more particular or specialized efforts we make in fulfilling guidance about maintaining a "chaste and holy life." In the long run, the purity of our endeavors is more than the sum total of specific outcomes we might amass during our lives.

In this context, the Báb cautions us that our ultimate desire to become spiritual should *not* be motivated by either our desire for future reward or fear of future punishment, but rather by our attraction to the joy of spiritual progress and by our love of the beauty of God: "That which is worthy of His Essence is to worship Him for His sake, without fear of fire, or hope of paradise" (The Báb, *Selections from the Writings of the Báb*, 3:2:2).

Perhaps we can accept this lofty exhortation at face value, but if we are honest with ourselves, this is an incredibly subtle objective. It is especially daunting during the beginning stages of our conscious efforts to transform ourselves by degrees into instinctively and habitually righteous individuals. In the beginning, we need more direct and specific feedback before we can begin to acquire the purity of motive the Báb describes.

A review of the overriding context for the Báb's observation might be a good place to begin a more comprehensive understanding and appreciation of this advice as it pertains to our previously stated objective of coming "to know and to worship God":

> Worship thou God in such wise that if thy worship lead thee to the fire, no alteration in thine adoration would be produced, and so likewise if thy recompense should be paradise. Thus and thus alone should be the worship which befitteth the one True God. Shouldst thou worship Him because of fear, this would be unseemly in the sanctified Court of His presence, and could not be regarded as an act by thee dedicated to the Oneness of His Being. Or if thy gaze should be on paradise, and thou shouldst worship Him while cherishing such a hope, thou wouldst make God's creation a partner with Him, notwithstanding the fact that paradise is desired by men.
>
> Fire and paradise both bow down and prostrate themselves before God. That which is worthy of His Essence is to worship Him for His sake, without fear of fire, or hope of paradise.
>
> Although when true worship is offered, the worshipper is delivered from the fire, and entereth the paradise of God's good-pleasure, yet such should not be the motive of his act. However, God's favour and grace ever flow in accordance with the exigencies of His inscrutable wisdom.
>
> The most acceptable prayer is the one offered with the utmost spirituality and radiance; its prolongation hath not

been and is not beloved by God. The more detached and the purer the prayer, the more acceptable is it in the presence of God. (The Báb, *Selections from the Writings of the Báb,* 3:2:2–4)

Perhaps the most important inference we can draw from reflecting on this weighty statement regarding the worship of God—whether we define it in terms of literal supplication or, more generally, as all those actions we invest with spiritual purpose—is the Báb's assertion that, ultimately, fear of punishment and hope for reward should not be the underlying motive for worship.

On a first reading, we get some sense of what He means—that once we attain the loftier levels of love and adoration of God, no ulterior motive is necessary. Everything we do stems from a desire for the existential delight of being in the spiritual presence of the Beloved, rather than from the desire to protect our souls from some undisclosed future torment or from the promise of some future reward. Any desire we have other than the unalloyed love of the Beloved is displaced and forgotten, along with concerns about the self. Our sole delight is service to humankind as we labor alongside our coworkers, those loving and faithful souls whose companionship sustains and reinforces all that we aspire to accomplish in fashioning a spiritual environment.

But if we are realistic, we might understandably question the extent to which we can achieve this condition during the physical stage of our existence, especially when all we strive to achieve often seems antithetical to the present-day environment—a moribund society mired in the depths of depravity, self-interest, and indifference.

I sincerely do not fear the fire, either literally or figuratively. I have read enough, studied enough, and conversed with the divine realm regularly enough to feel assured that so long as I sincerely desire grace and forgiveness and carry out all my good intentions with a sufficiency of noble actions, I will be pardoned, even for my most egregious mistakes and lost opportunities, however much I regret them and to whatever extent I will be made to regret them when I pass on. I am particularly fond of 'Abdu'l-Bahá's prayer in which he describes God as "He Who forgiveth even the most grievous of sins" ('Abdu'l-Bahá, in *Bahá'í Prayers*, p. 24).

I have no doubt I will be made aware of those willful trespasses—both those I remember and those I failed to notice. I am also certain that some significant portions of the assessment of my life will not feel very good, that this afterlife evaluation may cause me to feel remorse and sorrow, and so it should. But given an eternity to do better, I trust that as I pick up there where I leave off here, my Creator will, as an ever-forgiving Father of unconditional love, respond to my pleas for assistance and further growth with sufficient increments of grace and guidance. And yet I also am aware that, until that transition, I must seize upon those opportunities that yet remain and be ever vigilant in guarding against whatever subtle or gross failures might befall me along the way.

And do I hope for Paradise? If by Paradise we mean being plucked from this realm with its injustice, pain, and sadness, then I do indeed hope and long for such a transmigration. And if by attaining such a condition is meant that I no longer need concern myself with every part of my body that is daily demanding an ever greater portion of my attention, then I do desire it. And if attaining this Paradise means I need no longer worry about whether or not my sundry medications will adjust my organs to function as God intended, then, oh yes, I do indeed hope for such a condition.

Nevertheless, I am not ashamed to confess I find moments of detachment, delight, joy, and love here, now, in this place, in this aging temple. I must conclude, then, that in His exquisite elucidation of the condition we should strive to attain in worshipping God, the Báb is advising us to abandon the vain imagination of a heavenly paradise where we receive material or sensual gratification as a reward for mindlessly following someone else's creed. For if Paradise is not a physical experience but rather a sense of nearness to God, and if Hell is not physical torment but a sense of remoteness, regret, depression, and despair, then these fondest hopes are indeed attainable here and now, even as 'Abdu'l-Bahá observes in this chapter's epigraph.

THE BENEFITS OF THE FEAR OF GOD

There is another related theme that runs throughout the Bahá'í writings—that *until* we attain this purity of motive that the Báb describes and that Bahá'u'lláh mandates in His exhortation to "Observe My commandments, for the love of My beauty" (Bahá'u'lláh, The Kitáb-i-Aqdas, ¶4), we benefit from another process succinctly alluded to as "the fear of God," a condition that understandably confounds many.

For me, this theme alludes to a methodology and also a state of spiritual development, even though the phrase may at first sound enigmatic and contrary to the objective of positive reinforcement. If God is—as we have depicted Him—an entirely loving and ever-forgiving Creator, why should we fear Him, and why would the Manifestations cite this attitude as being a positive, desirable condition? Does this not seem contrary to the very motives we have just cited as being our goal in our spiritual attitude toward the afterlife?

And yet time and again, Bahá'u'lláh speaks of the "fear of God" and reward and punishment as being essential teaching devices, as "pillars" to uphold justice in society:

The Great Being saith: The structure of world stability and order hath been reared upon, and will continue to be sustained by, the twin pillars of reward and punishment. . . . (Bahá'u'lláh, *Gleanings*, no. 112.1)

* * *

218

O people of God! That which traineth the world is Justice, for it is upheld by two pillars, reward and punishment. These two pillars are the sources of life to the world. (Bahá'u'lláh, *Tablets of Bahá'u'lláh*, pp. 128–29)

* * *

Justice hath a mighty force at its command. It is none other than reward and punishment for the deeds of men. By the power of this force the tabernacle of order is established throughout the world, causing the wicked to restrain their natures for fear of punishment. (Bahá'u'lláh, *Tablets of Bahá'u'lláh*, p. 164)

From all we have previously examined, it seems clear that ultimately we should strive to achieve a state in which the act of manifesting virtue is existentially rewarding, where we follow the laws of God because we love the "Beauty" of the Creator. And by using the term *beauty* (which Socrates also uses in alluding to God as the "Good" and the "Beautiful"), the Bahá'í writings indicate that we become aware of the boundless perfections of God as well as the completely altruistic love and caring with which we have been created.

We gradually appreciate ever more fully that everything in creation as a whole, and in our personal lives as well, ultimately redounds to our bounty, to our spiritual development, and to our felicity. Our life, if lived well, does indeed have a just and happy ending. Therefore, in the above passages where Bahá'u'lláh speaks of the two pillars of reward and punishment, whether in this life or the life to come, He is stating, it would seem to me, that these incentives induce our initial motives for becoming good people and "God-fearing" individuals.

In this regard, Bahá'u'lláh explains that the Manifestations have employed the mythic images of "heaven" and "hell" to represent spiritual conditions of the afterlife solely for the purpose of conveying in accessible symbolic language the nature of certain spiritual or emotional states of being: "Even the materialists have testified in their writings to the wisdom of these divinely-appointed Messengers, and have regarded the references made by the Prophets to Paradise, to hell fire, to future reward and punishment, to have been actuated by a desire to educate and uplift the souls of men" (Bahá'u'lláh, *Gleanings*, no. 81.1).

In other words, individually and collectively, most of us benefit from, and even require, these emotional incentives of fear and hope in the beginning stages of our spiritual training. And while these images of cause and effect are never intended as literal conditions or physical abodes in terms of the destiny of our existence beyond the physical realm, they are useful and logically accurate representations of the spiritual condition—whether proximity or remoteness—awaiting each of us as a result of our response to the challenges of our life's journey.

But, as is also clear in the passages regarding reward and punishment, Bahá'u'lláh is describing literal tools that society needs to employ to maintain social justice and order by inducing and securing obedience to law. At the simplest level of society—the family—this "technique" would imply the wise application of reward and punishment to raising children. At the most expansive level of the global community, this same technique would allude to the principle of "collective security" as ordained and elucidated by Bahá'u'lláh regarding maintaining peace in a global commonwealth:

On the societal level, the principle of collective security enunciated by Bahá'u'lláh (see *Gleanings from the Writings of Bahá'u'lláh*, CXVII) and elaborated by Shoghi Effendi (see the Guardian's letters in *The World Order of Bahá'u'lláh*) does not presuppose the abolition of the use of force, but prescribes "a system in which Force is made the servant of Justice," and which provides for the existence of an international peace-keeping force that "will safeguard the organic unity of the whole commonwealth." (note in Bahá'u'lláh, The Kitáb-i-Aqdas, p. 240)

Thus in the beginning of our training, whether as individuals or as a community, the "twin pillars" may indeed allude to physical responses designed to guide our actions. We fear we may be deprived of certain freedoms or bounties if we disobey rules or laws by failing to live up to those standards of performance to which we have covenanted. We hope we will be rewarded by more freedom or other types of bounties should we fulfill or exceed the expectations that are our part of the same covenant.

DETACHMENT

It is our purpose, individually and collectively, to do well. We aspire to be helpful citizens and decent human beings. And because on some level we accept these standards as inherently enjoyable, we attempt to transform our motives from fear to attraction and love. This state of being for which we strive is perhaps most clearly portrayed by Bahá'u'lláh as the condition of "detachment."

This term most obviously relates to our rejection of physical comfort and material wellbeing as the dominating objectives in our lives or as the standards by which we gauge our progress. In one of my favorite passages about detachment, Bahá'u'lláh provides explicit images of those kinds of things to which His followers must gradually become inured:

Say: He is not to be numbered with the people of Bahá who followeth his mundane desires, or fixeth his heart on things of the earth. He is My true follower who, if he come to a valley of pure gold, will pass straight through it aloof as a cloud, and will neither turn back, nor pause. Such a man is, assuredly, of Me. From his garment the Concourse on high can inhale the fragrance of sanctity. . . . And if he met the fairest and most comely of women, he would not feel his heart seduced by the least shadow of desire for her beauty. Such an one, indeed, is the creation of spotless chastity. Thus instructeth you the Pen of the Ancient of Days, as bidden by your Lord, the Almighty, the All-Bountiful. (Bahá'u'lláh, *Gleanings*, no. 60.3)

But as we noted regarding the process of acquiring any important virtue, becoming detached is part of an ongoing process whereby we attain purity of motive—it cannot be mandated, nor does it result merely from the expression of our determination to succeed. Only by graduated steps of personal effort can we become detached, and each of these steps derives from our increasing attraction to the joy of "nearness" to the Beloved. Once this attraction becomes the dominating force in our lives, the notion of the "fear of God" takes on an entirely different meaning.

It should be clearly understood, however, that "detachment" in the context of the Bahá'í writings does not mean some form of asceticism or puritanical attitude toward the physical aspect of our lives. Neither is this condition meant to imply lethargy or apathy regarding taking action in the social or public sphere. Quite the contrary—"detachment" implies, instead, an enthusiastic and eager pursuit of justice and collaboration with others similarly inclined, while being focused on the collective wellbeing and advancement of civilization rather than assessing ourselves or our achievements using materialistic or egoistic standards.

The same concept of detachment applies with equal importance to the motive underlying our struggle to improve ourselves spiritually. Rather than being exhorted to strive for nearness to God because we fear for our own spiritual safety or wellbeing, we are cautioned to fear doing anything that might interfere with the health or development of this love relationship. We fear the loss of any opportunity we might have to assist in the promulgation of the spiritual principles so amply explicated and demonstrated by the Manifestation, and we become increasingly desirous of doing whatever we can to promote the curative plans that the Manifestation has designed to advance the spiritual infrastructure of human society.

In this context, the "fear of God" is still an apt allusion to a condition we desire to sustain, but it has assumed for us an entirely positive and benign connotation. We no longer sense in this term the fear of retribution for failure, nor does this concept induce in us an image of a Creator who is jealous, vindictive, wrathful, or capricious. Our fear of doing less than our full potential is thus an expression of our gratitude for the guidance and forgiveness of this Benign Father.

This condition of detachment, then, is what I believe to be one of the most important meanings of the "fear of God." This "fear" is nothing more or less than our awareness and acceptance of the fact that there is a Creator from Whom we emanated, and that our sole lasting source of achievement, wellbeing, and ease of heart can come only from obedience to the guidance He has devised to assist us. We are quite literally His offsprings, His loved ones whose safety and assistance He is constantly monitoring because He is, in truth, a "personal" God.

In one of the more than twenty occasions where Bahá'u'lláh exhorts us to "fear God" in Epistle to the Son of the Wolf, we find the following verse: "Fear ye God, and be not of them that have denied Him" (p. 38). In the context of this passage, the antithesis of the "fear of God" is disbelief in God. In sum, if we truly believe in God, then we understandably fear acting contrary to His plan for us by ignoring the guidance He conveys through His Manifestations, or else by becoming negligent in our efforts to attain nearness. In other words, if we believe in God, we "fear" the consequences of our actions in relation to Him because we know that this relationship is real, has actual consequences in our life, and is central to the core of our existence.

13 / THE EVIL WHISPERER AT WORK IN OUR LIVES

Cleanse thy heart from every blasphemous whispering and evil allusion thou hast heard in the past, that thou mayest inhale the sweet savours of eternity from the Joseph of faithfulness, gain admittance into the celestial Egypt, and perceive the fragrances of enlightenment from this resplendent and luminous Tablet, a Tablet wherein the Pen hath inscribed the ancient mysteries of the names of His Lord, the Exalted, the Most High. Perchance thou mayest be recorded in the holy Tablets among them that are well-assured.

—Bahá'u'lláh, *Gems of Divine Mysteries*, pp. 23–24

At this point, we may be considering not paying heed to any concerns we might have previously harbored about sin, Satan, the Devil, and hell. After all, from what we have surveyed, it seems that sin is simply an action that affects our progress negatively. We have concluded that we can always turn things around by using our free will any time we want. It may be more of a struggle the further we descend, but we can always apply our will more forcefully if it becomes necessary.

Even if we find ourselves in the depths of unbelief and immorality, the logic of the Bahá'í teachings about morality and spiritual development seems to indicate that it is still possible for us to correct our course, change our direction . . . possibly tomorrow, or maybe this evening. Of course, we could change directions right now, at this very minute! . . . if we weren't busy doing other stuff.

And if God is ever-forgiving and we don't happen to decide that it is worth the effort to turn things around right this minute . . . or tomorrow, or even before we depart from this plane of existence (which could also be tomorrow, or an hour from now, or at the next intersection), we could always cop a plea in the next stage of our life. And if the fear of God is not so much fear of His retribution but rather fear of the effect our misdeeds will have on our own felicity and future wellbeing, then won't God, who loves us unconditionally, come to our aid whenever we decide to change?

FAUSTUS' PACT WITH THE DEVIL

Isn't this the logical flaw in Marlowe's *Dr. Faustus*? In the final scene, when Faustus is dragged down to hell and wants to cry out to Jesus, the demons seem to restrain him. But doesn't he still have free will? He can still be redeemed if he simply follows through and pleads for Christ's assistance, and if he really means it, would not Christ come to his aid?

Of course, Faustus has signed in his own blood a contract with the Devil, but according to every version of theology we have thus far examined (Judaic, Christian, Islamic, Bahá'í), Satan cannot snatch our soul against our will. Therefore, this contract, even signed in his own blood, is binding only if he believes it is, only if he has a "fear of Satan" and accepts his destiny as a *fait accompli*. And according to what theological dogma can Faustus, who is an expert in the study of theology, not revoke his contract?

In the real world, as soon as he speaks of crying out to Christ, bells should sound and all other conversation and action should cease, as if he were in a properly run police station in the United States proclaiming, "I want a lawyer!"

> The stars move still, time runs, the clock will strike,
> The devil will come, and Faustus must be damned.
> O I'll leap up to my God! Who pulls me down?
> See, see where Christ's blood streams in the firmament!
> One drop would save my soul, half a drop: ah my Christ—
> Ah, rend not my heart from naming of my Christ;
> Yet will I call on him—O spare me, Lucifer!
> Where is it now? 'Tis gone: and see where God

Stretcheth out his arm, and bends his ireful brows!
Mountains and hills, come, come and fall on me,
And hide me from the heavy wrath of God.

(Marlowe, *The Tragical History of the Life and Death
of Doctor Faustus*, scene 13, ll. 67–77)

We need not immerse ourselves in the academic mire of debate about why Faustus is damned or what his flaw is, whether hubris in desiring inappropriate knowledge, or foolishness in how he becomes distracted from his quest for knowledge, or pride in thinking himself too great a sinner to be saved by God's grace. After all, at the end, when one of his scholar friends reminds him that "God's mercies are infinite" (scene 13, ll. 13–14), Faustus responds, "But Faustus' offense can ne'er be pardoned! The serpent that tempted Eve may be saved, but not Faustus" (scene 13, ll. 15–16).

Is Faustus just not smart enough to realize the flaw in what he has just said, or is he too distracted to appreciate the obvious logic of Christian doctrine that his own student is whispering in his ear? Is he simply so oppressed with guilt, shame, and despair that he has lost faith in the power of God to redeem him? Is he so prideful as to believe that his deeds are more grievous than those of all other sinners and that, therefore, he is beyond the power of God's redemption?

His final words seem to indicate that he is aware he could be saved. And when he considers calling on Christ as his redeemer, it would seem his intent alone should be sufficient to save him, if only he had the will to follow through and plead, together with patience and faith sufficient to shut up and let God's infinite redemption do its work. Or is he so far removed from the belief he once had that in his despair he succumbs to the cynical forces of darkness and completes his own damnation?

Of course, it is also possible that Marlowe's portrayal is simply not logically consistent within itself, nor must it be. Marlowe wrote a decent play, but it is fiction, after all, and not required to be precisely logical, especially since the theology on which it is based is itself convoluted. Marlowe's beliefs did not have to be logical for his play to be good drama.

The fact is that *The Tragical History of Doctor Faustus* is mostly a cautionary tale derived from the tradition of the then still-extant medieval morality plays. It is meant to frighten the audience into self-examination through the Aristotelian tragic emotions of pity and fear—pity for the "branch that might have grown full straight," and fear that we, the audience, might suffer the same fate if we are not sufficiently attentive to our own choices.

GOETHE'S GENIUS

Personally—and I can say this with impunity now that I am retired—I never liked Marlowe's play, even though I taught it many times, even acted in it, and thought Elizabeth Taylor was simply stunning as Helen of Troy in Richard Burton's 1967 version, although she didn't say a word.

I never found the play convincing. It makes too many assumptions about Faustus. This character simply does not strike me as being all that deep, all that desirous of acquiring knowledge about reality—metaphysical or otherwise. He is far too easily distracted by trivial delights, and not at all the fundamentally noble character we find in Goethe's Faust.

Goethe's examination of similar dynamics at work in his own masterpiece studies how the quest for knowledge at any cost, combined with a vulnerability that allows for passion and earthly affection, can bring about self-destruction. His Faust wants more than a moment's entertainment. He sincerely believes that superior knowledge might ultimately bring about the betterment of the human condition.

In Goethe's *Faust* part II, the dying and aged Faust is indeed saved from damnation because his underlying intentions, his fundamental motives, have been noble. He desires knowledge, but not to attain power or personal acclaim. He strives to achieve something worthwhile, reclaiming usable land by pushing back the sea with dikes and dams.

Mephistopheles, like the Tempter Satan in Job, tries to undermine Faust's efforts, but Faust himself, after experiencing a sense of blissful peace of mind, suddenly dies, whereupon angels appear and distract the lecherous demon while they ferry Faust's soul to a celestial wilderness. Once there, various symbolic and allegorical female figures plead for grace for the once noble Faust. They succeed in their campaign of mercy, and the spiritually reborn Faust is conveyed to the more lofty realms of the heavenly spheres.

To me, this ending is logically satisfying and, of course, it is also happier, and I am fond of happy endings. Goethe's work could not have ended in any other way, unless it were the product of some aberrant theology where salvation is the legalistic invention of deluded or misguided clerics. If by definition God is ever ready to respond to our sincere pleas for help, then Marlowe's Faustus was never beyond salvation or assistance, unless he simply refused to follow up on the obvious knowledge of God's infinite grace that his own friend had described only minutes before. He's only damned so long as he accedes to his fear that he cannot be helped and thereby refuses to try to deter his own damnation.

Of course, the ultimate flaw from the perspective of our discussion of the nature of reality is that hell is an internal condition, not a physical place. But the Elizabethan audience believed hell to be a literal, fiery dominion, even as various sects of a number of religions still do. Consequently, Marlowe's closing scene was doubtlessly effective and terrifying with all its flashing lights, smoke, and screams. It served its purpose in conveying the "fear of God," or perhaps more accurately "the fear of Satan," which is quite a different thing.

Possibly Marlowe himself believed that our relationship with God is predicated on legalisms, so that if we sign a pact with the devil we are bound by that agreement. We cannot go to "Sinners Anonymous" and work through our bad decisions.

ALL WE HAVE TO FEAR IS . . . OUR SELF

But if evil is not really a force in the universe, if evil is only a symbolic allusion to the effects of turning away from the active power of divine inspiration and assistance, then why need we worry? If there are no dark forces trying to usurp our will or tempting us to disavow our good intentions, then is fear itself all we have to fear? Was FDR right?*

Of course, he affirmed this hopeful axiom in 1933 at his inaugural address in the midst of the Great Depression. This was three years before the gruesome Spanish Civil War in which Hitler tested the *blitzkrieg* ("lightning war") techniques he would later use in his invasion of Poland in 1939.

Hitler is always there to remind us that turning away from the divine light of God's wisdom and guidance can have unimaginably devastating effects after all. Even if there is no essential power causing evil, even if evil and sin are simply the effects of rejecting goodness, the effects are no less severe. It would thus seem from our personal experience and from reviewing human history that this process of becoming obsessed with the insistent self can unleash a whirlwind, a maelstrom.

And what words with any less impact than these traditional scriptural allusions would carry any more effective weight in trying to depict the horror unleashed by "Satanic" individuals who seem thoroughly "Evil," "Pitiless," "Merciless," and "inhuman"?

I recently viewed a set of newly discovered high-definition color photographs taken as publicity photos during the height of Hitler's power and prestige in Germany. They are amazingly frightening to behold. Soldiers are proudly outfitted in imaginatively designed uniforms of varying fabrics, shiny leather boots, and polished buttons. Everything is orderly and neat. There are troops upon troops of adoring blond children, smiling in their own uniforms and saluting their leader.

---

* Franklin Delano Roosevelt.

Viewing these flawless pictures in the context of what we now know was going on behind the scenes and the firestorms that would follow on the heels of these celebratory gatherings, we are shocked that there is no ominous forewarning anywhere to be seen, no hint of evil or subterfuge. These people are truly delighted. They sincerely believe in this man and this cause. They have accepted the image of themselves as leading the way to the establishment of a worldwide homogeneity peopled by blue eyes, blond hair, and smiles. They are so beautiful that perhaps, they think, they should indeed rule the world. It is clear they have every confidence they will do so.

Had we been there among them, who is to say that we, too, would not have been swept up in the music and marching troops and brightness of that blue-sky day, with its singing and blaring brass. Perhaps we too would join in singing the famed lyrics to Haydn's anthem, "Germany, Germany over all!"

In spite of Jessie Owens' heroic exploits two years earlier, in spite of the strange odors that would soon begin to stream from the smoke stacks at nearby work camps, we also might have been caught up in this mindgame with the bright red banners waving the black twisted cross. We too might have been equally joyful, energized, and mindless, at least until one evening—as we settled down for sleep, with the music stopped and the uniforms pressed and closeted—when we might just for a moment question some part of this and experience a twinge in the gut, some hint of concern that something was just not quite right.

That's it! That's the point, if there is one, where personal responsibility kicks in, where innocence ends, where guilt begins, where sin in all its nonexistence ensues, unless we instantly instigate some course of action to set things right.

Look at those photos and into the tight shots of handsome faces, intelligent men standing beside the "evil one" in his Chaplinesque mustache, and try to peer inside those minds. When did they know? When did they figure out that what might have once seemed like salvation from the defeat and reparations of World War I, from the vast economic depression, was in fact a fast track to hell on earth and hell inside their hearts and minds?

Yes, we human beings are amazing creations. We have so few instincts. We can become accustomed to almost anything, at least for a while. It is often only later that we suffer from the reality of what we have done or seen, and experience that form of Post-Traumatic Stress Disorder (PTSD) which occurs when we try to realign our sanity with the insanity we have endured. But sometimes the contrast is too much. We can compartmentalize our lives and our "selves" only so much. At some point, we can be stretched no further. There is a sudden "Snap!" and a fracture. The shattered psyche then induces the only comfort it can manage on its own, the escape of insanity.

14 / THE HELL INSIDE

How high the reward of him that hath not deprived himself of so great a bounty, nor failed to recognize the beauty of his Best-Beloved in this, His new attire. Watch over yourselves, for the Evil One is lying in wait, ready to entrap you. Gird yourselves against his wicked devices, and, led by the light of the name of the All-Seeing God, make your escape from the darkness that surroundeth you. Let your vision be world-embracing, rather than confined to your own self. The Evil One is he that hindereth the rise and obstructeth the spiritual progress of the children of men.

—Bahá'u'lláh, *Gleanings*, no. 43.5

Almost all of us who are of a certain age have been to hell at some point in our lives. It may be associated with a place or a physical condition, but likely the most intense suffering we endured was probably experienced as an emotional state, an affliction of the psyche.

The horror of this sort of hell derives from the fact that the pain of the afflicted self is not like physical pain to which you know you can put an end, even if the solution might be to sever the afflicted part. By contrast, pain in the mind occurs precisely where we are, up here between the ears where our consciousness resides. How can we escape from our own "self"?

THE MIND IS ITS OWN PLACE

We have already cited Satan's famous observation from *Paradise Lost* in which the character, having fallen from the upper reaches of Paradise to the depths of Hell, confesses that the true torment is an internal condition of the mind, an inescapable awareness of unremitting despair, guilt, or depression: "The mind is its own place, and in itself / Can make a Heav'n of Hell, a Hell of Heav'n. / What matter where, if I be still the same . . ." (Milton, *Paradise Lost,* Book 1, ll. 254–56).

We may be able to escape an actual place, or we may be able to distract our mind from the horrid conditions of a prison or dungeon, but when the mind is itself the source of our misery or pain, the only solution is to somehow heal the self. Poet Richard Lovelace observed the same thought when he penned his famous lines "Stone walls do not a prison make, nor iron bars a cage. Minds innocent and quiet take / That for an hermitage"("To Althea from Prison," ll. 25–28, quoted in *The Norton Anthology of English Literature,* volume B, p. 1684).

However, when one is not innocent, discovering solace or refuge in some recess of the mind does not work so well. Take, for example, the bravado of Milton's Satan as he tries to rally his minions to continue in their rebellion against their Creator. As he will later confess in a soliloquy, inwardly he is fully aware that he would have more peace of mind and greater felicity were he to suppress his willful pride and relent in his attempt to deny the reality of God's essential goodness and supremacy. But in his stubborn pride, Satan implies that he would rather endure the decline of his own spiritual reality than submit to God, even though he acknowledges that the Creator merits his service and fealty.

As he pauses on the brink of entering Eden to tempt Adam and Eve, Satan confesses that God "deserved no such return / From me, whom he created what I was." But perhaps more revealing is Satan's statement that he detests the sun's light because it reminds him of the lost bliss of the heavenly abode he has willfully rejected:

> O thou that with surpassing glory crowned
> Look'st from thy sole dominion like the god
> Of this new world; at whose sight all the stars'
> Hide their diminished heads; to thee I call,
> But with no friendly voice, and add thy name,

O sun, to tell thee how I hate thy beams
That bring to my remembrance from what state
I fell, how glorious once above thy sphere;
Till pride and worse ambition threw me down
Warring in heav'n against heav'n's matchless King.

(Milton, *Paradise Lost*, Book 4, ll. 32–41)

THE MIND IS A DANGEROUS PLACE!

The argument about this condition is complex but worth a moment's reflection inasmuch as Satan's self-inflicted plight would seem to contradict Socrates' assertion that no one does evil with complete knowledge of the end in the beginning. As we noted in chapter 5, Socrates argues that in the final analysis, all the evil or injustice we contrive and carry out against others serves solely to injure our "selves"—not anyone else, at least not in the long run.

It would seem from this speech that Milton has devised a character who knows all this, who understands full well that he would be better off not carrying out his evil intentions. But because he willingly submits to his own pride, he refuses to submit to God.

I suspect Socrates would argue that Satan *thinks* he knows the end result of his machinations but that his own willful rebellion has already taken its toll on his ability to think clearly and to appreciate the long-term logical implications of what he is saying. That's the problem with "dabbling" in evil—while we may believe we could "quit any time we want," our will is deteriorating by degrees, as is our objectivity about the reality of our condition.

In this sense, will and reason develop or deteriorate in a manner analogous to the process affecting muscle development. The more we stress our muscles by exercising them with incrementally more strenuous tasks, the stronger they become. Conversely, the more we immerse ourselves into a state of lassitude or physical stagnation, the weaker our muscles become, even though we are not consciously aware of the loss until the muscles are tested.

So it is that Satan may *believe* he is still in control, that he could still stop at any time and ask for forgiveness, but what Milton has portrayed so artfully is a character whose reason and will gradually diminish the more he turns away from the light of knowledge and from those exercises that would sustain or strengthen his true power.

From a Bahá'í perspective, my imagined response by Socrates thus holds up. Indeed, in the Bahá'í writings there is an explicit assessment of exactly what is happening to Satan, a verity precisely applicable to what is indicated by his growing repulsion of the sun and its rays of light:

> This hatred of the light itself is irremediable and unforgivable; that is, it is impossible for such a soul to draw near to God. This lamp here is a lamp because of its light; without the light it would not be a lamp. A soul that abhors the light of the lamp is, as it were, blind and cannot perceive the light, and this blindness is the cause of eternal deprivation. ('Abdu'l-Bahá, *Some Answered Questions*, no. 31.4)

We might argue that because Satan still has sufficient logical perspective to *know* that what he is about to do will simply make him more miserable—and that it will serve to distance him further from the light—he is still in control, or believes he is. But the fact is that he does not seem to be aware that all he does or will do can ultimately serve only to diminish his own powers and further God's purposes for humankind. Clearly this is an outcome he does not, or cannot, anticipate. He seems relatively oblivious to the fact that, by degrees, he is losing the access he had as an archangel to wisdom and spiritual capacity. Milton symbolizes this decline by portraying Satan in the form of a slithering serpent.

Perhaps he will retain some reason, but not enough to appreciate how God's redemptive plan for the salvation of humankind will play out. Satan is unable to see the "end" in this "beginning"—

that because of the sin of Adam and Eve, God will send Christ to redeem humankind and thereby demonstrate His boundless love and forgiveness. It is in this sense that Satan is unable to foresee that the salvation of humankind will occur precisely *because* of his efforts, not in spite of them, that all his machinations will serve only to bring about exactly what God desires—human beings who understand the rationale underlying God's laws and guidance.

As a consummate artist and thinker, Milton doubtlessly was aware that the scene with which Book 4 begins marks the last opportunity for Satan to plead for forgiveness and give up his futile rejection of God's plan. Satan is, as we have previously mentioned, at a precise point of balance, the point of decision, and what tilts him the wrong way is a conscious decision that comes only after some forty lines of mulling over his condition when he realizes that the only path for redemption is through submission to the will of God: "is there no place / Left for repentance, none for pardon left? / None left but by submission: and that word / Disdain forbids me, and my dread of shame / Among the Spirits beneath, whom I seduced . . . " (Milton, *Paradise Lost,* Book 4, ll. 80–83).

So is that it? He disdains submission, even to a loving, just, and forgiving Being? It seems so—that he simply doesn't want to experience the shame of admitting to those he talked into rebelling with him that he has failed, or, having lost the battle, that he cannot find some way to get revenge, even though he knows whatever he tells them would be a lie.

HOW THE DELUDED MIND THINKS

If our observations are correct, then it may well be that at the beginning of Book 4 of *Paradise Lost,* we are privileged to observe the last opportunity Satan has to control his destiny. Theoretically he, like Faustus, can always be "saved," but here he makes a decision that we doubt he can ever reverse as he reflects about what course of action he should take at this critical point of balance. Therefore, Socrates might argue that at this point Satan is no longer thinking straight, is no longer in control of his reason or will. In effect, Socrates might argue that from this moment on, he will no longer be *capable* (even though it is theoretically feasible) of seeing the end in the beginning because he will never again have full or complete knowledge; ergo, Socrates is right that no one does evil with full or complete knowledge of its outcome.

If this is correct—if it is possible to wander so far from the light into the darkness of error that the wayfarer can lose track of which direction to turn in order to be saved—then eternal remoteness is possible. Furthermore, we must presume that it would be highly unlikely that a wayward, perverse, or self-deluded soul would even want to return to the light in the first place.

So it is that in this existential moment of choice, Satan decides he does not wish to undergo the discomfiture of admitting he's subservient to God and of being shamefaced before his wretched cohorts. In the course of these forty-odd lines, Satan makes a statement that defines his own view of hell, and it has nothing to do with the place to which he and his crew have been hurled. As we have mentioned, the true hell for Satan is a subjective state of being, an entirely internal condition: "Which way I fly is hell; myself am hell . . ." (Milton, *Paradise Lost*, Book 4, l. 70).

Satan now finds the light annoying and discomfiting because it reminds him of all he has lost. And while it is metaphorical, this is a vivid symbol of a declining internal condition we can understand if we have ever gone down this path, even a step or two. If we have ever wittingly and willingly and with "knowledge aforethought" (as the legal phrase goes) done something we knew to be wrong, sinful, or illegal (whatever term feels applicable), then we can identify with this problem of trying to set things right.

Perhaps, like Shakespeare's Macbeth, Satan feels that it would require more effort to go through the agonizing process of repenting and reforming than it would to go on with his diabolical plan and thereby win the approbation of his fallen colleagues. "Better to reign in Hell, than serve in Heaven" (Milton, *Paradise Lost,* Book 1, l. 263), Satan proudly proclaims as he tries to rally his miserably fallen angels.

In a similar moment of despairing resignation, Macbeth compares his own situation—he has already murdered to attain his goal of kingship—to crossing a stream of blood: "I am in blood / Stepped in so far that, should I wade no more, / Returning were as tedious as go o'er" (Shakespeare, *Macbeth*, act 3, scene 4, ll. 142–44). In other words, he might as well go through with his dastardly plot and gain the reward it seems to offer, because changing course and repenting would require at least the same amount of will and persistence as completing his plan.

Almost all groups or associations dedicated to helping those who suffer from what we loosely categorize as addictive behaviors employ a guided self-help process that begins where Satan leaves off—by acknowledging a personal pattern of behavior that is self-inflicted. The challenge, of course, is that to extricate oneself from the depths of despair and helplessness induced by such a condition, one must independently reach a point of awakening, some kind of *eureka* moment—or else possibly become awakened through the intervention of friends, relatives, or social workers.

But even with outside intervention, any enduring progress must derive from individual will and determination to change. All self-help must ultimately be self-motivated and must emanate from the persistent application of free will. And yet it is precisely the will that addictive behaviors tend to weaken or destroy. Consequently, spiritual reformation requires this same process. Once we have willingly "turned against the light" of spiritual sustenance and have set out on a course where we actively ignore or even disdain God's guidance or godliness itself, we have placed ourselves out of reach of forgiveness, inasmuch as forgiveness, by definition, cannot be imposed or coerced. Stated in terms of previously discussed axioms, God is always ready to forgive so long as we sincerely seek this gift and demonstrate our sincerity by willfully supplicating for His forgiveness—not just once, but in a pattern that must become habitual.

SOME CONCLUSIONS ABOUT HELL

In Part 5 of this book we will discuss an even more subtle issue regarding this process of how the human soul can alter its own condition and achieve ascent. This often discussed theological or ontological question revolves around whether or not the soul can, after this life, be forgiven or assisted if it dies in a condition of sin, decline, or denial. But in this conclusion of Part 4, we need only to recognize a handful of simpler verities about hell in relation to sin.

First, we have established that hell is not a physical place and that abiding in hell does not necessarily involve physical torture, though certainly in this life physical conditions can bring about hellacious states of being. Second, we have established that hell as a spiritual condition results from committing unjust or sinful acts consciously and through our own free will. Third, we have determined that all we need to know and all the powers we need to possess in order to avoid hell are readily available to us. Fourth, and possibly most weighty, we can conceive of a soul becoming so willfully degraded, so self-deluded and vain, that it could potentially remain forever debarred from light and redemption.

Surely the logical possibility of such a condition of eternal remoteness, even if only a state of obliviousness, recalls for us the notion of "the fear of God" in a most weighty and personal manner. For while we can hardly conceive of ourselves knowingly and deliberately falling so far or becoming so remote, our observations about the actions of present-day remorseless terrorists should give us pause to consider how such a precipitous descent can indeed occur. Furthermore, how can we possibly anticipate what tests will come our way and how we will respond to those unknown and unforeseen variables we may be called upon to confront?

Will we pen a poem on a scrap of paper if we become unjustly imprisoned? Will we recant our Faith if threatened with the loss of all we have worked our lives to acquire or attain? All we can know for certain is that right now, at this precise moment, we have a certain degree of free will, together with a certain degree of knowledge about what course of action we will most likely employ to steer clear of tumbling into an abyss of despair, cynicism, vanity, or the clutches of the insistent self.

PART 5: SALVATION AND THE HAPPY ENDING

15 / GUILT AND ATONEMENT

When the sinner findeth himself wholly detached and freed from all save God, he should beg forgiveness and pardon from Him. Confession of sins and transgressions before human beings is not permissible, as it hath never been nor will ever be conducive to divine forgiveness. Moreover such confession before people results in one's humiliation and abasement, and God—exalted be His glory—wisheth not the humiliation of His servants.

—Bahá'u'lláh, *Tablets of Bahá'u'lláh*, p. 24

At this point, we should have some broad idea of what constitutes sin or evil, as well as what the sources for such actions are and what effects they can have. In general, we have determined that something is sinful or evil when it deters us, or when we deter others, from striving to attain the purpose of coming to know and worship God. Conversely, what is good are those practices that help us fulfill our inherent mission by means of manifesting divine virtues in an ever more complete and refined manner. By such means we increasingly emulate the Creator in whose image we have been fashioned.

This same process causes us to become ever more joyous and ever more useful to other individuals, as well as to the collective human enterprise of creating a civilization conducive to justice, enlightenment, and spiritual development for all humankind. Implicit in this process, as well, is the methodology by which we can become redeemed from whatever sinful actions and inclinations we may have acquired or may be tempted to acquire along the way.

Virtually every world religion has some kind of ritual by which the believer can acknowledge sin or error and seek forgiveness from God. Most have some formal process whereby suppliants can become satisfied that they have been "cleansed," have made amends for error, and, therefore, have been absolved from the consequences of sin. Accordingly, the penitent, once officially shriven of the stain of sin, need not feel any further guilt or fear, unless or until another sin is committed.

THE BENEFITS OF GUILT

As we have mentioned earlier in our study, the concept of guilt is currently perceived by many largely as a socioreligious construct derived from centuries of being indoctrinated by various religious teachings about morality. From psychologists to sociologists, from high school counselors to theologians, guilt is now frequently portrayed as mostly needless, unhealthy, and unnecessary.

Understandably, those who view most moral codes as oppressive are going to think guilt inappropriate. The contemporary view of many is that we should be able to do whatever we want, so long as we are not actively abusing someone else. We should not be made to feel bad about anything we do because of someone else's notion of good and bad, of right and wrong. These constraints are viewed as conceptual inventions that we should accept as binding only if we choose to do so. From such a view, guilt should occur only when we voluntarily accept or adopt some extrinsic and possibly arbitrary standards as a gauge for our behavior.

If we have been raised in strict conditions of abiding by an explicit code of conduct, we will naturally feel guilty if we go against these expectations. But in most of our lives there will occur a point when we will be challenged to examine these standards independently, to decide if we wish to maintain or appropriate these standards for ourselves, or, instead, to search for some other code we find preferable, more logical, or better suited to our informed view of reality.

If we choose some other path or standard, then possibly what had become an ingrained sense of guilt at being disobedient to a prior code will disappear—if not all at once, then by degrees. But if we reject one set of moral standards and adopt a new one, then obviously we will subject ourselves once again to the possibility of having to deal with the onset of guilt.

The point here is the obvious fact that guilt is not inherently good or bad. As we implied earlier in chapter 4 and with our charts in chapter 7, "guilt" is simply a term we use to portray a thoroughly logical process of emotional feedback we experience if, reflecting on our performance, we find that we have fallen short of our expectations. And the intensity of that emotion depends on the extent to which we have accepted or internalized these standards—the degree to which we have made them our own.

Therefore, it might prove helpful for us to examine another chart to review this process, because guilt is not necessarily dependent on whether our expectations derive from within or without, whether we have accepted these expectations after careful consideration of alternatives, or whether we have inherited them mindlessly. The effects derive from the same sense of disparity regardless of the source from which we have acquired our sense of self:

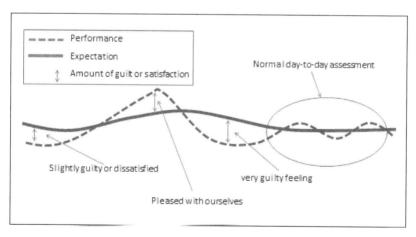

From the chart, we can see a graphic representation of the logic of guilt we experience as a result of our sense of the variance between our expectations and our performance. We observe that when we monitor ourselves on a regular basis—perhaps daily—we will have a normal and acceptable variance. We will feel better or worse about ourselves from day to day. Over time, we may find in this acceptable variance a sense of normalcy, a degree of stasis and peace of mind.

Or we may decide that we are becoming somewhat stagnant in relation to our overall aspirations. In this case, we may decide to make a change, perhaps a significant or dramatic alteration in what we expect from ourselves. As a result, we may become comfortable with our expectations being significantly higher than our performance, but because the expectation is self-imposed, we may feel more challenged than defeated. We may feel ourselves making progress rather than experiencing intense guilt.

Naturally, we could devise a myriad scenarios about how our sense of self derives from this interplay between expectations and actions, and an equal number of charts to demonstrate the value and persistence of our need to monitor ourselves with regard to all we wish to be, but most especially in terms of our ongoing internal dialogical process. Once we begin to realize the value of emotional feedback as one index of self-evaluation, we should no longer view guilt or any other emotion as "bad" or unhealthy, unless, of course, this feedback becomes oppressive or dysfunctional.

That is, our nervous system should be relatively transparent in its conveyance of accurate information about where we are in relation to reality—reality as we have in this discourse studied and accepted it. But for a variety of reasons, not the least of which is the result of having to live in an unhealthy environment, we may sometimes find our emotional feedback to be inaccurate. Consequently, we come to rely on a variety of emotional indices regarding our progress, in much the same way that a pilot relies on a multiplicity of sophisticated gauges to help him fly a plane successfully without direct sensory feedback.

Similarly, any emotions or feelings we derive from our nervous system need to reflect reality accurately in order for our conscious mind to respond appropriately. If our hand is burning, we want to know this information immediately so we can withdraw our hand from whatever is causing the burning sensation and thereby avoid injury. Whereas, if our hand were being burned and we felt no pain, then obviously there would be some sort of communications malfunction occurring in the nervous system—that physical messenger between reality and our perception of it, particularly our perception of our sense of self and wellbeing.

This analogy gets to the heart of the reason so many people in the mental health field are wary of religion and strong religious belief. If our beliefs impose on us unattainable or unnatural expectations (expectations not based on reality), they can be debilitating or even damaging to successful living. In extreme cases where our emotions convey inaccurate information about reality, we may need medical assistance to balance out our neurological system so that the neurotransmitters coursing through our brain convey more accurately how we are doing. When the neurotransmitters do their job properly, the brain becomes transparent as an intermediary between the essential self (the soul and the consciousness) and our relationship to external reality.

Again, the objective of assessing this process is not to feel one particular way, but to have clarity so that our emotions function as an accurate indicator among all the sophisticated physical systems that assist us to be successful in navigating the complex decisions we confront in our daily life.

THE SNAP*

What can happen when expectation from within or without far outstrip our performance over an extended period of time? Again, the logic is so simple that it hardly warrants graphic demonstra-

---

* This onomatopoetic term represents the fracturing of reason and restraint—the point when we feel we can no longer strive to set things right.

tion, but the chart below provides a visual referent that may provide feedback about how we are responding to our own reality:

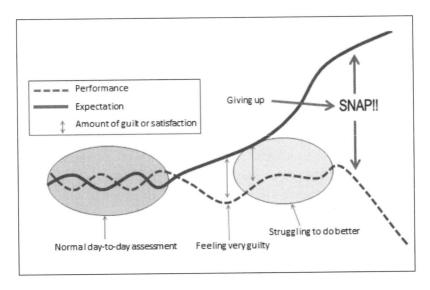

The scenario or plot indicated by this chart proceeds from left to
right as follows: We are doing pretty well. We are synchronizing our
performance with our expectations by monitoring ourselves daily.
We reflect on how we are doing systematically. We adjust our actions
or our expectations accordingly. Suddenly, we decide to assume a
dramatic increase in our expectations or aspirations for ourselves.

Perhaps we just got married and now must deal with being
unselfish, conciliatory, collaborative, and willing to compromise.
None of these are bad things, but it just so happens that we have
waited a long time to get married, and we are accustomed to living
alone, to doing things our own way. Never before have we had to
worry much about what anybody else thought or felt regarding our
decisions or actions.

Whereas before we could leave our clothes out, wash the dishes
later or tomorrow, and go wherever we wanted, whenever we

wanted, now we have the constraints of a relationship in which doing things unilaterally will likely harm its success. On some level, we may have known beforehand that some changes might be required when we got married. But the downside of having to change seemed, at the time, to be far outweighed by our love for the other person. We felt we would happily conform to any required adjustments or alterations in our routine.

It is unnecessary to spell out this scenario in great detail. One partner in the marriage could be a man whose mother always picked up his things, whose parents always paid his way, and who never instilled in him the self-discipline to be clean, neat, or refined on a regular basis. Conversely, the partner could be a woman who has been raised the same way but whose husband expects a mothering figure to carry out the myriad tasks that were done for him prior to getting married. Or, in a different scenario, the woman might be independent—a professional who has no intention of becoming a cook, housekeeper, and laundress while managing a full-time job where she enjoys a respected managerial position.

The reader can supply whatever story or details or combination of personalities would make for the most interesting plot. Ultimately, it is up to each couple to determine whether the marriage will be a situational comedy in which, over the course of time, they begin to consult and manage to divide up the daily tasks on a coequal basis, or whether this story will become a tragic and sudden implosion resulting in annulment or divorce.

The point is that we can raise our performance to meet changed expectations only so much at a time. And the more remote the possibility of our "catching up" to our expectations (or those we have accepted from somebody else), the more the "SNAP!" is likely to occur. Furthermore, the "SNAP!" can be as simple as an annulment or as horrific as a nervous breakdown, as salutary as a decision to have marriage counseling or as detrimental as descending to the depths of alcoholism and clinical depression.

RELIGION AND GUILT

Just as Socrates noted that the unexamined life is not worth living, neither is the unexamined or blind assumption of expectations worth having. Indeed, as our charts show, this kind of mindlessness can be lethal. So it is that religion has throughout the ages become one of the most pernicious and needless causes of guilt when one makes an attempt suddenly to convert to a set of beliefs that dictates virtually every aspect of a person's life.

Ironically, many people find comfort in a highly regimented religion because so little is left to individual choice. We can set aside the difficult and time-consuming process of exercising our free will. The attitude of such a convert may often be, "I don't want to think—just tell me what to do to be happy and saved, and I'll do it, no matter how illogical or mindless it might seem were I to consider each decision dispassionately in the light of reason."

It is in this context of "blind faith" that 'Abdu'l-Bahá cautions everyone to examine beliefs before accepting them. Otherwise these beliefs or this system of belief will ultimately falter and fail, possibly exactly when we need it the most, when its mettle must withstand the onslaught of grief or despair: "If religious beliefs and opinions are found contrary to the standards of science, they are mere superstitions and imaginations; for the antithesis of knowledge is ignorance, and the child of ignorance is superstition" ('Abdu'l-Bahá, *The Promulgation of Universal Peace*, p. 252).

What might seem to be the positive side of a highly codified and rigorous belief system is that we might be able to live up to the expectations it imposes, even if we do so mechanically and somewhat mindlessly. In such a system, every expectation is spelled out: how to worship, how to be good, and how to be forgiven. So we might understandably conclude that this type of belief, especially one that has existed so long that it has become ingrained in our social consciousness, would serve as a source of comfort without the guilt that has caused so many psychologists and psychiatrists to view religion with suspicion and concern. But such is not at all the case.

GUILT AND ATONEMENT IN JUDAISM

Guilt as an integral part of the religious experience is most tradi-
tionally associated with two particular religions that have a precise,
institutionalized methodology for dealing with actions that are
considered sinful or otherwise in breach of religious law or tradition: Judaism and Catholicism.

The notion of Jewish guilt is somewhat more mythical or material for comedy rather than fact, but we will leave that for Jewish
individuals to determine for themselves. The point is that Jewish
guilt is partly derived from the Jewish concept of *Teshuva*—the
remorse that occurs when one becomes aware of some sin or
wrongdoing (Yonah Ben Avraham of Gerona, *Shaarei Teshuva:
The Gates of Repentance*). In this context, remorse is not some nag-
ging undercurrent of relentless oppression but rather a conscious
awareness that one needs to atone for some particular deed or some
course of action. The process of atonement itself depends on the
degree of severity of the commandment that has been ignored or
violated, and whether the breach resulted from simple error or
from willfulness.

The process for atonement was devised or recommended by
renowned Jewish scholar Maimonides and involves alternative responses. If the sin or violation of law is simple error, then
atonement may consist of a sin offering (if a Temple is available)
followed by confession. If the sin is out of willful and conscious
disobedience, the atonement may consist of repentance plus confession plus Yom Kippur Temple Service plus tribulations plus
lashes or even execution, in the case of taking the Lord's name in
vain (ibid.).

Needless to say, much or most of this has now been altered or
eliminated altogether, such as Temple Service, lashes, and execution. Likewise, confession may be private if the sin or error is
between the believer and God. Another consideration in evaluating guilt in relation to atonement is whether one is an Orthodox, a
Conservative, or a Reform Jew. But in all three branches, tradition-

ally, one is relieved of guilt not solely through some personal relationship with God but rather by submitting to a process devised and overseen by an institution.

Not all Jews conform to whatever practices are suggested or required, but what we might term the "background noise" of guilt resulting from disobedience to laws and traditions can play on the conscience until the believer achieves personal reconciliation with the expectations. Rarely is there a "SNAP!" because in the contemporary world, so much of Jewishness and Judaism is a cultural thing, a way of life or a social milieu quite beyond whatever religious meaning a Jewish identity might imply or impose on the individual believer.

GUILT AND ATONEMENT IN CATHOLICISM

The process for penitence that is probably most universally well-known is that devised by the Roman Catholic Church, the "Sacrament of Penance and Reconciliation." While various expressions of concern for one's sins and attempts to become reconciled or redeemed were exercised early on in Christian religious history, that part of the sacrament with which we are most familiar—confession and penance—did not begin until around the eleventh century, more than a thousand years after Christ and more than four hundred years after the appearance of Muhammad (Thomas Bokenkotter, *A Concise History of the Catholic Church*).

I note the timeframe because when we examine this process and how it evolved, we quickly realize that not only is this sacrament a late addition to the heart of Christian practice, it also has only a tangential basis in Christian scripture. In both Christian and Muslim scripture, the resource for the penitent soul is personal and private prayer to God rather than a formal process overseen by clerics and involving the acknowledgement to another human being of one's shortcomings.

Nevertheless, the Catholic sacrament is worth a brief review because it involves a well-conceived paradigm that anyone desiring to become reconciled to his or her spiritual condition would do well to consider on a personal and private basis. The three parts of this exercise are contrition of heart, confession of mouth, and expiation of sin by means of penance or deed. Importantly, the Catholic Church does not recognize the validity of this process until and unless it is rehearsed under the guidance of a priest before whom personal assessment and reflection are combined with the confession of sins and the assignment by the curate of some penitential actions (Thomas Bokenkotter, *A Concise History of the Catholic Church*).

As a private exercise and internal assessment, this paradigm complies in general with what any religious teaching might encourage us to undertake. As we have noted earlier, before we can even consider what sort of spiritual condition we are in, we need to assess how our daily performance complies with the expectations we have devised or else assumed as a follower of a particular set of beliefs.

There is, however, a possibly pernicious and debilitating struggle against guilt that can insinuate itself into the Catholic regimen from two obvious sources. First, many laws in Catholic doctrine forbid virtually unavoidable human behaviors. For example, the sole legitimate motive for sexual intercourse between man and wife is for the purpose of procreation; hence the law against contraception. Second, the penitent can only feel redeemed or reconciled by going through the intermediary of the cleric as a Church official. In this sense, the individual is effectively emotionally bound to the institution.

There used to be a widely touted saying that a child raised within the strictures of the Catholic code would be a Catholic for life, the implication being that such a process is capable of maintaining an almost inescapable stranglehold on the conscience of a believer, particularly, an ineluctable sense of guilt. For if a believer cannot avoid violating the plethora of actions (or thoughts) designated by the Church as sinful, then the believer may also have instilled in his or her conscience the instinct that the only redemption from those sins is a sacrament administered according to certain strictures.

CONFESSION IS BAD FOR THE SOUL

Regardless of whether this system was devised benignly to provide believers with a means of reconciliation with their faith and a sanctioned method for relieving a sense of sin and guilt, or was instead contrived to make sure that no believer could escape emotional dependency on the church, the ultimate effect is that the believer may well become subjugated and helpless.

As we began discussing in chapter 4, Bahá'u'lláh exhorts us to evaluate ourselves daily, to bring ourselves to account (Bahá'u'lláh, The Hidden Words, Arabic, no. 31). During this internal evaluation, we may find ourselves failing enough to wish to acknowledge our failure, beseech God for assistance to do better, and ask His forgiveness for falling short of our avowed objectives or for some particular violation of His laws and exhortations. Certainly this process might involve confession, but to God, not to an institution or a representative of an institution—clearly a more direct and efficacious method of receiving assistance from the only valid source capable of providing it.

Bahá'u'lláh confirms that supplication to God for forgiveness is purely a private matter. Anything we "confess" to God is also an entirely private matter. Bahá'u'lláh strictly forbids the practice of formal confession of sins, asserting that God does not wish our humiliation or abasement:

> When the sinner findeth himself wholly detached and freed from all save God, he should beg forgiveness and pardon from Him. Confession of sins and transgressions before human beings is not permissible, as it hath never been nor will ever be conducive to divine forgiveness. Moreover such confession before people results in one's humiliation and abasement, and God—exalted be His glory—wisheth not the humiliation of His servants. Verily He is the Compassionate, the Merciful. (Bahá'u'lláh, *Tablets of Bahá'u'lláh*, p. 24)

Clearly, then, the process of recognizing our shortcomings and reconciling ourselves to God by beseeching His forgiveness is not only allowable but exhorted. Likewise, inasmuch as the Bahá'í writings also instruct the believers, "Let deeds, not words, be your adorning" (Bahá'u'lláh, Hidden Words, Persian, no. 5), the follow-through or completion of this process of reconciliation—as well as the proof of the sincerity of our contrition—will be the reformation of our deeds and actions.

While among the revealed prayers of Bahá'u'lláh there is a great number of supplications that acknowledge our shortcomings and plead for assistance, one particular prayer (contained in the same tablet in which He forbids confession) is a somewhat long supplication for forgiveness:

> O God, my God! I implore Thee by the blood of Thy true lovers who were so enraptured by Thy sweet utterance that they hastened unto the Pinnacle of Glory, the site of the most glorious martyrdom, and I beseech Thee by the mysteries which lie enshrined in Thy knowledge and by the pearls that are treasured in the ocean of Thy bounty to grant forgiveness unto me and unto my father and my mother. Of those who show forth mercy, Thou art in truth the Most Merciful. No God is there but Thee, the Ever-Forgiving, the All-Bountiful.
>
> O Lord! Thou seest this essence of sinfulness turning unto the ocean of Thy favour and this feeble one seeking the kingdom of Thy divine power and this poor creature inclining himself towards the daystar of Thy wealth. By Thy mercy and Thy grace, disappoint him not, O Lord, nor debar him from the revelations of Thy bounty in Thy days, nor cast him away from Thy door which Thou hast opened wide to all that dwell in Thy heaven and on Thine earth.
>
> Alas! Alas! My sins have prevented me from approaching the Court of Thy holiness and my trespasses have caused me

to stray far from the Tabernacle of Thy majesty. I have committed that which Thou didst forbid me to do and have put away what Thou didst order me to observe.

I pray Thee by Him Who is the sovereign Lord of Names to write down for me with the Pen of Thy bounty that which will enable me to draw nigh unto Thee and will purge me from my trespasses which have intervened between me and Thy forgiveness and Thy pardon.

Verily, Thou art the Potent, the Bountiful. No God is there but Thee, the Mighty, the Gracious. (Bahá'u'lláh, *Tablets of Bahá'u'lláh*, p. 24)

The Bahá'í law regarding confession should not be understood to imply that we cannot mention our wrongdoings to another, especially if we are seeking professional advice or assistance. In the notes to the translation of The Kitáb-i-Aqdas, we find the following explanation about our freedom to talk with others about our personal dilemmas: "However, if we spontaneously desire to acknowledge we have been wrong in something, or that we have some fault of character, and ask another person's forgiveness or pardon, we are quite free to do so. The Universal House of Justice has also clarified that Bahá'u'lláh's prohibition concerning the confession of sins does not prevent an individual from admitting transgressions in the course of consultations held under the aegis of Bahá'í institutions. Likewise, it does not preclude the possibility of seeking advice from a close friend or of a professional counsellor regarding such matters" (editorial note in Bahá'u'lláh, The Kitáb-i-Aqdas, p. 194).

SINNERS BY NATURE OR NURTURE?

At first glance, there may be some parts of this prayer that might be disconcerting to someone studying the Bahá'í teachings for the first time. Principal among these might be those confessional phrases where the suppliant acknowledges his or her failure with such epithets as "this essence of sinfulness," "this feeble one," and this "poor creature." The supplicant then asserts: "My sins have prevented me from approaching the Court of Thy holiness and my trespasses have caused me to stray far from the Tabernacle of Thy majesty. I have committed that which Thou didst forbid me to do and have put away what Thou didst order me to observe."

If God (and Bahá'u'lláh as His Emissary) do not wish us to suffer humiliation or abasement, then why is the supplicant directed to describe himself or herself in such terms of submissiveness and obeisance? The answer here again is that this is not a public pronouncement and that the believer is not forced to recite this prayer. It is designed as a tool for assistance for those who feel it appropriate and helpful to use. Bahá'u'lláh revealed this prayer specifically to reconcile one who has committed some error and who wishes to be forgiven. Since this confession or conversation is entirely private and spoken only to God, then no humiliation is attached, even if humility before the Divine Presence is inevitably an important condition any time we are in a state of supplication.

Thus one articulates in frank terms and without equivocation the fact that a sin has been committed and that this pattern of behavior will inevitably cause one to become remote and to stray from the path that the Manifestation has delineated to help the believer become secure and continue advancing spiritually.

This same sort of acknowledgement is found in the Long Obligatory Prayer revealed by Bahá'u'lláh for all believers to recite on a daily basis, whether or not they feel that they have committed some palpable error that day. One passage in particular seems to imply that all believers turn to God under the shadow of failure and remorse: "O God, my God! My back is bowed by the burden of my sins, and my heedlessness hath destroyed me. Whenever I ponder my evil doings and Thy benevolence, my heart melteth within me, and my blood boileth in my veins. By Thy Beauty, O Thou the Desire of the world! I blush to lift up my face to Thee, and my longing hands are ashamed to stretch forth toward the heaven of Thy bounty" (Bahá'u'lláh, *Prayers and Meditations*, p. 322).

I remember many years ago having a lengthy discussion with a young Bahá'í about her discomfiture regarding this part of the prayer. I suppose the passage never bothered me as much because I have always felt myself to be a work in progress regarding the basic goals and guidelines about being a spiritual person.

But this young woman was rigorous in her dedication to following laws and exhortations of Bahá'u'lláh to the best of her ability, and she asked me why she should acknowledge her "sinfulness" when she did not feel she had done anything wrong. I think the statement in the prayer also grated on her subconscious because it recalled on some level what she had experienced as a believing Baptist who had been constantly reminded that she was "born in sin" and could be saved solely by believing that Christ had paid for her sins by dying on the cross—something she neither understood nor accepted. Indeed, the belief in the essential nobility of human nature was one of the first things that had attracted her to the Bahá'í Faith. "Noble have I created thee," says God in the Arabic Hidden Words, no. 22, "yet thou hast abased thyself. Rise then unto that for which thou wast created."

'Abdu'l-Bahá goes into great detail about the symbolic meaning of the biblical account of the fall of Adam to explain that the spiritual implications of this story have *nothing* to do with the spurious notion of "original sin." He explains that the story is a symbolic allusion to the nature of the relationship between the individual soul and the physical body it must associate with while dwelling in a physical environment: "Adam is the spirit of Adam and Eve His self; the tree is the material world and the serpent is attachment to it. This attachment, which is sin, has been transmitted to the descendants of Adam" ('Abdu'l-Bahá, *Some Answered Questions*, no. 30.11).

'Abdu'l-Bahá observes that if the story were interpreted as being literally true—as it is by many Jews and Christians—"it would be sheer injustice and absolute predestination" ('Abdu'l-Bahá, *Some Answered Questions*, no. 30.10). He goes on to explain that the idea of the advent of Christ being the cause of the redemption from hell of all the descendants of Adam "is beyond the pale of every rule and principle, and no rational person can ever accept it" (ibid).

In other words, Christ did indeed come to save humankind from this attachment to the world and to free humankind from this sin of worldliness. But the importance of His advent is not the singular event of His martyrdom. As a Manifestation of God, He came from the realm of the spirit to take on a physical form in order to speak about how spiritual purposes underlie all our physical experience. And like all Manifestations, He also served to manifest through His own behavior a pattern of life that the aspiring Christian should attempt to emulate.

The concept of "original sin" is thus entirely false. Sin is not and never was an essential or inherent attribute of the human soul. We are created pure and unsullied, and our sins and transgressions are, as we have described, actions relative to what we could or should be. And, as we have repeatedly noted from the outset, we never become completely "sinless" or "flawless" in that we never attain some final state or condition of perfection.

In this sense, while we may not have recently committed any explicit breach of law—spiritual or otherwise—we all fall short of what we could achieve and what we hopefully will attain in the future. These phrases can thus be understood as acknowledging the reality that all of us will always be works in progress, that we can always improve, both in our objective of coming to know God and of expressing that knowledge in ever more expansive and creative acts of service.

A portion of a prayer of the Báb states this condition of relative attainment exquisitely, even as it also demonstrates a profound observation about human nature—namely, that without the mandate of the Manifestation that we pray daily, we might well not consider it a priority except in times of great need or despair: "O my God! Thou hast inspired my soul to offer its supplication to Thee, and but for Thee, I would not call upon Thee. Lauded and glorified art Thou; I yield Thee praise inasmuch as Thou didst reveal Thyself unto me, and I beg Thee to forgive me, since I have fallen short in my duty to know Thee and have failed to walk in the path of Thy love" (The Báb, in *Bahá'í Prayers*, p. 6).

This prayer also states succinctly the wisdom in God's sending us successive Teachers to enable us to fulfill our inherent purpose of learning about God and of acquiring and strengthening the spiritual powers of prayer and meditation. By this means we can maintain a dialogue with God while also learning those guidelines that sustain us in following the sure path to our ascent. Yet, as the prayer then acknowledges, we all fall short of doing the best we are capable of doing because we are all in a state of becoming.

It is extremely important that we not interpret any of these passages to imply that this condition of always being in a state of relative success must keep us somber, depressed, and constantly struggling with a sense of guilt and heaviness of heart at having done less than is possible. On the contrary, an accurate understanding of this axiom should induce in us delight and utmost joy in the realization that we always have more to learn and further to grow in this eternal journey. If we are presently solaced and joyful because of the guidance and comfort we receive, how much more felicity awaits us if we continue on this path. One important definition of the Bahá'í concept of salvation is forward motion assisted by the daily monitoring of our progress.

It is in this context that sin and sinfulness are neither inherent nor unavoidable. We are not born in sin, nor are we naturally base creatures who must renounce the world and all its joys and pleasures. But the daily articulation of the fact that we are forever a work in progress is one important method by which we hear ourselves reciting the verities that keep us on the right track, as the following prayer by 'Abdu'l-Bahá articulates so beautifully:

O Thou forgiving Lord! Thou art the shelter of all these Thy servants. Thou knowest the secrets and art aware of all things. We are all helpless, and Thou art the Mighty, the Omnipotent. We are all sinners, and Thou art the Forgiver of sins, the Merciful, the Compassionate. O Lord! Look not at our shortcomings. Deal with us according to Thy grace and bounty. Our shortcomings are many, but the ocean of Thy forgiveness is boundless. Our weakness is grievous, but the evidences of Thine aid and assistance are clear. Therefore, confirm and strengthen us. Enable us to do that which is worthy of Thy holy Threshold. Illumine our hearts, grant us discerning eyes and attentive ears. Resuscitate the dead and heal the sick. Bestow wealth upon the poor and give peace and security to the fearful. Accept us in Thy kingdom and illumine us with the light of guidance. Thou are the Powerful and the Omnipotent. Thou art the Generous. Thou art the Clement. Thou art the Kind. ('Abdu'l-Bahá, in *Bahá'í Prayers*, p. 81)

This is, in fact, a hope-filled prayer, inasmuch as every statement acknowledging our condition of relative progress is coupled with a powerful assertion of God's assistance, forgiveness, and grace to secure our advancement so long as we desire it.

I don't remember what my response was to the young woman so many years ago. I don't think it was very profound. She went on to dedicate her life to serving humankind as a Bahá'í in Central and South America, and through the various avenues that her profession in humanitarian agencies afforded her. I feel certain that in her well-lived life, she came up with her own creative solution to that personal quandary of hers.

As for me, I take comfort daily in believing that God is forgiving, even though He is aware of our most secret thoughts. He is our confidant in all things. So if we "are all sinners," He is the "Forgiver of sins." Our "shortcomings are many" and our "weakness is grievous," but the ocean of God's forgiveness "is boundless," and "the evidences" of God's assistance "are clear," for God is "the Generous," "the Clement," "the Kind."

The beauty of this counterpoint melody in the recitation of how the special needs of every individual will be met with unstinting generous gifts of the Beloved is that it is fully capable of solacing the suppliant. We are forthrightly acknowledging that we can do better and that we wish to improve, but each articulation of our failings is followed by the assurance that God is ever-forgiving and every ready to provide us with whatever assistance we need. As a result, the overall tenor and balance of this prayer and of the Long Obligatory Prayer, are, for me, much the same: we can make no progress without God's continuous nurture, but His aid is relentless and plenteous. All that is required of us is the wisdom and the will God has bestowed on us to seize it.

16 / TESTS, SUFFERING, AND SALVATION

Thy might beareth me Witness! The companions of all who adore Thee are the tears they shed, and the comforters of such as seek Thee are the groans they utter, and the food of them who haste to meet Thee is the fragments of their broken hearts.

—Bahá'u'lláh, *Prayers and Meditations*, p. 155

The Bahá'í writings are replete with statements affirming that tests and suffering promote spiritual development. In fact, some passages imply that the difficulties we encounter are *essential* tools for our progress. Of course, implicit in these observations is the assumption that when we are confronted with these tests, we respond with increased determination and with reliance on the spiritual safeguards of prayer, dedication, and devotion.

As we have already observed, these tests—whether physical, mental, or spiritual—can be usefully compared to how increased physical stress helps an athlete enhance endurance and strength. Without such stress, the athlete would make no progress, and without developing the capacity to face and overcome tests and difficulties, neither would the aspirant to spiritual development. At the same time, Bahá'u'lláh abolishes those practices—formerly endorsed by some followers of previous revelations—that supposedly induced spiritual powers and mystic insight by means of self-inflicted pain, deprivation, and severe penance.*

---

* "Mortification" may include flagellation, fasting, or extreme forms of labor.

Upholding the value of suffering yet abolishing penance, monasticism, asceticism, and other methods of self-induced affliction is not a contradiction. To appreciate in full the distinction between these two points of view, we need to understand the Bahá'í view of the part tests and suffering play in our spiritual development and how we are to react when they occur.

For example, there are Bahá'í prayers in which the believer can actually ask for tests in order to be strengthened, yet there are also prayers beseeching God to deliver us from tests or to help us avoid travail. How can these ostensibly contradictory attitudes be reconciled, and what part does suffering play in the Bahá'í concept of edification, of redemption, or "salvation"?

THE LOGIC OF ABOLISHING SELF-INDUCED SUFFERING

If tests and suffering help promote spiritual development, why is it not logical that we should expose ourselves to those traditional practices that cause us to endure suffering? After all, do we not admire the biographies of those historical figures who endured a life of poverty, austerity, and deprivation and who, as a result, produced insightful works about the life of the spirit? Did not Bahá'u'lláh Himself spend two years in seclusion in the mountains of Kurdistan, living off little and sometimes dwelling in caves? Shoghi Effendi has written, "Attired in the garb of a traveler, coarsely clad, taking with Him nothing but his *kashkul* (almsbowl) and a change of clothes, and assuming the name of Darvish Muhammad, Bahá'u'lláh retired to the wilderness, and lived for a time on a mountain named Sar-Galu, so far removed from human habitations that only twice a year, at seed sowing and harvest time, it was visited by the peasants of that region" (Shoghi Effendi, *God Passes By*, p. 187).

Did not Christ fast in the wilderness for forty days prior to beginning His ministry? Did not Gandhi win the hearts and minds of his nation through a life of poverty and fasting? Did not Bahá'u'lláh, like the Manifestations before Him, create a period of fasting for His followers as a spiritual exercise, as portrayed in the following prayer revealed specifically for this month-long period?*

> These are the days whereon Thou hast bidden all men to observe the fast, that through it they may purify their souls and rid themselves of all attachment to any one but Thee, and that out of their hearts may ascend that which will be worthy of the court of Thy majesty and may well beseem the seat of the revelation of Thy oneness. Grant, O my Lord, that this fast may become a river of life-giving waters and may yield the virtue wherewith Thou hast endowed it. Cleanse Thou by its means the hearts of Thy servants whom the evils of the world have failed to hinder from turning towards Thine all-glorious Name, and who have remained unmoved by the noise and tumult of such as have repudiated Thy most resplendent signs which have accompanied the advent of Thy Manifestation Whom Thou hast invested with Thy sovereignty, Thy power, Thy majesty and glory. (Bahá'u'lláh, *Prayers and Meditations*, p. 79)

It would seem that one purpose of this prayer is to teach the suppliant how experiencing this self-imposed deprivation of food and drink from sunrise to sunset for nineteen successive days will help bring about spiritual transformation. The believer prays "that this fast may become a river of life-giving waters and may yield the virtue wherewith Thou hast endowed it" and that the fast may cleanse "the hearts of Thy servants whom the evils of the world have failed to hinder from turning towards Thine all-glorious Name. . . ."

---

* A period of nineteen days during which Bahá'ís abstain from food and drink from sunup to sundown.

MODERATION, MOTIVE, AND METHOD

To begin to clarify the distinction between what Bahá'u'lláh demonstrated in His own actions and ordained in His laws—as opposed to some of the ascetic practices in various other religious traditions (hermits, mendicants, Sufis, monks, priests, and so on)—we need first to examine several axioms related to the attitude or motive with which we should approach our relationship to the things of this world, as this interplay affects our spiritual advancement.

We have already suggested that the source of most waywardness or sin is the ego or the insistent self when that aspect of self becomes attached to those pleasures and rewards that derive from a life lived in the world. The desire to escape such temptations, to entertain no thought but spiritual considerations, may in past ages have seemed a straightforward method for conquering the "insistent self." Therefore, various categories of ascetics isolated themselves from family, friends, or any sort of physical diversion or comfort.

We cannot presume to evaluate the benefits such exercises may have had on these individuals as examples of detachment and devotion in the past—Bahá'u'lláh throughout His revealed works stresses the importance of expressing faith with social action, as we have already noted several times. Repeatedly the Bahá'í writings state that words without deeds are hollow and useless: "The essence of faith is fewness of words and abundance of deeds; he whose words exceed his deeds, know verily his death is better than his life" (Bahá'u'lláh, *Tablets of Bahá'u'lláh*, p. 152).

On the one hand, if the examples set by ascetics who strove to set aside the comforts and pleasures of the physical world and focus solely on a life of the spirit were followed by all the people of the world, society would cease to exist. For example, there would be no infrastructure, food and power supply, schools, communication systems, or civil forces to uphold obedience to civil law. Simply put, such practices by a few individuals might serve as examples of what the human being could do without, something like Thoreau's experiment at Walden Pond.* But as an overall pattern of life for the body politic, such methods would be clearly impractical and unnecessary.

Living a decent life by helping to create a moral and productive family and by assisting in the creation of a vital and healthy community are themselves practices often fraught with sufficient tests without our needing to go about seeking additional ones. Ordinary occupations are usually already quite challenging, especially when coupled with the unforeseen changes and chances of life. In sum, most people hardly require self-imposed stress to expand their capacity.

A second axiom that ties this principle to how one should approach life in general is the idea integrated into every part of the Bahá'í concept of human purpose that life is inherently and necessarily a social or collective enterprise: "All men have been created to carry forward an ever-advancing civilization," says Bahá'u'lláh (*Gleanings*, no. 109.2). And the means by which civilization is carried forward is the organic process of creating healthy families abiding in healthy communities.

In other words, each of us is obliged to participate in this process by constructing an essential building block or social "God Particle," a family fashioned according to the explicit guidelines established by Bahá'u'lláh in His Most Holy Book and in the miscellaneous teachings He reveals about love, justice, and community.

A third and equally essential axiom is perhaps at the heart of all other guidance related to our attitude about the world and our relationship to physical reality as a source of spiritual redemption on a daily basis. In part, this axiom relates to the principle of moderation. This principle, for example, is extremely important in matters of justice and in our attitude about law. Indeed, in some instances, justice is virtually synonymous with moderation:

---

* Henry D. Thoreau, *Walden: or, Life in the Woods*, 1854.

Whoso cleaveth to justice, can, under no circumstances, transgress the limits of moderation. He discerneth the truth in all things, through the guidance of Him Who is the All-Seeing. The civilization, so often vaunted by the learned exponents of arts and sciences, will, if allowed to overleap the bounds of moderation, bring great evil upon men. Thus warneth you He Who is the All-Knowing. If carried to excess, civilization will prove as prolific a source of evil as it had been of goodness when kept within the restraints of moderation. Meditate on this, O people, and be not of them that wander distraught in the wilderness of error. The day is approaching when its flame will devour the cities, when the Tongue of Grandeur will proclaim: "The Kingdom is God's, the Almighty, the All-Praised!"

All other things are subject to this same principle of moderation. Render thanks unto thy Lord Who hath remembered thee in this wondrous Tablet. All-Praise be to God, the Lord of the glorious throne. (Bahá'u'lláh, *Gleanings*, no. 164.2–3)

Thus the axiom about our relationship to the world and worldliness seems to lie in the principle of moderation. We are obliged to participate *in* the world instead of trying to become spiritually enlightented by renouncing it through ascetic practices or self-deprivation, yet we are cautioned to be constantly monitoring whether our participation is a means to an end (the spiritualization of ourselves, our families, our communities, and civilization), or an end in itself (indulging ourselves in sensual pleasure, power, or fame).

'Abdu'l-Bahá, in one of his talks, portrays this balance as the major characteristic of the exemplary followers of the Manifestations who live "in" the world, but who are not "of" the world: "Saints are men who have freed themselves from the world of matter and who have overcome sin. They live in the world but are not of it, their thoughts being continually in the world of the spirit.

Their lives are spent in holiness, and their deeds show forth love, justice and godliness. They are illumined from on high; they are as bright and shining lamps in the dark places of the earth. These are the saints of God" ('Abdu'l-Bahá, *Paris Talks*, no. 18.4).

Of course, implicit in using this standard of balance or moderation is the gradual strengthening of our evaluative powers of discernment or judgment—"He discerneth the truth in all things." As we evolve and change, possibly even on a daily basis, so must our faculty of judgment become more acute and sagacious in its capacity to weigh all the variables involved in a given decision or course of action. As we examine reality anew each day, so must we reevaluate where that point of balance might lie. After all, what was moderate for us yesterday may be excessive for us today.

Here again we see the vast distinction between what Bahá'u'lláh has ordained and the elaborate code of law that various religious traditions have become. And we also observe that at the heart of this axiom about balance and the faculty of discernment is an unfailing touchstone by which we can assess the efficacy of our relationship to any worldly activity, a standard or point of reference set forth in a statement of Bahá'u'lláh about our license to enjoy the things of this world so long as we allow nothing to interfere with our relationship with God, the love and worship of whom is the central purpose of our creation:

> Should a man wish to adorn himself with the ornaments of the earth, to wear its apparels, or partake of the benefits it can bestow, no harm can befall him, if he alloweth nothing whatever to intervene between him and God, for God hath ordained every good thing, whether created in the heavens or in the earth, for such of His servants as truly believe in Him. Eat ye, O people, of the good things which God hath allowed you, and deprive not yourselves from His wondrous bounties. Render thanks and praise unto Him, and be of them that are truly thankful. (Bahá'u'lláh, *Gleanings*, no. 128.4)

THE WORLD AND THE SELF

The Bahá'í writings are replete with what I remember one Bahá'í categorizing as "delicious paradoxes." They are palatable because there is always a logical method by which seemingly contradictory guidance can be happily reconciled. But at the heart of this reconciliation is the self, the personal obligation to assess one's individual condition in order to make good choices—and not merely once or twice, but unrelentingly on a daily basis.

The reason we are thus challenged to think for ourselves is easily explained by the simple fact that no two of us have precisely the same experiences or encounter the exact same challenges in life. Each of us has a unique combination of variables at work in our lives, and therefore we are each faced with weighing for ourselves the exigencies of a given choice in the context of its special circumstances.

In this sense, to assert that each day is a new beginning may sound naïve or trite, but it is amazingly accurate. Consequently, the "good choice" or the "right path" may require constant and continuous monitoring because reality itself is never static. Here, once again, we need to call to mind the importance of acquiring and refining our tools of judgment and assessment. This axiom also reminds us again how valuable these capacities are in navigating our way through life, as opposed to following a fixed or exacting "code" of conduct or an elaborate canon of spiritual guidance. Put simply, authentic spiritual advancement necessarily requires that we think and make decisions for ourselves because each person must "manfully struggle against the natural inertia that weighs him down in his effort to arise" (Shoghi Effendi, *Citadel of Faith*, p. 148).

Therefore, the standard cited above regarding how we should become involved in the world without becoming obsessed with worldliness does not imply a single decision about some crucial matter that we can make once for all time. When our fiscal or physical or social conditions change, it may be warranted that we become *more* attentive to worldly affairs rather than detached from them. Whereas, if by some means our life becomes more "comfortable" financially, for example, we may be able to become increasingly detached from such concerns. For me, this is the underlying meaning in the following passage from a prayer of 'Abdu'l-Bahá in which we beseech God for sufficiency that we may not become dependent on any other resource: "Give us our daily bread, and grant Thine increase in the necessities of life, that we may be dependent on none other but Thee, may commune wholly with Thee, may walk in Thy ways and declare Thy mysteries. Thou art the almighty and the Loving and the Provider of all mankind" ('Abdu'l-Bahá, in *Bahá'í Prayers*, p. 23).

It is precisely in this context that Bahá'u'lláh gives us a working definition of what He means by *attachment* to "the world," as opposed to *detachment* and its focus on the "life to come." The standard, of course, is the extent to which our necessary and important relationship to physical reality transmutes from spiritual exercises into "worldliness" or possibly even to "sin": "Know ye that by 'the world' is meant your unawareness of Him Who is your Maker, and your absorption in aught else but Him. The 'life to come,' on the other hand, signifieth the things that give you a safe approach to God, the All-Glorious, the Incomparable. Whatsoever deterreth you, in this Day, from loving God is nothing but the world. Flee it, that ye may be numbered with the blest" (Bahá'u'lláh, *Gleanings*, no. 128.4).

While implicit in this passage, it is nevertheless worth noting that the allusion to the "safe approach to God" should not be interpreted as referring exclusively to the Bahá'í Faith or its teachings. There is nothing in the Bahá'í writings to indicate that righteousness or spiritual development is the sole prerogative of those who have recognized and accepted the station and teachings of Bahá'u'lláh. All the axioms we have thus far cited may be valid for whatever spiritual path one has discovered and accepted.

MERCY VERSUS JUSTICE

We now approach the crux of our discussion—how we can be redeemed, saved, or justified, whether we are Bahá'ís or followers of any of the other revealed religions. As we have asserted repeatedly from the start, because we are organic and essentially spiritual creations, we never experience a precise point of attainment. We are forever works in progress. But we still may want to know if we will ever achieve some state or condition where we need no longer fear gross failure, abrupt regression, or some sudden unexpected test that might cause us to question or doubt our faith.

We have already examined the passage about how, at the moment of transition to the next stage of our lives, we might temporarily fall into "the nethermost fire" of doubt, an experience I associate with a sort of transitional panic attack. But here we are speaking about our progress in this life and whether or not it is possible to attain a condition of certitude and confidence such that we are mostly secure from failure, a condition that might be equated with what some religious traditions refer to as being "saved" or "justified."

In the Bahá'í writings, there are several axiomatic statements and principles at work in comprehending the Bahá'í view relating to this encompassing subject. First and foremost among these is that we are utterly and forever dependent on God's mercy, forgiveness, grace, and love, as opposed to His strict justice—unless, of course, we define God's "justice" as implying "that which is fitting or expected from a merciful and loving Creator." In other words, because God is inherently forgiving and gracious—these are inalienable characteristics of His essential nature—it is "fitting" or "just" that He is kind to us, His creation.

At the same time, the Bahá'í texts also employ the usual definition of "justice" as "that which is earned or deserved." Therefore, if God were to bestow on us only what we were due according to some strict standards of cause and effect or *"quid pro quo,"* none of us would fare very well. We noted this point in the previous chapter when we discussed our confession of relative "sinfulness" in the Long Obligatory Prayer.

In discussing justice in its ordinary meaning versus the mercy ("bounty") of God, 'Abdu'l-Bahá makes the following logical distinction: "Know that justice consists in rendering to each his due. For example, when a workman labours from morning till evening, justice requires that he be paid his wage, but bounty consists in rewarding him even when he has done no work and expended no effort. So when you give alms to a poor man who has made no effort and done nothing for your benefit to deserve it, this is bounty. Thus, Christ besought forgiveness for those responsible for His death: This is called bounty" ('Abdu'l-Bahá, *Some Answered Questions*, no. 76.1).

RESOLUTION AND THE CONTINUITY OF LIFE

The operation of this principle of forgiveness, mercy, and bounty is not confined to our life in this physical portion of our existence. The Bahá'í writings state that even after we have passed on to the next stage of our journey, we will have access to redemption and transformation.

Again, this axiom affirms that God's grace exceeds His justice in His relationship with us. In this connection, 'Abdu'l-Bahá affirms, "It is even possible for those who have died in sin and unbelief to be transformed, that is, to become the object of divine forgiveness. This is through the grace of God and not through His justice, for grace is to bestow without desert, and justice is to give that which is deserved" ('Abdu'l-Bahá, *Some Answered Questions*, no. 62.7).

'Abdu'l-Bahá points out that the progress of the soul in the next world can also be assisted by other means: "through the intercession and prayers of other human souls, or through the significant contributions and charitable deeds which are offered in its name," or "purely through the grace and bounty of the Lord" ('Abdu'l-Bahá, *Some Answered Questions*, no. 66.6). But, of course, *all* progress of every human being at *any* stage of life is accomplished "purely through the bounty and grace of the Lord," whether that grace is channeled through the advent of each successive Manifestation, or in the daily life of the individual believer through reflection, meditation, and prayer.

From these statements, however, we can infer that this forgiveness, even in the next stage of our lives, is contingent on one particular action on the part of the penitent soul seeking salvation—supplication for acceptance and pardon. And to have value, as we noted in the previous chapter, this supplication must be accompanied by our recognition of failure and by our desire and decision to change and to follow an appropriate course of action. And, of course, we presume that an omniscient God would be instantly capable of detecting whether we are sincere in this process of repentance striving for salvation: "And just as they can seek illumination here through supplication, so too can they plead there for forgiveness and seek illumination through prayer and supplication. Thus, as souls can progress in this world through their entreaties and supplications, or through the prayers of holy souls, so too after death can they progress through their own prayers and supplications, particularly if they become the object of the intercession of the holy Manifestations" ('Abdu'l-Bahá, *Some Answered Questions*, no. 62.7).

When Shoghi Effendi discusses this same principle, he, like 'Abdu'l-Bahá, confirms that "God's Mercy exceeds His Justice, and that through the repentance of a soul, the prayers and supplications of other souls, and the goodness of God, even a person who has passed away in great spiritual darkness can be forgiven, educated spiritually in the next world and progress" (from a letter written on behalf of the Guardian to an individual believer, February 7, 1947, in *Lights of Guidance*, p. 187).

The concept of being "educated" in the next world is a particularly heartening and illuminating term in this context. It obviously implies that we will undergo the same sort of educational process we delight in during the physical stage of our experience. Of course, it should not be surprising that these spiritual laws and axioms continue in the metaphysical or spiritual environment, since that is where they occur in this life—in the abstract thoughts of the mind, which itself is but a metaphysical power or faculty of the soul.

Indeed, there are many passages in which it is made clear that in the "afterlife" we will not be allocated to some static condition. Change, as has been noted, is a principle of all life, whether it be physical or metaphysical in essence: "It is therefore clearly established that motion, whether advancing or declining, is necessary to existence. Now, as the human spirit continues after death, it must either advance or decline, and in the next world to cease to advance is the same as to decline. But the human spirit never transcends its own degree: It progresses only within that degree" ('Abdu'l-Bahá, *Some Answered Questions*, no. 63.2).*

To conclude, then, Shoghi Effendi makes the following comparison between the experience in the afterlife of a devoted believer and someone who has died in sin or unbelief: "you might say that a wonderful believer is like a diamond blazing in the sun, an unawakened soul like one in a dark room. But we must couple this concept with the other part of the teachings, that God's mercy exceeds His justice, and that soul can progress in the world beyond; the unillumined soul can become brilliant" (Shoghi Effendi, in *Lights of Guidance*, p. 477).

So to answer the question with which we began this chapter, the fact is that both in this life and in the life to come, we are capable of

---

* "Man, having reached the human station, can progress only in perfections and not in station, for there is no higher station to which he can find passage than that of a perfect man. He can progress solely within the human station, as human perfections are infinite. Thus, however learned a man may be, it is always possible to imagine one even more learned" ('Abdu'l-Bahá, *Some Answered Questions*, no. 64.6).

achieving infinitely progressive stages of assurance, enlightenment, certitude, and delight. But all stages of our progress are relative and contingent; there is no final point where we need no longer strive for spiritual growth, even if that effort becomes completely joyful in and of itself. As we discussed in chapter 6, Bahá'u'lláh speaks about entering the "City of Certitude" as a spiritual condition available to us. And yet, once we have entered this celestial city, is it not conceivable that we might, whether through willfulness or negligence, become bereft of this same certitude, even if only temporarily?

Needless to say, these are among the many questions we cannot answer in any definitive manner. But what we can with surety determine is that it is clearly much better for us if we take advantage of the opportunities for development on this plane of existence when the array of tests that come our way cause us to focus on our inherent purpose, strengthen our resolve to advance, and thereby enable us to welcome the transition to the next stage of our lives as we become released from "the world" and begin our further development in "the life to come."

17 / THE LIMITLESS FORGIVENESS OF GOD

Likewise apprehend thou the nature of hell-fire and be of them that truly believe. For every act performed there shall be a recompense according to the estimate of God, and unto this the very ordinances and prohibitions prescribed by the Almighty amply bear witness. For surely if deeds were not rewarded and yielded no fruit, then the Cause of God—exalted is He—would prove futile. Immeasurably high is He exalted above such blasphemies! However, unto them that are rid of all attachments a deed is, verily, its own reward. Were We to enlarge upon this theme numerous Tablets would need to be written.

—Bahá'u'lláh, *Tablets of Bahá'u'lláh*, p. 189

The remedy for a disease may incur pain, but because we know that the end result will be the restoration of health and relief from even greater pain, we readily endure temporary discomfort. As we have discussed throughout this book, this is the value of knowing the end result of a process at the outset. So it is that the judicious athlete welcomes the stress of training and feels his endurance and powers increase, as what at first seemed difficult and strenuous gradually produces the reward of feeling healthy and strong.

Another useful analogy about learning to follow the right path can be found in our understanding about nutrition. Once we accustom ourselves to a strictly healthy diet—perhaps after years of eating unhealthily—foods that might at first have seemed distasteful begin to have immense appeal, and, conversely, the junk food we once adored may now seem repulsive. These simple analogies demonstrate that habituation to a healthy regimen, whether physical or spiritual, will in time free us from an attraction to what might deter our health and felicity, just as our initial resistance to the regimen is replaced by an existential joy in pursuing those exercises that induce health in all its forms.

WHERE JUSTICE OCCURS

As we contemplate the end of this life and our departure from it, we may in our youth look upon our inevitable passing with trepidation. But for those who have endured a long life and are experiencing the gradual diminishing of the physical temple and its powers, the departure from this world may well be a most welcome relief. 'Abdu'l-Bahá expresses this relief in the following description:

> When thou lookest about thee with a perceptive eye, thou wilt note that on this dusty earth all humankind are suffering. Here no man is at rest as a reward for what he hath performed in former lives; nor is there anyone so blissful as seemingly to pluck the fruit of bygone anguish. And if a human life, with its spiritual being, were limited to this earthly span, then what would be the harvest of creation? Indeed, what would be the effects and the outcomes of Divinity Itself? Were such a notion true, then all created things, all contingent realities, and this whole world of being—all would be meaningless. God forbid that one should hold to such a fiction and gross error. ('Abdu'l-Bahá, *Selections from the Writings of 'Abdu'l-Bahá*, no. 156.9)

As 'Abdu'l-Bahá continues in this same discourse, he comments that the rewards for a noble life are rarely experienced before our departure from the physical stage of our existence. As we noted before, it often seems that in this earthly life the selfish and the unjust prosper at the expense of those who strive to live decently. Therefore, if we look for justice in this life, at least in some final sense, we will rarely if ever find it. The process of justice is fulfilled in the continuation of our lives, and were it not so, belief in God would be virtually impossible:

For just as the effects and the fruitage of the uterine life are not to be found in that dark and narrow place, and only when the child is transferred to this wide earth do the benefits and uses of growth and development in that previous world become revealed—so likewise reward and punishment, heaven and hell, requital and retribution for actions done in this present life, will stand revealed in that other world beyond. And just as, if human life in the womb were limited to that uterine world, existence there would be nonsensical, irrelevant—so too if the life of this world, the deeds here done and their fruitage, did not come forth in the world beyond, the whole process would be irrational and foolish.

Know then that the Lord God possesseth invisible realms which the human intellect can never hope to fathom nor the mind of man conceive. When once thou hast cleansed the channel of thy spiritual sense from the pollution of this worldly life, then wilt thou breathe in the sweet scents of holiness that blow from the blissful bowers of that heavenly land. ('Abdu'l-Bahá, *Selections from the Writings of 'Abdu'l-Bahá*, no. 156.10–11)

CONSEQUENCE AND JUSTICE

As we discussed in the previous two chapters, Bahá'u'lláh's law against penance abrogates the notion that the only way we can become cleansed of sin is by following some course of action ordained and overseen by a priest, cleric, or institution. However, the abrogation of these processes does not mean that our acts have no consequences, whether positive or negative.

In light of the various axiomatic statements about the continuity of the soul and of our opportunity for further development—especially when assisted by God's forgiveness, mercy, and enlightenment—it becomes absolutely clear that the only thing we have to fear is ourselves: our choices, our actions, or our loss of constancy.

Put quite directly, the Bahá'í writings assure us that while God's assessment of our performance is tempered with unfailing grace and fathomless forgiveness, there is still an explicit relationship between our performance in this early physical stage of our existence and what we experience as we continue our lives in the realm of the spirit. Thus, while it may take into consideration all the struggles we have endured—as well as the myriad variables of which we may not have been conscious—a judgment of how we did while operating through the veils of material signs and symbols still takes place at the moment of our transition: "It is clear and evident that all men shall, after their physical death, estimate the worth of their deeds, and realize all that their hands have wrought" (Bahá'u'lláh, *Gleanings*, no. 86.4).

Therefore, as we near the conclusion of our study of reality and the human soul, it is timely that we now examine some of the parameters that govern what we will experience in the process of evaluating our physical lives. As we have already noted, even if we have done poorly and wasted opportunities for growth and development, we can still ask for forgiveness and strive for progress and enlightenment. However, it is crucial that we not infer from such assurance that our present actions have no permanent consequence, even if the Bahá'í writings do imply that we can always make amends for our bad choices and misdeeds after we have departed this realm.

As we discussed in great detail in the second section, the Bahá'í teachings affirm that the afterlife is not physical and thus all allusions to hell and heaven are descriptions of spiritual conditions of remoteness or proximity (which are themselves but metaphorical expressions of metaphysical conditions). However, these conditions have emotional results, and as we also discussed, an emotional experience can be just as powerful as any purely physical sensation.

Despair, depression, guilt, and self-loathing are often more dreaded conditions—over the long haul—than even the most grievous physical pain, especially since physical pain stops forever at death, whereas these internal spiritual and emotional conditions may be capable of enduring indefinitely. And given that the afterlife is a timeless realm, such a prospect certainly warrants our concern. It is in the context of these considerations that Bahá'u'lláh describes the parameters of those feelings we will experience upon examining our lives when we depart this material realm and "estimate the worth" of our deeds.

On one extreme are the detachment and immeasurable joy we feel if we have devoted ourselves to God's purposes for us. The other extreme is immeasurable despair if we have willfully failed in our obligations and have rejected the Manifestation or rebelled against His Cause and guidance: "I swear by the Daystar that shineth above the horizon of Divine power! They that are the followers of the one true God shall, the moment they depart out of this life, experience such joy and gladness as would be impossible to describe, while they that live in error shall be seized with such fear and trembling, and shall be filled with such consternation, as nothing can exceed" (Bahá'u'lláh, *Gleanings*, no. 86.4).

Of course, it is important to note that the term "followers" here may not be confined to Bahá'ís, even as the Muslim phrase "people of the Book" alludes to all those who worship God through the paths revealed by any of the Manifestations. Likewise, the phrase "they that live in error" is not a reference to a particular category or degree of sin. As we have so often noted, all individual lives are distinct and must necessarily be evaluated in the context of the myriad circumstances affecting each unique soul. As we have also noted, the condition of the soul in the afterlife is always changing, and those who may have lived in error may undergo significant change after they have experienced an awareness of the bounties they had foregone during their physical existence.

RECOMPENSE

In discussing the cause-and-effect relationship between how one does in this life and what one experiences in the afterlife, the Bahá'í writings frequently employ two distinct terms. The term "recompense" is most often applied to those experiences that will bring about a form of justice for those who have done well, or for those who have experienced injustice and are thus due some form of repayment for their nobility of character or unjust suffering.

For example, Bahá'u'lláh states that the reward will be significant for those who strive to recognize God through the Manifestation and couple that learning with obedience to His laws. Additionally, Bahá'u'lláh affirms that a special recompense awaits those who shed even a single drop of blood for this Cause: "Say: O ye lovers of the One true God! Strive, that ye may truly recognize and know Him, and observe befittingly His precepts. This is a Revelation, under which, if a man shed for its sake one drop of blood, myriads of oceans will be his *recompense*" (Bahá'u'lláh, *Gleanings*, no. 3.2) [italics added].

Bahá'u'lláh uses the term "recompense" similarly in describing the reward that will accrue to those who have been faithful and firm, while those around them have proven frail and perfidious: "O My servant, who hast sought the good-pleasure of God and clung to His love on the Day when all except a few who were endued with insight have broken away from Him! May God, through His grace, *recompense* thee with a generous, an incorruptible and everlasting reward, inasmuch as thou hast sought Him on the Day when eyes were blinded" (Bahá'u'lláh, *Gleanings*, no. 15.2) [italics added].

Of particular interest in the following passage is Bahá'u'lláh's observation that for those who have attained the loftier levels of detachment, the joy inherent in performing a good deed "is its own reward":

As to Paradise: It is a reality and there can be no doubt about it, and now in this world it is realized through love of Me and My good-pleasure. Whosoever attaineth unto it God will aid him in this world below, and after death He will enable him to gain admittance into Paradise whose vastness is as that of heaven and earth. Therein the Maids of glory and holiness will wait upon him in the daytime and in the night season, while the daystar of the unfading beauty of his Lord will at all times shed its radiance upon him and he will shine so brightly that no one shall bear to gaze at him. Such is the dispensation of Providence, yet the people are shut out by a grievous veil. Likewise apprehend thou the nature of hell-fire and be of them that truly believe. For every act performed there shall be a *recompense* according to the estimate of God, and unto this the very ordinances and prohibitions prescribed by the Almighty amply bear witness. For surely if deeds were not rewarded and yielded no fruit, then the Cause of God— exalted is He—would prove futile. Immeasurably high is He exalted above such blasphemies! However, unto them that are rid of all attachments a deed is, verily, its own reward. Were We to enlarge upon this theme numerous Tablets would need to be written. (Bahá'u'lláh, *Tablets of Bahá'u'lláh*, p. 189) [italics added]

ATONEMENT

While Bahá'u'lláh has abolished or abrogated all laws of penance, the concept of atonement, implicit in the passages we have already discussed, obviously portrays a causal relationship between our performance here and our experience in the afterlife. Explicit in the second half of the previous passage is the notion of some sort of atonement for our sins or failures—partly to instruct us, but also, we might infer, to enable us to understand and appreciate the notion of justice at all levels of reality: "For surely if deeds were not rewarded and yielded no fruit, then the Cause of God—exalted is He—would prove futile."

This assurance is important whether we feel ourselves to be victims or victimizers. Justice will ultimately be done, we are told. Therefore, the passage seems to imply that we should fear not if we are victims, nor should we think that we have escaped retribution as a victimizer, even if we have managed to avoid the punishment of civil justice in this life.

This assurance, this fact about reality in relation to the human soul, is incredibly important as we go about the job of trying to fashion and implement a spiritually based form of global governance. As a global community, we will always be only *relatively* successful. Even should we create a social environment where, as 'Abdu'l-Bahá describes it, the worst punishment will be the state of being considered lawless or untrustworthy, we can be certain there will still be those who will be defiant, those who will rebel against their own best interests and against the common weal. Free will allows for bad choices, and only individual dedication can ensure that one refrains from making them, even when the social environment collectively upholds spiritual standards.

One of the terms Bahá'u'lláh most frequently uses to allude to the process of experiencing some recompense for negative actions is the verb *atone* or the noun *atonement*, though neither of these is referring exclusively to the afterlife. For example, in the following passage from Bahá'u'lláh's powerful and lengthy Súriy-i-Mulúk (Surah of the Kings), He speaks about recompense and atonement in terms of the continuity of history. In particular, He refers to the fact that God is well aware of the trials that have afflicted the Manifestation, and that the people who perpetrated these actions will be made to atone: "The day is approaching when God will have raised up a people who will call to remembrance Our days, who will tell the tale of Our trials, who will demand the restitution of Our rights from them that, without a tittle of evidence, have treated Us with manifest injustice. God, assuredly, dominateth the lives of them that wronged Us, and is well aware of their doings. He will, most certainly, lay hold on them for their sins. He, verily, is the fiercest of avengers" (Bahá'u'lláh, "The Súriy-i-Mulúk," *The Summons of the Lord of Hosts*, ¶53).

Then, referring to the fact that earlier in this same tablet He has recounted the wrongs inflicted upon Manifestations of the past and what subsequently was the recompense imposed on those who perpetrated this injustice, Bahá'u'lláh explains that He has recited these accounts to inspire the present-day rulers and peoples to repent and atone for their wrongdoings while they still have the power to do so: "Thus have We recounted unto you the tales of the one true God, and sent down unto you the things He had preordained, that haply ye may ask forgiveness of Him, may return unto Him, may truly repent, may realize your misdeeds, may shake off your slumber, may be roused from your heedlessness, *may atone* for the things that have escaped you, and be of them that do good" (Bahá'u'lláh, "The Súriy-i-Mulúk," *The Summons of the Lord of Hosts*, ¶54) [italics added].

Following this caution, Bahá'u'lláh speaks as a "warner," like Muhammad before Him, and explains to the kings and rulers (the "concourse of Ministers of State") that their fate is not sealed, but that it is contingent on their response to Bahá'u'lláh's exhortation, because God is forgiving and the "greatness of His mercy surpasseth His wrath":

> Let him who will, acknowledge the truth of My words; and as to him that willeth not, let him turn aside. My sole duty is to remind you of your failure in duty towards the Cause of God, if perchance ye may be of them that heed My warning. Wherefore, hearken ye unto My speech, and return ye to God and repent, that He, through His grace, may have mercy upon you, may wash away your sins, and forgive your trespasses. The greatness of His mercy surpasseth the fury of His wrath, and His grace encompasseth all who have been called into being and been clothed with the robe of life, be they of the past or of the future. (Bahá'u'lláh, *Gleanings*, no. 66.13)

Still another weighty example of Bahá'u'lláh's use of the term *atone* to designate recompense for failure is a passage in the midst of one of His most powerful exhortations to the peoples of the world about the purpose and brevity of physical life in light of the single most important task before us. In exquisite poetic language, Bahá'u'lláh bids us ("mortal birds") to bestir ourselves from slumber and attachment to the world in order to make use of the brief "hours and moments" of our lives that remain. Otherwise, He cautions, how will we atone for such a failure in the future?

> Night hath succeeded day, and day hath succeeded night, and the hours and moments of your lives have come and gone, and yet none of you hath, for one instant, consented to detach himself from that which perisheth. Bestir yourselves, that the brief moments that are still yours may not be dissipated and lost. Even as the swiftness of lightning your days shall pass, and your bodies shall be laid to rest beneath a canopy of dust. What can ye then achieve? How can ye *atone* for your past failure? (Bahá'u'lláh, *Gleanings*, no. 151.4) [italics added]

NO SIN IS BEYOND THE GRACE AND FORGIVENESS OF GOD

Finally, we come to a concept that seems totally alien to the abiding logic underlying everything we have thus far noted about the nature of reality. In particular, this concept seems contrary to the laws governing the relationship between physical and spiritual reality as we have delineated them from the Bahá'í texts. This is the matter of whether or not there could be such an action, whether physical or spiritual, that could be considered an unforgivable or unpardonable sin.

The logical answer according to the Bahá'í scripture is quite simple. If God is ever-forgiving, then there is no point at which one is beyond His grace. Consequently, the idea that there could be an action one could commit that would be beyond the capacity of God to forgive is an implicit constraint or limitation of the powers of a Being Who, by definition, is beyond limitations. Logically, then, the only way anyone could be beyond the grace or forgiveness of God would be through the willful rejection of that forgiveness or the refusal to seek divine assistance, a point 'Abdu'l-Bahá makes clear in the following passage:

This hatred of the light itself is irremediable and unforgivable; that is, it is impossible for such a soul to draw near to God. This lamp here is a lamp because of its light; without the light it would not be a lamp. A soul that abhors the light of the lamp is, as it were, blind and cannot perceive the light, and this blindness is the cause of eternal deprivation.

It is evident that souls receive grace from the outpourings of the Holy Spirit which are apparent in the Manifestation of God, and not from the individual personality of Manifestation. It follows that if a soul fails to partake of the outpourings of the Holy Spirit, it remains deprived of God's grace, and this deprivation itself is equivalent of the denial of divine forgiveness. ('Abdu'l-Bahá, *Some Answered Questions*, no. 31.4–5)

Yet, in this same vital discourse, 'Abdu'l-Bahá explains two further points that clarify why it is only through willful rejection of God's forgiveness and grace that one would be eternally banished from reformation and redemption. Indeed, it is for this reason that he says such rejection is "equivalent" to the "denial of divine forgiveness," and not that it *is* denial.

First, 'Abdu'l-Bahá explains that even those who have "opposed the Manifestations of God" are not automatically made to endure "eternal deprivation":

That is why there have been many souls who opposed the Manifestations of God, not realizing that They were Manifestations, but who became Their friends once they had recognized Them. Thus, enmity towards the Manifestation of God was not the cause of eternal deprivation, for they were enemies of the candleholder and knew not that it was the seat of God's effulgent light. They were not enemies of the light itself, and once they understood that the candleholder was the seat of the light, they became true friends. ('Abdu'l-Bahá, *Some Answered Questions*, no. 31.6)

In other words, we can become redeemed and forgiven for any action if we become aware of how our actions (whether physical or spiritual) have deprived us of the truth about the divine nature of reality and what we must do to gain access to God's grace and guidance.

In this sense, there can be no sin that could be properly categorized as "unpardonable" or "unforgivable," not in the sense these terms are commonly used and not so long as we do not willfully and wittingly reject or abhor the "light itself." And yet, as 'Abdu'l-Bahá makes clear in the final paragraph of this same discussion, it is possible for us to become the cause of our own "eternal deprivation," not because any specific action is beyond forgiveness and not because God's grace is ever limited or withheld, but simply because it is possible for one to become so depraved as to detest and reject the light itself: "Our meaning is that remoteness from the candleholder is not the cause of eternal deprivation, for one may yet be awakened and guided aright, but that enmity towards the light itself is the cause of eternal deprivation and has no remedy" ('Abdu'l-Bahá, *Some Answered Questions*, no. 31.7). And, as 'Abdu'l-Bahá notes in the previously cited passage, the eternality of this deprivation endures only so long as the soul maintains its enmity. Should it somehow ever awaken from its state of detestation, then clearly guidance and grace would be available.

Theoretically, then, no individual—however sinful or depraved—is beyond the infinite grace and forgiveness of God, though perhaps, through our experience in the world with those whose souls seem to have become depraved or willfully callous, we can conceive of those who might eternally refuse to exert the effort necessary for redemption.

THE CONSEQUENCE OF OUR ACTIONS

As this chapter's epigraph states, all our actions bear fruit or have consequences. And in terms of everything we have thus far discussed, all those who have died in sin have a chance for atonement and forgiveness. We also have pondered the passage in which Bahá'u'lláh describes how, after our passing to the next stage of our existence, we go through a process of examining how we did in this stage. This evaluation or judgment makes us aware of both the ways in which we served others, thereby fulfilling our inherent charge, as well as the opportunities we lost by being inattentive or possibly negligent and perverse. Having learned all we can from this life review, we can assume that we then continue more or less from where we left off.

However, what is not necessarily apparent from these passages is what we have just acknowledged—that some form of atonement for some of our actions may be necessary for us to appreciate sufficiently the consequences of what we have done, to experience the appropriate remorse and shame for "sinful" or "inappropriate" acts, and thereby to establish the foundation for our spiritual advancement.

For while God is loving and infinitely forgiving—a perfect Guide and Educator—He wisely determines what we need to experience in order to make further progress, or in some cases, to make any progress at all. And merely to acknowledge or become subjectively aware that something we have committed, or omitted, is reprehensible may not establish in us the same necessary foundation as experiencing the appropriate emotional response of guilt and remorse we should have felt at the time we committed the malfeasance or nonfeasance.

Therefore, many of our frailties and less offensive sins might be acknowledged but require no atonement—they might be instantly pardoned or forgiven—even if we are made aware that we committed what we should not have. But some sins may be sufficiently severe that merely becoming intellectually and even subjectively aware of them might be an inadequate result to bring about the necessary reformation of our character so that we may make progress in our eternal journey. Even if we understand to some extent the gravity of what we have inflicted, we may still be required to experience something akin to the emotional pain or mental anguish we caused others to endure before we are subjectively appreciative of the nature of our failings.

To cite but one example that bears out the logic of this process, 'Abdu'l-Bahá notes that if a murderer is punished for his crime in this life, he will not then be required to endure punishment in the afterlife. In this instance, too, we see both the relationship between our deeds here and our atonement in the afterlife, as well as the variables that might affect what sort of experience we will be made to endure in order to learn from our actions. But clearly underlying the process is that we learn from our experiences and become changed thereby, not that some impersonal or mechanical codified process be employed to determine the outcome of our lives.

Surely God is aware of all we do and is capable of determining to what extent we are responsible and culpable for each action. God is equally capable of determining how ready we are to move on after we have reflected on our performance and the degree to which we may need to go through some process of awakening so that we might become aware of the harm we have perpetrated. By this means, and with God's further grace and guidance, we might become sincerely remorseful, regret the opportunity we lost to live better, and supplicate God with our whole heart for pardon and forgiveness, as well as eternal assistance as we strive for reformation and spiritual development.

Yet, as 'Abdu'l-Bahá notes, it is conceivable that one might not make such supplications if, for whatever reason, one possesses "hatred of the light itself," a condition which may be temporary, or not. Certainly it seems unlikely that one could be so debased or negligent as to reject his or her own salvation and reformation, but since it is logically feasible and since 'Abdu'l-Bahá describes this condition, we must presume that it can and does occur.

Needless to say, this subject is inexhaustible, but the central point is clear. Both in this life and in the continuation of our lives after this one, all existence is relative, whether we are discussing the heights we can attain or the depths to which we can descend. In a simple but sublimely useful discussion of how this concept of relative existence applies in relation to the afterlife of those who have striven to become good versus those who have become totally depraved in their indifference to matters of the spirit, 'Abdu'l-Bahá uses the following analogy:

> Entrance into the Kingdom is through the love of God, through detachment, through sanctity and holiness, through truthfulness and purity, through steadfastness and faithfulness, and through self-sacrifice.
>
> It follows clearly from these explanations that man is immortal and everlasting. Those who believe in God, who cherish His love, and who have attained certitude, enjoy the blessing which we call life eternal; but those who are veiled from God, though they be endowed with life, yet they live in darkness and their life, in comparison with that of the believers, is non-existence.
>
> Thus, the eye is alive and so too is the fingernail, but the life of the fingernail in relation to that of the eye is nonexistence. The stone and man both exist, but in relation to man the stone has no existence or being. For when man dies and his body is disintegrated and destroyed, it becomes like the stone, the earth, and the mineral. It is therefore clear that even though the mineral exists, it is nonexistent in relation to man.
>
> Likewise, those souls who are veiled from God, although they exist both in this world and in the world to come, are non-existent and forgotten in relation to the sanctified existence of the children of the divine Kingdom. ('Abdu'l-Bahá, *Some Answered Questions*, no. 67.7–10)

We might wish to presume that all of us will continue to grow spiritually, to develop and serve, but obviously we will do so according to our own particular powers and station. And for many of us, some form of remedial learning may be required. Obviously, the more willfully negligent we have become regarding our spiritual "self" during our physical existence, the more education we will require in the afterlife.

We cannot imagine what experiences would be required for a serial killer, an unconscionable thief, or an abuser of children to be pardoned in the next world—after all, we are not God and thus do not possess the powers required to make such a judgment. But we most certainly can appreciate that various sins cannot be instantly forgiven or simply "pardoned," for then these souls would not have learned sufficiently about the gravity of what they deliberately perpetrated and what grief, pain, and suffering they caused others. We can imagine that possibly, before all else, these souls will be made to know through some subjective means what they have caused others to experience.

According to the laws of Bahá'u'lláh, capital punishment is one of the options that may be imposed by civil authority in a society run according to Bahá'í law, though every crime is considered according to the particular exigencies of the case. We might think that in the context of creating a spiritually-based and infinitely more advanced and enlightened civilization, the Creator would deem capital punishment inappropriate. However, it must be made clear that the society Bahá'u'lláh is portraying where such a penalty could be imposed is quite distinct from our contemporary society. Where capital punishment is presently employed, whether in the United States or elsewhere, there are major inequities regarding equal access to legal protection and defense. In addition, it has long been noted that in the United States, such punishment is racially biased and that, especially in cases adjudged prior to DNA testing, the danger of the innocent being unjustly tried and wrongly executed is hardly a mere possibility.

In short, as with many of the laws set forth by Bahá'u'lláh in the Kitáb-i-Aqdas, the implementation of this law as one of several possible punishments for a murder awaits a time and a social environment where a significantly more evolved system of justice prevails. It should also be noted in this context that one of the reasons a more evolved society would consider what to some seems a regressive or egregious form of punishment is that the world-view of such a society will include a belief in the continuity of the soul after death.

The importance of this perspective or belief is obvious. When we accept that our spiritual existence continues after this physical life and that sometimes people are so detrimental to society that they need to be removed from it, then the punishment in some contexts is not only reasonable, it is the only sensible alternative. Shoghi Effendi has responded to this question with the following observation: "In the Aqdas Bahá'u'lláh has given death as the penalty for murder. However, He has permitted life imprisonment as an alternative. Both practices would be in accordance with His Laws. Some of us may not be able to grasp the wisdom of this when it disagrees with our own limited vision; but we must accept it, knowing His Wisdom, His Mercy and His Justice are perfect and for the salvation of the entire world" (Shoghi Effendi, quoted in Bahá'u'lláh, *The Kitáb-i-Aqdas*, p. 204).

Naturally, the first objection advanced by many to such a law is, that it is possible for a jury to convict an innocent person. Shoghi Effendi's response to this reasonable objection is likewise contingent on the fact that in a Bahá'í society where the continuity of life is an accepted fact of reality, the possible execution of an innocent person would be taken no less seriously, but there would be the obvious consolation that the innocent victim of this injustice would be provided due recompense in the world to come, perhaps along the lines of a religious martyr or a soldier who has given his or her life to secure or safeguard the freedom of society: "If a man were falsely condemned to die, can we not believe Almighty God would compensate him a thousandfold, in the next world, for this human injustice? You cannot give up a salutary law just because on rare occasions the innocent may be punished" (Shoghi Effendi, quoted in Bahá'u'lláh, *The Kitáb-i-Aqdas*, p. 204).

In this context, we see that afterlife justice works both ways, in recompensing those who have suffered injustice and in rectifying the failure or inability of society to punish the perpetrator. One very transparent window into the logic of this relationship that welds together the physical life with its continuation in the spiritual realm can be glimpsed in 'Abdu'l-Bahá's statement that if a murderer is executed or punished by society, then he is reconciled for that act: "As to the question regarding the soul of a murderer, and what his punishment would be, the answer given was that the murderer must expiate his crime: that is, if they put the murderer to death, his death is his atonement for his crime, and following the death, God in His justice will impose no second penalty upon him, for divine justice would not allow this" (from 'Abdu'l-Bahá, *Selections from the Writings of 'Abdu'l-Bahá*, no. 150.1).

Finally, we come to the notion of what would seem to be perhaps an eternally unpardonable sin according to the Bahá'í perspective of reality, that of being a Covenant-breaker. As we noted earlier, this appellation is not designating someone who has simply broken a law (which is part of Bahá'u'lláh's Covenant), but rather someone who, similar to Milton's Satan, knows that the Manifestation is God's representative, accepts that truth, but rebels against it and proceeds actively and persistently to work against the Manifestation or the institution He has created to secure His Covenant in perpetuity. Surely it would seem that forgiveness is not possible for someone who has effectively and knowingly warred against God.

The answer is that, as we stated in our early description of reality, only one act can eternally deprive a soul of forgiveness and assistance—the refusal of the soul to turn to God in humble obeisance and ask for His help, and then follow whatever course of action the road back requires. This verity applies both while the soul is enduring its brief association with the physical world, and afterward as it exists in the unveiled reality of the placeless realm.

Nowhere is this axiom more amply and logically set forth than in a final portion of Bahá'u'lláh's Most Holy Book where He states to His perfidious half-brother, Mirza Yahya, that were he to repent of his actions and plead for forgiveness, God would assist him to become redeemed. To put this assurance in context, it is being offered to one who had tried to usurp Bahá'u'lláh's authority, had hired an assassin to have Him killed, and who had poisoned Bahá'u'lláh so that His hand was palsied for the rest of His life:

> Say: O source of perversion! Abandon thy wilful blind-ness, and speak forth the truth amidst the people. I swear by God that I have wept for thee to see thee following thy self-ish passions and renouncing Him Who fashioned thee and brought thee into being. Call to mind the tender mercy of thy Lord, and remember how We nurtured thee by day and by night for service to the Cause. Fear God, and be thou of the truly repentant. Granted that the people were confused about thy station, is it conceivable that thou thyself art similarly confused? Tremble before thy Lord and recall the days when thou didst stand before Our throne, and didst write down the verses that We dictated unto thee—verses sent down by God, the Omnipotent Protector, the Lord of might and power. Be-ware lest the fire of thy presumptuousness debar thee from attaining to God's Holy Court. Turn unto Him, and fear not because of thy deeds. He, in truth, forgiveth whomsoever He desireth as a bounty on His part; no God is there but Him, the Ever-Forgiving, the All-Bounteous. We admonish thee solely for the sake of God.

> Shouldst thou accept this counsel, thou wilt have acted to thine own behoof; and shouldst thou reject it, thy Lord, ver-ily, can well dispense with thee, and with all those who, in manifest delusion, have followed thee. Behold! God hath laid hold on him who led thee astray. Return unto God, humble, submissive and lowly; verily, He will put away from thee thy

sins, for thy Lord, of a certainty, is the Forgiving, the Mighty, the All-Merciful. (Bahá'u'lláh, The Kitáb-i-Aqdas, ¶184)

18 / RESURRECTION AND COLLECTIVE SALVATION

"Hath the Hour come?" "Nay, more; it hath passed, by Him Who is the Revealer of clear tokens! Verily, the Inevitable is come, and He, the True One, hath appeared with proof and testimony. The Plain is disclosed, and mankind is sore vexed and fearful. Earthquakes have broken loose, and the tribes have lamented, for fear of God, the Lord of Strength, the All-Compelling." Say: "The stunning trumpet blast hath been loudly raised, and the Day is God's, the One, the Unconstrained." "Hath the Catastrophe come to pass?" Say: "Yea, by the Lord of Lords!" "Is the Resurrection come?" "Nay, more; He Who is the Self-Subsisting hath appeared with the Kingdom of His signs."

—Bahá'u'lláh, Epistle to the Son of the Wolf, pp. 131–32

We could hardly think our discourse on salvation complete without discussing and clarifying the emotionally charged, eschatological terms such as "the Last Judgment," "the Second Coming," "the Resurrection," "The Day of Days," and other gut-wrenching allusions to the end of time and to some form of collective salvation or damnation. The relevance of these concepts to our discussion is that several of these terms imply some direct connection between individual salvation or judgment and the collective judgment of humankind when an apocalyptic "end time" occurs. These terms are employed in the authentic scriptures of Judaism, Christianity, Islam, the Bábí, and the Bahá'í Faiths, and they actually have important meanings.

This chapter's epigraph is an extremely fascinating and powerful excerpt from a tablet of Bahá'u'lláh entitled "Muballigh," which means the "teacher" or the "proclaimer." It was revealed in honor of Hájí Muhammad Ibráhím and, according to Adib Taherzadeh, it represents a dialogue between "the voice of Truth and the voice of those who are bereft of true understanding . . ." (Taherzadeh, *The Revelation of Bahá'u'lláh*, 4:153). In this dialogue, questions are asked regarding Islamic prophecies concerning the promised "Day of God" or "Resurrection," and the Voice of Divine authority responds that all has been fulfilled and that the Day of Days has arrived with the advent of the Báb and Bahá'u'lláh. But let us examine the expectation of some prior revelations leading up to this moment to appreciate what these allusions to an "End Time" or "Day of Judgment" mean.

THE FUNDAMENTALS OF A BAHÁ'Í ESCHATOLOGY

Concepts of eschatology (theological discourse about the "End Time" or "Last Judgment") frequently relate individual salvation to a collective process where the living, as well as those who have died, are resurrected and judged, whereupon a division or judgment is made in which the "saved" are segregated from the "damned." For example, the aforementioned "Apostles' Creed" (chapter 12) of some Christian sects states that this event or process will involve the return of Christ to judge "the living and the dead."* Some Islamic versions of the Last Judgment likewise involve the return of Christ.

The Bahá'í writings also speak vividly about an unavoidable calamitous upheaval that the human body politic must experience before it will become "awakened," united, and galvanized to go about the God-given task of fashioning a just and equitable planetary civilization: "O ye peoples of the world! Know, verily, that an unforeseen calamity followeth you, and grievous retribution awaiteth you. Think not that which ye have committed hath been effaced in My sight. By My beauty! All your doings hath

---

* Please see the Apostles' Creed at http://www.vatican.va/archive/ccc_css/ archive/catechism/credo.htm.

My pen graven with open characters upon tablets of chrysolite"
(Bahá'u'lláh, The Hidden Words, Persian no. 63).

However, totally unlike the more literalist interpretations of
Jewish, Christian, and Islamic prophecies regarding this Judgment
and Resurrection, the Bahá'í authoritative texts interpret most of
these prophecies as being figurative images, parables, analogies, or
symbolic representations of historical events. Indeed, the Bahá'í
texts assert that most of these prophecies have already occurred or
else are well under way.

The Bahá'í writings do portray an upheaval or calamity as having both literal/physical components as well as symbolic/spiritual
implications. Likewise, this period of transformation and reformation of our global community is portrayed as a process, a series of
events, not merely a single apocalyptic catastrophe. What is most
distinctive about the Bahá'í interpretation of this turning point in
human history is that it portrays this process, this "End Time," as
neither the termination of human existence nor the extinction of
our planet; quite the opposite is the case.

The Bahá'í vision of the future is optimistic, a happy ending, as
it were. This traumatic reformation will serve not only to enable
us to understand that the earth is one community, but it will also
serve to cleanse world civilization of those prejudices and traditions that, until now, have been impediments to constructing an
enduring world peace and a global infrastructure. This process of
transition will further serve as a major impetus to instigate and
catalyze the unity of humankind under the aegis of a series of
collaborative systems—a world commonwealth, a unified religious
perspective, and a cooperative civilization the likes of which the
world has yet to envision, let alone experience.

Therefore, if we presume to assert that our examination of the
Bahá'í view of reality is complete in terms of the notion of sin and
salvation, we must in this concluding chapter at least touch on this
concept of collective judgment and redemption, especially as this
event or process applies to our individual objectives in relation to

our collective spiritual destiny. To repeat a previously cited statement by Bahá'u'lláh about collective human purpose: "All men have been created to carry forward an ever-advancing civilization" (Bahá'u'lláh, *Gleanings*, no. 109.2).

Stated succinctly, the Bahá'í vision of a collective salvation should not be understood as a mere afterthought or as tangentially related to how we view the path to individual spiritual redemption. As we have repeatedly observed, throughout the Bahá'í writings, as well as in the scriptures of previous religions, individual development is always predicated on, and inextricably linked to, social objectives. As we have noted, the simple fact is that spiritual attributes derive from and are necessarily practiced and exercised in social relationships with others.

ESCHATOLOGY IN JUDAISM AND CHRISTIANITY

A number of religions have eschatological prophecies. For example, if the Mayan calendar is correct as some have interpreted it, this book should never have made it to press. If you are reading it, then the end of the world didn't happen, and the publisher liked what I wrote. Hinduism, Buddhism, Zoroastrianism, and Judaism all have prophecies alluding to some great upheaval or "End Time." Some interpret these passages as referring to the end of an age or era, but others believe these to be an ominous foreshadowing of the end of human civilization or of planet Earth itself.

According to some of these prophetic or visionary scriptures and traditions, the saved will be given a new body and will be taken to a physical heaven of material delights. The damned, on the other hand, will be taken to a physical place of punishment and deprivation, a hell or some equally abysmal abode. Furthermore, according to most faith traditions that uphold such a doctrine, this judgment is final, and these conditions for the two groups are eternally fixed and binding. There is no further process of atonement or development—the "judgment" is final and everlasting.

There are substantial variations regarding how these prophecies are interpreted. For example, the terms "living" and "dead" are often portrayed in a literal sense, while others interpret these terms as alluding to spiritual conditions. Likewise, there is variability of interpretation about what is intended by the concepts of the "Time of the End." Do terms referring to the "end times" allude to the end or extermination of our planet and all human civilization, or are these terms predicting the end of a particular period or era, a time when some important transformation of human society and understanding will occur? Likewise, some interpret the concept of a "last judgment" as a permanent relegation of every soul to some eternal and changeless place or condition, while others believe these terms allude to the immediate response of humankind to some momentous challenge that will occur during a time of critical change.

THE MESSIAH

In Judaism, we find allusions to the Messianic expectations, to the raising of the dead, to the end of war, to a peaceful coalition of all peoples in the service of God. In the allusions to these events among various books in the Hebrew Bible (the *Tanakh*), we find passages prophesying the advent of the Messiah and the propitious results from His coming. But while there is much about the impact of the advent of the Messiah, we find nothing about a collective judgment in which the good and faithful are sent to heaven and the wicked are doomed to hell.

While the Jews expected the "reign" of the Messiah to be a literal fulfillment of the prophecies in the Old Testament, the fulfillment of this expectation was more figurative and symbolic than literal. For example, while Jesus was, according to the genealogy in Matthew, descended from David and Abraham, He ascended to the "throne of David" (Isaiah 9:7) only in a spiritual sense, which was not at all what most Jewish clerics expected.

Indeed, most of the Messianic prophecies seemed to foretell observable changes in governance, justice, and world order. The attendant results of the advent of the Messiah are familiarly summarized in Charles Jennens' libretto for Handel's masterpiece oratorio *The Messiah*. Most of the prophetic "proofs" of Christ as Messiah in this magnificent opus are taken by Jennens from the book of Isaiah, with a few from the Psalms.

Other important Messianic expectations we might understandably infer as having been fulfilled literally—such as the Jews returning to their homeland (Isaiah 11:12).* What seems too vague for explicit interpretation is the important notion of the spiritual salvation or resurrection of humankind. The prophecy of an apocalyptic upheaval is explicit. Daniel's allusion to "the abomination that maketh desolate" appears in three verses, each ostensibly foretelling some catastrophic end time in which humankind will experience the wrath of God.**

While in virtually every sect and denomination of Christianity believers accept the advent of Christ as fulfilling the Jewish prophecies about the Messiah ("He Who is Anointed"),† a variety of interpretations are applied to two major eschatological themes derived from Christian scripture—theories surrounding the so-called "Second Coming" of Christ, and theories of interpretation regarding the calamitous turmoil of Armageddon portrayed in the Book of Revelation—both of which involve Christ's judgment of "the living and the dead."‡

---

* The Jewish state of Israel was created in 1948.

** See Daniel 9:27, 11:31, and 12:11.

† The "anointed" is deemed to be referring to Christ's anointing in the Jordan River as a follower of John the Baptist.

‡ From the "Apostles' Creed" as translated in the *Book of Common Prayer* of the Church of England.

THE SECOND COMING

The notion of a Second Coming derives from two main sources. First, there are explicit statements made by Christ in His so-called "Olivet discourse" alluding to His return.* This talk, recounted in all three synoptic gospels (Matthew, Mark, and Luke, but most fully in Matthew), begins with Christ warning of the calamities of the "end time" that will occur prior to His return. He states that unless those times are shortened (by God's grace for the sake of the "elect") the world would be utterly destroyed:

> When ye therefore shall see the abomination of desolation, spoken of by Daniel the prophet, stand in the holy place, (whoso readeth, let him understand). Then let them which be in Judaea flee into the mountains. Let him which is on the housetop not come down to take anything out of his house, neither let him which is in the field return back to take his clothes.
>
> And woe unto them that are with child, and to them that give suck in those days! But pray ye that your flight be not in the winter, neither on the Sabbath day, for then shall be great tribulation, such as was not since the beginning of the world to this time, no, nor ever shall be. And except those days should be shortened, there should no flesh be saved: but for the elect's sake those days shall be shortened. (Matthew 24:13–22)

Some Protestant sects, such as the Puritans, tried wholeheartedly to define exactly who these "elect" might be. They believed this allusion to be a literal reference to a specific number of individuals, similar to what seems to be implied in the Book of Revelation.

---

* The "Olivet Discourse" refers to Christ's sermon on the Mount of Olives.

Many Christian religions have focused on the "signs" Christ establishes in this discourse, portents that His return is imminent because certain events have taken place or presently seem to be in process:

> Immediately after the tribulation of those days shall the sun be darkened, and the moon shall not give her light, and the stars shall fall from heaven, and the powers of the heavens shall be shaken. And then shall appear the sign of the Son of man in heaven: and then shall all the tribes of the earth mourn, and they shall see the Son of man coming in the clouds of heaven with power and great glory.
>
> And he shall send his angels with a great sound of a trumpet, and they shall gather together his elect from the four winds, from one end of heaven to the other. (Matthew 24:29–31)*

Christ follows the portrayal of these events with the enigmatic parable of the fig tree and the even more enigmatic statement that "This generation shall not pass, till all these things be fulfilled" (Matthew 24:34).

Paul places a great deal of emphasis on what seems to have been his own expectation that the return was imminent during his day, his "generation." He seems to have taken this caution quite literally and advised his "generation"—the members of the various Christian congregations to whom he wrote his numerous epistles—that they should not marry (unless absolutely necessary) nor undertake any other distracting endeavors. Rather, they should prepare themselves for Christ's imminent return.

---

* Bahá'u'lláh provides an exhaustive interpretation of these same three verses in the first hundred pages or so of His principal doctrinal work, The Kitáb-i-Íqán.

THE LAST JUDGMENT AND THE NEW JERUSALEM

The Book of Revelation is the primary source of the most imaginative speculation about the calamitous events that will precede the return of Christ. This work is also the principal inspiration for literalist versions of the judgment that will be imposed on humankind.

In his description in the Book of Revelation of a complex symbolic dream, John* recounts four visions in which, he affirms, he is privileged to behold the plan of God in order to assist humankind in preparing for the future. Most likely of Jewish background, John cites numerous passages from the Hebrew Bible, primarily from prophecies in Isaiah, Ezekiel, Daniel, and Psalms. His focus, however, is on the war between God and Satan, and his ultimate objective is to portray in detail the establishment of the "New Jerusalem," a process that will take place after Jesus, as God's vicegerent, conquers Satan, evil, and sin.

The use of evocative imagery, allegory, and symbol all invite imaginative interpretation of John's visions with their vividly drawn figures, such as the Four Horsemen of the Apocalypse, the Seven Trumpeters, the Seven-Headed Beast of the Sea, the Archangel Michael, and the Whore of Babylon. Clearly these are intended as symbolic or allegorical figures, but lacking any authoritative interpretation of St. John's narrative, Christian scholars as well as ordinary believers have, through the ages, attempted to discern in the historical signs of the times how the narrative applies to contemporary events.

In recent popular culture, for example, these diverse signs and symbols have become a rich, if abysmally perverted, resource for cinematic fictional horror stories and for televangelists plying their trade to vast audiences caught up in the emotional tumult of the age. Unfortunately, much of the authentic usefulness of the

---

* His exact identity has produced an abundance of scholarly speculation.

work—which was doubtlessly intended as a warning about the future—has mutated into a pastiche of unholy nonsense about evil spirits, infernal monsters from the vasty deep, little children afflicted with demonic possession, and indestructible serial killers who appear, donning hockey masks, when we say the wrong words into a mirror.

Fortunately, as we will mention later, the Bahá'í texts offer logical and helpful interpretations and elucidations of these same biblical prophecies from both the Old and New Testaments. One of the richest repositories of these is the section of 'Abdu'l-Bahá's *Some Answered Questions*, titled "Some Christian Subjects" ('Abdu'l-Bahá, *Some Answered Questions*, pp. 119–202). The general thrust of these discussions is that most of these events have already occurred, and that what remains to take place, while extremely relevant to our discussion about sin and salvation, ultimately has a most happy ending.

While speculation will undoubtedly abound until, as Paul says, "old things are passed away" and "all things are become new" (II Corinthians 5:17), more than a few Christians have come to agree with Christ's own statement regarding the Second Coming and the judgment of humankind, namely, that "of that day and hour knoweth no man, no, not the angels of heaven, but my Father only" (Matthew 24:36). For while we should always be spiritually prepared for any eventuality, there can be no sure way to predict what Christ Himself asserts is entirely unpredictable.

ESCHATOLOGY IN ISLAM

The Last Judgment or Day of Resurrection is a major theme of the Qur'án and Islamic traditions (hadíths). Yet a similar sort of dispute about interpreting these prophecies occurs among Islamic scholars. In a most general sense, these disputes similarly focus on whether or not passages are to be understood as literal or figurative.

But there is in Islam another sort of finality or end point in human history associated with the advent of Muhammad. Most

Muslims believe that because Muhammad describes the Qur'án and Islam as a "complete" revelation and Himself as the "seal" of the Prophets, there will be no further revelations from God. Therefore, all references to an end time or Day of Days—events that must transpire after Muhammad—could have no other meaning than some allusion to the Last Judgment and the end of the world.

Many Muslims thus interpret Christ's allusions to His return as a reference to the revelation of Muhammad as the Counselor Who comes in Christ's name:* "I have yet many things to say unto you, but ye cannot bear them now. Howbeit when he, the Spirit of truth, is come, he will guide you into all truth, for he shall not speak of himself; but whatsoever he shall hear, *that* shall he speak, and he will shew you things to come. He shall glorify me, for he shall receive of mine, and shall shew *it* unto you" (John 16:12–14).

However, most Muslims cannot accept that Muhammad's own allusions to a transformative Day of Days is likewise a foreshadowing of a future revelation—not if He is the "seal" of the Prophets, the last Manifestation with the final revelation from God. Both Muslims and Bahá'ís believe that some of the Christian prophecies were fulfilled with the advent of Muhammad, but only Bahá'ís believe that others of these have now been fulfilled with the advent of the Báb and Bahá'u'lláh.

Since most Muslims do not believe there will be a further revelation, they hold that the "Day of Days" alluded to throughout the Qur'án will occur with the advent of the "Last Judgment" associated with the end of creation. Most Muslims also believe that at that time, the good will be admitted to a physical heaven and the evil consigned to a physical hell according to exacting and precise assessment of deeds as assayed by God Himself: "When the Earth is shaken to her (utmost) convulsion, and the Earth throws up her burden (from within), and man cries (distressed), 'What is

---

* See Munqidh Bin Mahmoud Assaqqar, *The Promised Prophet of the Bible.*

the matter with her?'—on that Day will she declare her tidings, because thy Lord will have given her inspiration. On that Day will men proceed in companies sorted out, to be shown the Deeds that they (have done). Then shall anyone who has done an atom's weight of good, see it! And anyone who has done an atom's weight of evil, shall see it" (Surah 99:1–8).

Of course, not all Muslims accept these passages as being literally true. There are numerous passages in the Qur'án where Muhammad alludes to God's eternal mercy, grace, and forgiveness. And yet, balanced against this hope is always the theme that no sinful deed is left unrecorded in the "Book of Deeds": "Truly those in sin are the ones straying in mind, and mad. The day they will be dragged through the Fire on their faces, (they will hear:) 'Taste ye the touch of Hell!' . . . All that they do is noted in (their) Books (of Deeds). Every matter, small and great, is on record. As to the Righteous, they will be in the midst of Gardens and Rivers in an Assembly of Truth, in the Presence of a Sovereign Omnipotent (One)" (Surah 54:47–55).

Like Christ, Muhammad affirms that only God knows when this Day of Days will occur, but Muhammad alludes to several signs of the approach of that time. Among the most frequently cited are twin trumpet blasts, the first of which will dumbfound the peoples and render them unconscious, while the second will resurrect humankind:

The Trumpet will (just) be sounded, when all that are in the heavens and on earth will swoon, except such as it will please Allah (to exempt). Then will a second one be sounded, when behold, they will be standing and looking on! And the Earth will shine with the glory of its Lord. The Record (of Deeds) will be placed (open). The prophets and the witnesses will be brought forward, and a just decision pronounced between them, and they will not be wronged (in the least). And

to every soul will be paid in full (the fruit) of its deeds, and
(Allah) knoweth best all that they do. (Surah 39:68–70)

ESCHATOLOGY IN THE BAHÁ'Í TEXTS

It would require volumes to explicate in full what the authoritative Bahá'í texts accomplish by way of prophesying the future and
interpreting logically and usefully all the major prophecies of the
past.* But let us review some of the more salient points we have
raised for the purpose of discussing the relationship between individual and collective salvation.

For example, according to the Bahá'í teachings, a judgment is
imposed upon humankind whenever a Manifestation appears.
Those living at that time and in the part of the globe for which
the Manifestation has come will be tested in the sense that each
individual will be challenged to recognize the new Prophet and,
if they recognize Him, further challenged to follow whatever laws
and guidance He reveals as the path for that "Day" or "Age," even
should this guidance seem radically different from, or contrary to,
the guidance of the past.

The advent of the Báb and Bahá'u'lláh represent the "Last" of
these tests in the sense that during the course of the dispensation
of Bahá'u'lláh—which Bahá'u'lláh asserts will endure no less than
a thousand years and will minister collectively to all the peoples of
the world—humankind will come to understand the abiding logic
of the divine process by which God has progressively enlightened
human civilization. And yet, until this unity and progression of
religions is universally understood and accepted, all people will be
tested as to whether or not they can discern this truth and, once
having appreciated the wisdom of God's Divine plan, assist in the

---

* For a full explication of this discussion in the Bahá'í texts, see John S.
Hatcher, *The Arc of Ascent*, "From the Lesser Peace to a Golden Age: Stages in
the Evolution of a World Commonwealth," pp. 235–76.

construction of the global commonwealth by which means our world will become transformed and unified.

In the first chapter of this book, in our discussion about the nature of reality, we clarified some of the major aspects of the Bahá'í prophecies regarding the destiny of human civilization on planet Earth and how this long-awaited stage is depicted in the Bahá'í texts as the "maturation of humankind." In this context, it is little wonder that Bahá'ís consider this transformative period as fulfilling the "Day of Days" or the "Day of Resurrection," the dispensation during which the whole of humanity will become awakened to the underlying reality of creation and will be revived by this optimistic perspective about the propitious destiny of human history. We have likewise discussed how this vision accords with the plan of God for human advancement. Now let us sum up the solutions proffered in the Bahá'í authoritative texts to the enigmatic prophecies from the Hebrew Bible, the Christian Bible, and the Qur'án regarding the collective resurrection or salvation of humankind.

While the reader would do well to examine the texts firsthand, it is sufficient here for us first to set forth simply and sequentially some specific interpretations regarding what these writings have to offer by way of elucidating such eschatological concepts as a world-engulfing upheaval, the Second Coming of Christ, the Day of Resurrection, and the Last Judgment.

THE TWIN MANIFESTATIONS

Let us begin with a glance at 'Abdu'l-Bahá's discussion of those prophecies that allude to the advent of two Prophets (or two Manifestations). For example, in his discussion of prophecies from the Book of Daniel in *Some Answered Questions*, 'Abdu'l-Bahá states that the followers of all three Abrahamic religions of Judaism, Christianity, and Islam await the advent of "two Manifestations" who "must be contemporaneous." He observes these same three religions also await some form of collective Resurrection followed by a Last Judgment:

All the peoples of the world are awaiting two Manifestations, Who must be contemporaneous. This is what they all have been promised. In the Torah, the Jews are promised the Lord of Hosts and the Messiah. In the Gospel, the return of Christ and Elijah is foretold. In the religion of Muhammad, there is the promise of the Mahdi and the Messiah. The same holds true of the Zoroastrians and others. . . . Our meaning is that all have been promised the advent of two successive Manifestations. It has been prophesied that, through these twin Manifestations, the earth will become another earth; all existence will be renewed; the contingent world will be clothed with the robe of a new life; justice and righteousness will encompass the globe; hatred and enmity will disappear; whatever is the cause of division among peoples, races, and nations will be obliterated; and that which ensures unity, harmony, and concord will be promoted. ('Abdu'l-Bahá, *Some Answered Questions*, no. 10.8)

'Abdu'l-Bahá goes on to assert that this "End Time" will not herald the end of the world, but will instead witness the transformation of our planet into a spiritually grounded global commonwealth. Indeed, while there will doubtlessly be a climactic series of events to help galvanize the will of the nations, peoples, and rulers to instigate a unified world community, the outcome, as we have noted, will be the promised "ever-advancing civilization": "this world will mirror forth the heavenly Kingdom; and the earth below will become the throne of the realm above. All nations will become one nation; all religions will become one religion; all mankind will become one family and one kindred; all the regions of the earth will become as one; racial, national, personal, linguistic, and political prejudices will be effaced and extinguished; and all will attain everlasting life under the shadow of the Lord of Hosts" ('Abdu'l-Bahá, *Some Answered Questions*, no. 10.8). 'Abdu'l-Bahá then explains that the notion of the end time is an allusion to a turning point in human history, not the end of humankind or planet Earth. This turning point, he explains, is the confluence of two eras—the conclusion the "Prophetic Cycle" (the universal cycle that began with Adam and ended with Muhammad), and the inauguration of a new universal era or cycle in which humankind will come to understand and implement the unity of purpose that has been the underlying principle of all prior revelations throughout human history.

The point that marks this confluence occurred in 1844 when the Báb declared His station as the long-awaited Qá'im or Mahdi of Shi'a Islam, and His revelation as the Day of Resurrection foretold by all previous religions. But His principal mission, the Báb asserts, is to herald the advent of the "Latter Resurrection" (The Báb, *Selections from the Writings of the Báb*, 1:2:4)—the Revelation of Bahá'u'lláh.

THE TWIN TRUMPET BLASTS

The first Trumpet Blast, as foretold in the Qur'án,* occurred at the Conference at Bada<u>sh</u>t when Ṭáhirih appeared unveiled before the assembled attendees, an event symbolizing the end of the Islamic dispensation: "The trumpeter was a lone woman, the noblest of her sex in that Dispensation, whom even some of her co-religionists pronounced a heretic. The call she sounded was the death-knell of the twelve hundred year old law of Islam" (Shoghi Effendi, *God Passes By*, p. 54).

---

* "The Trumpet will (just) be sounded, when all that are in the heavens and on earth will swoon, except such as it will please Allah (to exempt). Then will a second one be sounded, when behold, they will be standing and looking on! And the Earth will shine with the glory of its Lord: the Record (of Deeds) will be placed (open); the prophets and the witnesses will be brought forward: and a just decision pronounced between them; and they will not be wronged (in the least)" (Qur'án 39:68–69).

This milestone event and fulfillment of prophecy was followed twenty years later by the Second Trumpet Blast in 1868 when Bahá'u'lláh proclaimed to the world at large that His Revelation was the fulfillment of the "Day of Days," the "Latter Resurrection," and that He was the fulfillment of the promised advent of the "Lord of Hosts" of the Judaic Psalms, the "Spirit of Truth" and "Son of Man" alluded to by Christ, the "Glory of God" promised in the Book of Revelation, the "Great Announcement" prophesied by Muhammad in the Qur'án, the "Qayyúm" who will follow the "Qá'im" prophesied by Siyyid Kázim, and "He Whom God shall make manifest" as foretold by the Báb (Shoghi Effendi, *God Passes By*, p. 97).

These interpretations and elucidations are of immense value for those who wish to trace the gradual unfolding of the fulfillment of these prophecies in the scriptural works from Judaism, Christianity, and Islam. 'Abdu'l-Bahá explicates in significant detail how the numerical symbols in these prophecies accurately establish the dates for the appearance of the Báb and the advent of the "Day of Days." But rather than rehearse what 'Abdu'l-Bahá has already accomplished so clearly and completely,* let us simply list a few of the major examples of how he unlocks or unseals the meanings to those symbols that have baffled so many for so long.

Among the most interesting and revealing explanations in his discussions of these prophecies are those that clarify what so many contemporary Christian evangelicals perceive as a literal war waged by Satan and his minions. For example, 'Abdu'l-Bahá explains that the beast that will ascend from the bottomless pit to make war

---

* See 'Abdu'l-Bahá, *Some Answered Questions*, no. 10.8–22 for explanation of how the years are calculated prophesying the advent of the Báb and Bahá'u'lláh. See no. 11.1–15.9 for explication of the major symbols about the advent of this transformative period as foreshadowed in Revelation chapter 11, Isaiah chapter 11, and Revelation chapter 12.

against the "two witnesses" is, like many prophecies in this section of the Book of Revelation, referring to the dispensation of Muhammad. The witnesses, he explains, are Muhammad and the Imam 'Alí, and the beast refers to the "Umayyads, who assailed these witnesses from the pit of error" ('Abdu'l-Bahá, *Some Answered Questions*, no. 11.20).*

Of similar interest to me is 'Abdu'l-Bahá's explication regarding the "new Jerusalem" (Revelation 21:2), an image that has evoked so much inspiration and speculation among various Christian sects over the past centuries. Both here and elsewhere, 'Abdu'l-Bahá states that the "New Jerusalem," or the descent of the "Holy City," is referring to the law of God whenever it is revealed by a new Manifestation. In this particular passage, 'Abdu'l-Bahá says, the allusion is to the advent and revelation of Muhammad. The specifics of this interpretation are worth repeating here to demonstrate the rich repository of insights that are available in 'Abdu'l-Bahá's discussions, thereby resolving, for those who accept his explanations, ages of endless conjecture and contention:

> Furthermore, the religion of God is likened to an adorned bride who appears with the utmost grace, as it has been said in chapter 21 of the Revelation of John: "And I John saw the holy city, new Jerusalem, coming down from God out of heaven, prepared as a bride adorned for her husband." And in chapter 12 it is said: "And there appeared a great wonder in heaven; a woman clothed with the sun, and the moon under her feet, and upon her head a crown of twelve stars." This woman is that bride, the religion of God, that

---

* The passages from the Book of Revelation are from 11:7. The Umayyads were a clan within the same Quraysh tribe as Muhammad, but the longstanding antipathy between the Umayyads and the Hashemite clan (to which Muhammad belonged) grew extremely intense after Muhammad declared His revelation and station as a Prophet of God.

descended upon Muḥammad. The sun with which she was clothed, and the moon which was under her feet, are the two governments which are under the shadow of that religion, the Persian and the Ottoman, for the emblem of Persia is the sun and that of the Ottoman Empire is the crescent moon. Thus the sun and the moon allude to two governments under the shadow of the religion of God. Afterwards it is said: "upon her head a crown of twelve stars." These twelve stars represent the twelve Imáms, who were the promoters of the religion of Muḥammad and the educators of the nation, and who shone as stars in the heaven of guidance. ('Abdu'l-Bahá, *Some Answered Questions*, no. 13.4)

Since our concern here is focused on allusions to the resurrection and collective salvation of humankind, we can conclude by reviewing two main prophecies regarding this present time in religious history. We can most profitably focus on the critical role that we are destined to play in this turning point in human history, and we can begin to appreciate history itself as a divine process rather than as a random assortment of natural disasters, wars, empires, tyrants, and a sprinkling of heroes who, more often than not, seem to end up suffering at the hands of bad people.

The first of these prophecies we have already mentioned—the two trumpet blasts. The first blast is the revelation of the Báb, Whose brief but crucial appearance prepared humankind for a break with the past and all its baggage of misunderstanding about the purpose and relationship among the religions of the world. As we have noted, the critical nature of this "point" in human history designates the confluence of two universal cycles—the ending of the Prophetic or Adamic cycle, and the beginning of the Cycle of Bahá —thereby fulfilling the expectation of universal peace as prophesied in all previous revelations.

The second trumpet blast is the revelation of Bahá'u'lláh, which is nothing less than the vision of a holistic plan whereby the diverse peoples of the world can become a coordinated commonwealth of just and peaceful communities. This second trumpet blast has awakened the sleepers, resurrected those who have been spiritually dead, listless, or recalcitrant, and set in motion a sequence of plans whereby the "new Jerusalem" can descend in its full splendor.

By the impetus of this resurrecting force, combined with Bahá'u'lláh's revealed organizational plan, Christ's prayer will be fulfilled—that God's kingdom will become manifest on earth in physical form, even as it is manifest in the celestial realm in metaphysical form.

THE CALAMITY AND THE RESURRECTION

As we have discussed, the Bahá'í texts do indeed confirm the validity of past prophecies regarding some world-engulfing crises that will demonstrate the inadequacy and obsolescence of divisive doctrines and religious and governmental systems. This process, which has already begun, will provide additional motive force to underscore the urgency for us to create the global commonwealth Bahá'u'lláh described to world leaders.

Perhaps the most powerful description in the Bahá'í texts of the scope and ultimately propitious nature of this world-engulfing process is the beginning passage in Shoghi Effendi's work *The Promised Day is Come* in which he portrays the current crises as a vast tempest cleansing the world of archaic notions in preparation for the acceptance of a federation of world governments:

> A tempest, unprecedented in its violence, unpredictable in its course, catastrophic in its immediate effects, unimaginably glorious in its ultimate consequences, is at present sweeping the face of the earth. Its driving power is remorselessly gaining in range and momentum. Its cleansing force, however much undetected, is increasing with every passing day. Humanity, gripped in the clutches of its devastating power, is smitten

by the evidences of its resistless fury. It can neither perceive its origin, nor probe its significance, nor discern its outcome. Bewildered, agonized and helpless, it watches this great and mighty wind of God invading the remotest and fairest regions of the earth, rocking its foundations, deranging its equilibrium, sundering its nations, disrupting the homes of its peoples, wasting its cities, driving into exile its kings, pulling down its bulwarks, uprooting its institutions, dimming its light, and harrowing up the souls of its inhabitants. (Shoghi Effendi, *The Promised Day is Come*, p. 3)

The solution or outcome which Shoghi Effendi describes as "unimaginably glorious in its ultimate consequences" is portrayed in full throughout a number of Bahá'í texts as a series of stages—most prominently, perhaps, in Shoghi Effendi's *The World Order of Bahá'u'lláh*. Stated briefly, these stages consist of the various phases of a Lesser Peace, followed in time by an ever-evolving Most Great Peace—what is sometimes referred to in the Bahá'í writings as The Golden Age of Bahá'u'lláh.

The sequence of these stages will proceed first with a binding pact or agreement among the nations of the world. 'Abdu'l-Bahá describes the fundamental ingredients of this pact as follows: "The fundamental principle underlying this solemn Pact should be so fixed that if any government later violate any one of its provisions, all the governments on earth should arise to reduce it to utter submission, nay the human race as a whole should resolve, with every power at its disposal, to destroy that government. Should this greatest of all remedies be applied to the sick body of the world, it will assuredly recover from its ills and will remain eternally safe and secure" ('Abdu'l-Bahá, *The Secret of Divine Civilization*, ¶120).

Shoghi Effendi describes the federated government that will emerge from this pact as most probably containing four major constituent parts or agencies: a world legislature or parliament, a world or international executive, a supreme world tribunal, and an international force to assist the world executive in carrying out the decisions of the world legislature.*

Naturally the question arises as to what will cause the nations of the world and their leaders willingly to participate in constructing this commonwealth, and the answer discussed at length in the Bahá'í texts is that at some point, the aforementioned "tempest" will reach such a pitch and become so ubiquitous and urgent that gathering together to make such a pact and construct such a federation will be the only possible solution to maintain the body politic.

Over time, as this secular commonwealth develops in concert with the already established worldwide Bahá'í community, it will become apparent that the spiritual and social principles underlying and driving the global Bahá'í polity should be conjoined with secular governance. The resulting planetary construct will not be a theocracy, but a single commonwealth established according to universal suffrage and upholding the major spiritual principles articulated by Bahá'u'lláh as requisite remedies for the needs of this new age: the equality of women and men; the elimination of the extremes of poverty and wealth; the establishment of universal compulsory education; the unity of science and religion in responding to the needs of an advancing global community. These and various other salutary components are spelled out in detail in the Bahá'í prescription for a government portrayed by Shoghi Effendi as containing aspects of various forms of governance, but as being an entirely new creation:

> The Bahá'í Commonwealth of the future, of which this vast Administrative Order is the sole framework, is, both in theory and practice, not only unique in the entire history of political institutions, but can find no parallel in the annals

---

* See Shoghi Effendi, *The World Order of Bahá'u'lláh*, pp. 40–41, 203.

of any of the world's recognized religious systems. No form of democratic government; no system of autocracy or of dictatorship, whether monarchical or republican; no intermediary scheme of a purely aristocratic order; nor even any of the recognized types of theocracy, whether it be the Hebrew Commonwealth, or the various Christian ecclesiastical organizations, or the Imamate or the Caliphate in Islam—none of these can be identified or be said to conform with the Administrative Order which the master-hand of its perfect Architect has fashioned.

This new-born Administrative Order incorporates within its structure certain elements which are to be found in each of the three recognized forms of secular government, without being in any sense a mere replica of any one of them, and without introducing within its machinery any of the objectionable features which they inherently possess. It blends and harmonizes, as no government fashioned by mortal hands has as yet accomplished, the salutary truths which each of these systems undoubtedly contains without vitiating the integrity of those God-given verities on which it is ultimately founded. (Shoghi Effendi, *The World Order of Bahá'u'lláh*, pp. 152–53)

HOW TO GET THERE FROM HERE

Every day the news from around the world confirms the validity of this vision and the dire necessity for it to become realized—whether in the immediate need to secure the wellbeing and basic necessities for powerless and oppressed peoples, in the relentless tensions among nation states and religious sects, or in the global urgency for securing natural resources, watersheds, crops, and protecting the air we breathe. No less obvious is the call for complete revision of educational systems, health systems, available foodstuff, and sources of energy.

Already major steps have been made toward economic alliances as we now fully realize that, whether we desire it or not, an interdependent global economy has emerged. We can no longer avoid the collective necessity of assisting immigrants in want of the basic necessities of life. Gradually our world-view has assumed a more diverse global perspective since the depolarization of the planet. The "Cold War" that characterized the post-war world for almost half a century has vanished, but in its place a more diverse array of conflicts has emerged with exponentially greater complexity and danger.

So it is that we all have readily available to us this new vision, this new knowledge, this new need, and this new opportunity. We all agree that tyranny and oppression are no longer acceptable forms of government, even if the final eradication of such injustice is not fully accomplished. As archaic systems gradually and systematically diminish in their ability to function as a global infrastructure, we wait for largely isolationist and dysfunctional national governments to intelligently address problems that far exceed their capacity to respond with creativity, coherence, and collaboration.

Regardless of what form the upheaval or tempest deriving from this breakdown in increasingly deficient social and political systems may take, we are beginning to see how it will demonstrate at least two major verities about our emerging global community.

First, it will demonstrate to all humankind, including world religious and political leaders, that our present approaches are inadequate to maintain order, let alone establish justice, peace, and progressive social structures. If our present systems are insufficient to forestall the rapid onset of decline in a sustainable global polity, then we certainly cannot believe that the same flawed and divisive systems will be capable of responding to ever more encompassing and complex challenges.

But while this ordeal or series of world-engulfing crises will demonstrate with unavoidable clarity the inadequacy of our present approach to governance and social order, a second prophesied force, more powerful than the first, will demonstrate the methods by which a new identity, coupled with a new methodology, can immediately be employed to redeem a disheartened humanity and the dismantled patchwork of diverse and uncoordinated national systems. Out of this turmoil will most certainly emerge a unified desire to create and uphold a system of peace, justice, and spiritual reformation—the very "redemption" and "resurrection" so long foretold and so forthrightly articulated by Bahá'u'lláh in His message to the world leaders: "The earth is but one country, and mankind its citizens" (Bahá'u'lláh, *Gleanings*, no. 117).

BIBLIOGRAPHY

WORKS OF BAHÁ'U'LLÁH

Epistle to the Son of the Wolf. Wilmette, IL: Bahá'í Publishing Trust, 1988.

Gems of Divine Mysteries. Haifa, Israel: Bahá'í World Centre, 2002.

Gleanings from the Writings of Bahá'u'lláh. Wilmette, IL: Bahá'í Publishing, 2005.

Prayers and Meditations by Bahá'u'lláh. Translated by Shoghi Effendi. 1st ps ed. Wilmette, IL: Bahá'í Publishing Trust, 1987.

Tablets of Bahá'u'lláh Revealed after the Kitáb-i-Aqdas. Compiled by the Research Department of the Universal House of Justice. Translated by Habib Taherzadeh et al. Wilmette, IL: Bahá'í Publishing Trust, 1988.

The Hidden Words. Translated by Shoghi Effendi. Wilmette, IL: Bahá'í Publishing, 2002.

The Kitáb-i-Aqdas: The Most Holy Book. 1st ps ed. Wilmette, IL: Bahá'í Publishing Trust, 1993.

The Kitáb-i-Íqán: The Book of Certitude. Translated by Shoghi Effendi. Wilmette, IL: Bahá'í Publishing, 2003.

The Seven Valleys and the Four Valleys. Translated by Marzieh Gail in consultation with Ali-Kuli Khan. Wilmette, IL: Bahá'í Publishing Trust, 1991.

The Summons of the Lord of Hosts. Wilmette, IL: Bahá'í Publishing, 2006.

WORKS OF THE BÁB

Selections from the Writings of the Báb. Compiled by the Research Department of the Universal House of Justice. Translated by Habib Taherzadeh et al. Wilmette, IL: Bahá'í Publishing Trust, 2006.

WORKS OF 'ABDU'L-BAHÁ

'Abdu'l-Bahá in London: Addresses & Notes of Conversations. London: Bahá'í Publishing Trust, 1987.

Paris Talks: Addresses Given by 'Abdu'l-Bahá in 1911. Wilmette, IL: Bahá'í Publishing, 2011.

Selections from the Writings of 'Abdu'l-Bahá. Wilmette, IL: Bahá'í Publishing, 2010.

Some Answered Questions. Collected and translated by Laura Clifford Barney. Newly revised by a committee at the Bahá'í World Center. Haifa, Israel: Bahá'í World Center, 2014.

The Promulgation of Universal Peace: Talks Delivered by 'Abdu'l-Bahá during His Visit to the United States and Canada in 1912. Wilmette, IL: Bahá'í Publishing, 2012.

The Secret of Divine Civilization. Translated from the Persian by Marzieh Gail in consultation with Ali-Kuli Khan. Wilmette, IL: Bahá'í Publishing, 2007.

WORKS OF SHOGHI EFFENDI

The Advent of Divine Justice. Wilmette, IL: Bahá'í Publishing Trust, 2006.

Bahá'í Administration: Selected Messages, 1922–1932. Wilmette, IL: Bahá'í Publishing Trust, 1998.

Citadel of Faith: Messages to America 1947–1957. Wilmette, IL: Bahá'í Publishing Trust, 1980.

Directives from the Guardian. http://www.gutenberg.org/files/19270/19270-h/19270-h.html.

Letters from the Guardian to Australia and New Zealand 1923–1957. Sydney: Halstead Press, 1970.

The Promised Day is Come. 1st pocket-sized ed. Wilmette, IL: Bahá'í Publishing Trust, 1996.

The World Order of Bahá'u'lláh. First pocket-sized edition. Wilmette, IL: Bahá'í Publishing Trust, 1991.

WORKS OF THE UNIVERSAL HOUSE OF JUSTICE

Century of Light. Haifa, Israel: Bahá'í World Center, 2001.

COMPILATIONS

Bahá'í Prayers: A Selection of Prayers Revealed by Bahá'u'lláh, the Báb, and 'Abdu'l-Bahá. Wilmette, IL: Bahá'í Publishing Trust, 2002.

Compilation of Compilations. Mona Vale: Bahá'í Publications Australia, 1991.

OTHER WORKS

Alighieri, Dante. *The Divine Comedy.* New York: Random House, 1932.

Bahíyyíh Khánum. *Bahíyyíh Khánum: The Greatest Holy Leaf.* Haifa, Israel: Bahá'í World Centre, 1982.

Balyuzi, Hasan. *Muhammad and the Course of Islam.* Oxford: George Ronald, 1976.

Ben Avraham, Yonah. *Shaarei Teshuva: The Gates of Repentance.* Trans. Shraga Silverstein. Jerusalem, Israel: Feldheim Publishers, 1971.

Bin Mahmoud Assaqqar, Munqidh. *The Promised Prophet of the Bible.* http://www.scribd.com/doc/217806/The-Promised-Prophet-of-the-Bible.

Bokenkotter, Thomas. *A Concise History of the Catholic Church.* New York: Doubleday, 2005.

Brown, Peter. *The Rise of Christendom: Triumph and Diversity, A.D. 200–1000.* West Sussex, UK: John Wiley & Sons, Inc., 2013.

Esslemont, John. E. *Bahá'u'lláh and the New Era: An Introduction to the Bahá'í Faith.* 5th ed. Wilmette, IL: Bahá'í Publishing Trust, 1980.

Fletcher, Joseph. *Situation Ethics: The New Morality.* Louisville, KY: Westminster John Knox Press, 1997.

Goethe, Johann Wolfgang von. *Faust I & II.* Edited and translated by Stuart Atkins. Princeton, NJ: Princeton UP, 1984.

Hatcher, John S. *The Arc of Ascent.* Oxford: George Ronald, 1993.

———. *The Ascent of Society: The Social Imperative in Personal Salvation.* Wilmette, IL: Bahá'í Publishing, 2007.

———. *The Face of God among Us: How God Educates Humanity.* Wilmette, IL: Bahá'í Publishing, 2010.

———. *The Purpose of Physical Reality.* Wilmette, IL: Bahá'í Publishing, 2005.

Hornby, Helen, comp. *Lights of Guidance: A Bahá'í Reference File.* 6th ed. New Delhi: Bahá'í Publishing Trust, 1999.

Milton, John. *The Complete Poetical Works of John Milton.* Edited by Douglas Bush. Boston: Houghton Mifflin Company, 1965.

Momen, Wendi, ed. *A Basic Bahá'í Dictionary.* Oxford: George Ronald, 1989.

Plato. *The Republic.* Ed. G.R.F. Ferrari. Trans. Tom Griffith. New York: Cambridge UP, 2000.

Shakespeare, William. *The Complete Works of Shakespeare.* Edited by Harden Craig. Chicago: Scott, Foresman and Company, 1951.

Sonn, Tamara. *Islam: A Brief History.* West Sussex, UK: John Wiley & Sons, Inc., 2010.

Taherzadeh, Adib. *The Revelation of Bahá'u'lláh: Baghdad, 1853–63.* Vol. 1. Oxford: George Ronald, 1975.

————. *The Revelation of Bahá'u'lláh: Adrianople, 1863–68.* Vol. 2. Oxford: George Ronald, 2006.

————. *The Revelation of Bahá'u'lláh: 'Akká, the Early Years 1868–77.* Vol. 3. Oxford: George Ronald, 1983.

————. *The Revelation of Bahá'u'lláh: Mazra'ih & Bahji, 1877–92.* Vol. 4. Oxford: George Ronald, 1988.

The Holy Bible. Nashville: Thomas Nelson Publishers, 1984.

The Holy Qur'án. Trans. Abdullah Yusuf Ali. Elmhurst, New York: Tahrike Tarsile Qur'án, Inc., 2001.

The Norton Anthology of English Literature. 8th edition, Volume B. New York: W. W. Norton & Company, 2006.

Thoreau, Henry D. *Walden: or, Life in the Woods.* New York: Cosimo Classics, 2009.

Tolkien, John R. R. *The Lord of the Rings: The Two Towers.* New York: Ballantine Books, 1965.

Vitullo Martin, Julia, and J. Robert Moskin, eds. *The Executive's Book of Quotation.* New York: Oxford UP, 1994.

For more information about the Bahá'í Faith,
or to contact Bahá'ís near you,
visit http://www.bahai.us/
or call
1-800-22-UNITE

PUBLISHING

BAHÁ'Í PUBLISHING AND THE BAHÁ'Í FAITH

Bahá'í Publishing produces books based on the teachings of the Bahá'í Faith. Founded over 160 years ago, the Bahá'í Faith has spread to some 235 nations and territories and is now accepted by more than five million people. The word "Bahá'í" means "follower of Bahá'u'lláh." Bahá'u'lláh, the founder of the Bahá'í Faith, asserted that He is the Messenger of God for all of humanity in this day. The cornerstone of His teachings is the establishment of the spiritual unity of humankind, which will be achieved by personal transformation and the application of clearly identified spiritual principles. Bahá'ís also believe that there is but one religion and that all the Messengers of God—among them Abraham, Zoroaster, Moses, Krishna, Buddha, Jesus, and Muḥammad—have progressively revealed its nature. Together, the world's great religions are expressions of a single, unfolding divine plan. Human beings, not God's Messengers, are the source of religious divisions, prejudices, and hatreds.

The Bahá'í Faith is not a sect or denomination of another religion, nor is it a cult or a social movement. Rather, it is a globally recognized independent world religion founded on new books of scripture revealed by Bahá'u'lláh.

Bahá'í Publishing is an imprint of the National Spiritual Assembly of the Bahá'ís of the United States.

Light of the Kingdom
BIBLICAL TOPICS IN THE BAHÁ'Í WRITINGS
JoAnn Borovicka
$20.00 US / $22.00 CAN
Trade Paper
ISBN 978-1-61851-101-0

A comprehensive and eye-opening guide to biblical topics as they are addressed in the Bahá'í writings.

In *Light of the Kingdom,* author JoAnn Borovicka explores questions relating to the Bible and its significance and meaning from a Bahá'í perspective. The purpose of the book is to provide an introductory compilation of the wealth of insights on biblical topics offered in the Bahá'í Writings. To this end, it starts with an overview of Bahá'í teachings about the Bible in general, and then explores Bahá'í guidance on a variety of topics as they arise from the first book of the Old Testament through the last book of the New Testament. The result of years of exploration and research, the book provides samples of Bahá'í guidance on a wide range of biblical topics in a way that is accessible to anyone regardless of their prior knowledge of the Bible or the Bahá'í Faith.

What Good Will Come

Jana Hannigan
Illustrated by Henry Warren
$14.00 US / $16.00 CAN
Hardcover
ISBN 978-1-61851-103-4

A heartwarming story that will help children learn problem solving and discover the importance of relying on God during times of tests.

Pasha Dev lives in Delhi, India with his beloved cat, Mustafa. The two enjoy a good life in Pasha's simple apartment, but one evening during a rainstorm Mustafa goes missing, and Pasha ends up sleeping next to the window he has left open in the hope that Mustafa will return. When Pasha wakes the following morning, he finds that he has come down with a cold and that Mustafa has not returned. Still, Pasha must travel to the Bahá'í House of Worship, where he will serve as the keeper of people's shoes—a responsibility he takes very seriously. During his day of service, Pasha worries about Mustafa and faces some challenges that leave him with some riddles to solve. Along the way, he learns to put his faith in prayer and God, and comes to realize that tests and challenges can lead to some exciting, life-changing opportunities.

The First Gift

Judith A. Cobb
Illustrated by Wendy Cowper-Thomas
$8.95 US / $10.95 CAN
Trade Paper
ISBN 978-0-87743-708-6

A heartwarming story that will help young children begin to understand their spiritual reality.

The First Gift tells the story of six-year-old Griffin, who attends Bahá'í children's class, where he learns that he has a soul that was given to him by God. But where is his soul? Intrigued, Griffin asks his brother Paul for more detail, but Paul is in a hurry and can only tell him briefly that his soul is God's first gift to him. Griffin checks everywhere he can think of—his pockets, the car he rides home in, his bedroom. When he doesn't find his soul, he worries that he doesn't have one after all. His mother, sensing something is wrong, begins to talk to him, learns of his fears, and comforts him with an explanation of his soul that is based on the Bahá'í teachings. After talking to his mother, Griffin feels better and understands more clearly how he received his soul as well as God's love.

Fountain of Wisdom

A COLLECTION OF WRITINGS FROM BAHÁ'U'LLÁH

Bahá'u'lláh

$24.00 US / $26.00 CAN

Hardcover

ISBN 978-1-61851-104-1

A timeless collection of writings penned by the Prophet-Founder of the Bahá'í Faith with a universal message that all humanity is one race, destined to live in peace and harmony.

Fountain of Wisdom: A Collection of Writings from Bahá'u'lláh is a collection of the writings of Bahá'u'lláh, the Prophet-Founder of the Bahá'í Faith, in which He explains some of the "precepts and principles that lie at the very core of His Faith." Revealed during the final years of His ministry, the sixteen tablets contained in this volume cover a wide range of topics and place emphasis on principles such as the oneness and wholeness of the human race, collective security, justice, trustworthiness, and moderation in all things.